BURNING BRIDGES

TURKEY'S RETURN TO ISLAMIC AUTHORITARIANISM

JAY ALAN SEKULOW

American Center
for Law & Justice
P.O. Box 90555
Washington, D.C. 20090-0555
www.ACLJ.org

The Centre for the Study of Law & Public Policy at Oxford is an autonomous organisation not affiliated with the University of Oxford.

Printed in the United States by Cushing-Malloy, Ann Arbor, Michigan
Cover design by American Center for Law and Justice

TABLE OF CONTENTS

A Word
from the Author

I am grateful for your role as a member of the American Center for Law & Justice, and I am happy to send you this unique resource. It is a presentation that the ACLJ team and I made at the Centre for the Study of Law & Public Policy at Oxford.

We launched this Centre to (a) educate global leaders on a number of critically important issues, including the dangers of radical Islam and anti-Semitism across the globe, and (b) train them to respond effectively. Our goal is to work in the academic arena reflecting your values in order to bring influence to bear among policymakers, world leaders, attorneys, and more.

In my recent *New York Times* Best Sellers, *Rise of ISIS* and *Unholy Alliance*, I explored the conditions allowing the Islamic State (ISIS) to gain a foothold and begin its reign of terror and looked at how Russia and Iran are positioning themselves as a global force against the West. In this new collection of studies, we examine the nation of Turkey, exploring that country's relationship as a bridge between East and West, Islam and Christianity. Most importantly, we study the possibility of Turkey becoming more radically Islamic and the implications of such a shift: Could Turkey become a future home of terrorism, like Iran, Afghanistan, and Pakistan?

This important volume will help you understand the climate of the Middle East today, and Turkey's critical and tenuous role — particularly Turkey's potential impact on the stability of the region.

Jay Alan Sekulow

The following articles were produced as a joint endeavor with the Centre for the Study of Law & Public Policy at Oxford and are current as of 2016. We recognize that as the issues continue to develop, content presented herein may be superseded by more current facts and events. For more information on this issue and others, please visit ACLJ.org.

PRESIDENT'S INTRODUCTION

The Centre for the Study of Law & Public Policy at Oxford (the Centre) was launched in 2014 as the education and policy arm of the American Center for Law & Justice (ACLJ). With the world facing the scourge of terrorism, religious persecution, and other serious systemic and systematic abuses of human rights, we could think of no better way to assist world leaders in winning the fight than to educate them through an organisation dedicated to providing invaluable insight into issues of law and the intersection of politics and public policy on a global scale.

The Centre was formed to host scholarly conferences and produce scholarly papers on a wide range of current global issues, including religious freedom, counter-terrorism, international affairs, and national security, issues which the global community must deal with on a daily basis. The Centre brings together established and emerging leaders and subject-matter experts from around the world to discuss serious issues of global importance, pursue innovative solutions to such issues, and produce scholarly papers as a catalyst for further discussions and solutions.

The Centre held its inaugural symposium in March 2015 at Harris Manchester College, University of Oxford. Recent events bear poignant witness to the importance of the Centre's inaugural conference. Capturing global headlines during the fall of 2016, these events include the assassination of the Russian Ambassador to Turkey by an Islamic militant and the imprisonment on false charges of Pastor Andrew Brunson. At the time of this writing, Pastor Brunson faces grave danger in a Turkish prison where he is being held simply because of his Christian beliefs. The government of Turkey—led by an Islamic party—has begun increased crackdowns on Christians; and Pastor Andrew, if convicted, may face years in prison based on extremely serious—and false—charges. The ACLJ represents Pastor Brunson's family.

The title of our 2015 Symposium was *Persecution, Peace, and Reconciliation*. The presentations centred on Turkey and its role and influence in the Middle East. The keynote speaker was Mr Aykan Erdemir, Member of the Turkish Parliament and leader of the main Turkish opposition political party. Baroness Berridge of the Vale of Catmose, Member of the House of Lords, joined us and made welcoming remarks. Moreover, at least twenty symposium participants from six different countries on four different continents presented papers at the inaugural symposium, discussing various issues related to the Republic of Turkey, including, inter alia, religious freedom in Turkey; its history as the seat of the Ottoman Empire and the Islamic Caliphate; its growing Islamisation under the AKP; its relationship with other countries in the region, including Israel, Iran, Syria, and Cyprus; its role in fighting terrorism; and so on.

The Centre's inaugural symposium at Harris Manchester College was a resounding success. In light of that success, the Centre will meet annually at different venues around the world. At these meetings, participants will prepare, submit, and present scholarly papers on the particular topic chosen for that particular year. Scholarly papers were selected to be published in the *Journal of the Centre for the Study of Law & Public Policy at Oxford*.

This book, *Burning Bridges: Turkey's Return to Islamic Authoritarianism*, represents the best papers from the Centre's Journal and provides readers with well-researched, well-reasoned, scholarly papers on issues of vital concern. It is consistent with our objective to provide educators and policy-makers with salient information and the tools needed to craft policies on both domestic and international levels in order to fight religious persecution, terrorism, and other human rights abuses as well as to promote the rule of law in international affairs. Our hope is that this book, along with other scholarly papers and books, including the recent *New York Times* bestseller, *Unholy Alliance: The Agenda Russia, Iran and Jihadists Share for Conquering the World*, will encourage robust discussions among educators, policy-makers, and subject-matter experts alike regarding cutting-edge issues. The Centre's goal is to make the world a safer place for the oppressed and marginalised.

Dr Jay Alan Sekulow
President, Centre for the Study of Law & Public Policy at Oxford
Chief Counsel, American Center for Law & Justice and European
Centre for Law & Justice

FOREWORD: VIEWING TURKEY THROUGH AN AUTHORITARIAN MIST?

HARRY G. HUTCHISON

As David Benjamin has stated, "Turkey has long aspired to serve as a bridge between civilisations: between East and West, between Europe and Asia, between Islam and Christianity"[1]. On the other hand, present circumstances intrude on this ambition. Amidst complicating factors, fault lines are surfacing in Turkey's often-vexed relationship with Israel, the United States, Russia, Iran, Syria, Hamas and NATO. Additional complications arise due to Turkey's current autocratic turn that threatens to pull it further from its Western alliances and return it to its pre-modern past, a history that has often placed the nation at the centre of the troubled Middle East[2].

Among the most alarming events is fresh evidence that Russian President Vladimir Putin continues to outflank the United States. For example, Russia has taken a progressively more active role in Syria, a move that has been aided and abetted by Russia's improving relations with Iran. This move has been financed, at least in part, by billions of dollars flowing to Iran—the leading state sponsor of terror—because of the recently concluded nuclear deal and the corresponding relaxation of sanctions. Tangible corroboration of improved relations between Iran and Russia materialized in August of 2016, when Russia startled the West by launching bombers from a new base located in Iran, thus enabling Putin to strike more quickly with heavier bombardments

---

[1]   David Benjamin, *Turkey's Support for Hamas: A Bridge Too Far?*
[2]   Yaroslav Trofimov, *Turkey's Autocratic Turn*, THE WALL STREET JOURNAL, December 10, 2016 available at http://www.wsj.com/articles/turkeys-autocratic-turn-1481288401.

against U.S.-backed rebels in Syria[3].

In reality, the seeds of Russia's involvement in Syria and a reduction in Western influence in the Middle East were triggered when a young man set himself on fire to protest the oppressive regime in Tunisia in December 2010[4]. That moment sparked the first Arab Spring uprising and then spread like wildfire throughout the Middle East, culminating in a crackdown by Syrian president Bashar al-Assad, which led to a bloody civil war[5]. As a consequence of the ebb and flow of war, the Assad regime has increasingly relied on external support to retain power, primarily from Russia and Iran. Although both countries have long competed to expand their influence in the region, more recently, they have cooperated with one another. These developments coincide with the march of radical Islamic jihadists, who target the West and western political influence[6].

Apparently, these players are unified by a common purpose to constrain American influence around the globe[7]. This objective may be advanced by the emergence of what *Wall Street Journal* columnist Bret

---

[3]   Rowan Scarborough, The Washington Times, August 18, 2016 *available at* http://www.washingtontimes.com/news/2016/aug/18/vladimir-putin-ups-ante-in-challenge-of-us-dominan/

[4]   Jay Sekulow, Unholy Alliance: The Agenda Iran, Russia, and Jihadists Share for Conquering the World 161 (2016).

[5]   *Id.* at 162. Since the outbreak of war in 2011, more than three hundred thousand Syrians have been killed, and almost half the Syrian population has been forced to flee their homes in search of an escape from some of the worst humanitarian crises since World War II. *Id.*

[6]   *See e.g.*, Harry G. Hutchison, *Russian Strategic Quadrangle vs. United States*, American Center for Law and Justice, August 25, 2016, Blogpost available at http://aclj.org/middle-east/the-russian-strategic-quadrangle-russia-iran-turkey-and-radical-islam-team-up-to-thwart-the-united-states [hereinafter, Hutchison, *Russian Strategic Quadrangle*]. The quadrangle consists of Russia, Syria, Iran, Turkey and possibly China, which may then serve to strengthen the West's mortal enemy, radical Islam. *See id.* Recent evidence includes Russia's proposal to conduct joint naval exercises with the Chinese navy, a move that would encroach on Japan's territorial waters. *Id.*

[7]   *Id.*

Stephens calls the New Dictators Club[8]. This forecast may be particularly true if Syria operates as a catalyst, which levels out the often-turbulent historical relationship between Russia and Iran. The prospect of increasing cooperation between Russia and Iran can be understood by virtue of both nations' longing to increase their own power and influence in the Middle East[9]. This aspiration has become emboldened by the fact that Russia in particular, and perhaps Iran, believe that they are pushing against a largely open door[10] due to the Obama Administration's weakness in ceding power and influence to those willing to fill the vacuum[11]. American fecklessness issues forth from President Obama's demonstrable unwillingness to lead[12], coupled with his Administration's disorientation in the face of an ongoing reordering of the Middle East following the recent release of funds to Iran as a result of the Iran nuclear deal[13]. A newly bolstered Iran now has additional resources to finance and accelerate change within the Persian Gulf. Reacting to the changed circumstances on the ground, Turkey may find quite convenient the prospect of an alliance with nations that can be seen as past and future rivals[14]. This remains true despite its expressed distaste

---

[8]   Bret Stephens, *The New Dictators Club: An echo of the 1930s in the budding alliance of Russia, Iran, Turkey and China* THE WALL STREET JOURNAL, August 17, 2016, available at http://www.wsj.com/articles/the-new-dictators-club-1471908089. Ominously, this club echoes events that took place during the 1930s and 1940s when the governments of Japan, Italy and Germany pledged mutual support. *Id.* Within a span of five years, seventy million people would be killed as the result of an authoritarian effort to build a brave new world. *Id.*

[9]   SEKULOW, *supra* note___ at 165.

[10]   Charles Krauthammer, *The Price of Powerlessness*, THE WASHINGTON POST, August 18, 2016 available at https://www.washingtonpost.com/opinions/the-price-of-powerlessness/2016/08/18/f61d2c34-6575-11e6-96c0-37533479f3f5_story.html?utm_term=.952169af129f.

[11]   *Id.*

[12]   *Id.* Krauthammer's analysis tracks with the analysis offered by ACLJ Chief Counsel Jay Sekulow. *See e.g.*, SEKULOW, *supra* note___ at 10 (arguing that America's withdrawal from the Middle East has allowed Iran, Russia, and ISIS the opportunity to grown in strength).

[13]   Hutchison, *Russian Strategic Quadrangle*, *supra* note___.

[14]   Tiffany Barrans, *Turkey-Iran Relations: Pragmatic Economics & the Ideological Ceiling to Strategic Relations* 1 J. CTR. FOR STUDY OF L. & PUB. POL'Y AT OX-

for Russia and Iran's ally, Syrian president al-Assad. An alliance with former rivals may be a price Turkey is willing to pay to maintain its influence within the region, despite evidence that the unholy alliance of Russia and Iran is prepared to accommodate radical Islamic jihad whenever necessary to complicate the geopolitical picture for the West in the future. At the same time, history shows that while the bodies of children wash up on Greece's shores and despite evidence indicating that ISIS fighters have used the Turkish border as a transit point to the war-torn Middle East, the Turkish government—in an apparent effort to hedge its bets between Europe and NATO, on one hand, and its Middle Eastern friends, on the other—has been hesitant to fully invest the nation's political and ideological capital in the ongoing conflict with ISIS[15].

Complicating this complex picture are implications issuing forth from Turkish President Recep Erdoğan's increasing affection for authoritarianism, a position that has been reinforced by the recent failed coup and Russia's purported role in ensuring the coup's failure[16]. Whether the news reports regarding the coup are true or false, it seems clear that Russia is prepared to take full advantage of this situation as President Erdoğan continues to consolidate power. Despite Erdoğan's landslide victory in Turkey's first direct presidential election in 2014, which extended his 12-year grip on power[17], his ability to implement

FORD 27, 27 (2015); The Centre for the Study of Law & Public Policy at Oxford Research Paper No. 15-4. Available at SSRN: http://ssrn.com/abstract=2719980 (suggesting that the relationship between Turkey and the Islamic Republic of Iran has been mired with centuries of ideological and geopolitical friction and that even during waves of pragmatic cooperation, these unlikely friends will find themselves limited by ideological tension).

[15] Andrew Ekonomou, Robert Ash & Harry G. Hutchison, *Introduction*, 1 J. Ctr. For Study of L. & Pub. Pol'y at Oxford, iii, iii (2015); The Centre for the Study of Law & Public Policy at Oxford Research Paper No. 15-2; George Mason Legal Studies Research Paper No. LS 16-02. Available at SSRN: http://ssrn.com/abstract=2719971.

[16] *Hours Before Military Coup Attempt, Turkey Warned by Russia—Reports*, available at https://sputniknews.com/russia/20160721/104337382/russia-warned-turkey-coup-attempt.html.

[17] Joe Parkinson and Emre Peker, *Turkey Election: Erdogan Wins Landmark*

authoritarian rule has been thwarted by Turkey's democratic forces. During his victory speech, he called for societal reconciliation despite the hardening of divisions across the country; ominously, he warned his political enemies against undermining Turkish security[18].

Against this background, Russia's desire to reset the Turkish-Russian relationship has been previously blocked by the fallout from the Turkish military decision to shoot down a Russian military jet in November 2015[19]. Initial reporting after the downing of the Russian jet indicated that this event could make it more difficult for world leaders to convince Russia to join the U.S.-led, anti-Islamic State coalition, which includes Turkey[20]. Russian assistance in thwarting this summer's coup attempt appears to change everything by pulling Turkey even further into Russia's orbit[21] as Erdoğan now has a ready-made crisis that provides the justification to pursue his enemies on grounds of national security. Hence, despite Turkey's misgivings about working with one of Syria's allies, and even though both Turkey and Iran have had deep-seated differences, the evidence on the ground suggests the possible formation of a strategic partnership comprised of formerly rivalrous

Victory, The Wall Street Journal, August 11, 2014 available at http://www.wsj.com/articles/turks-cast-votes-in-presidential-election-witherdogan-primed-for-win-1407658125.

[18] *Id.*

[19] Natasha Bertrand, *Russia may be preparing a 'long-term, game-changing move' with Turkey*, Business Insider, August 5, 2016 available at http://www.businessinsider.com/russia-turkey-relations-coup-2016-8 (noting that "[e]fforts to reset the Turkish-Russian relationship after Turkey shot down a Russian warplane . . . have been underway since before July's attempted coup").

[20] Dion Nissenbaum, Empe Peker and James Marson, *Turkey Shoots Down Russian Military Jet*, The Wall Street Journal, November 24, 2016 available at http://www.wsj.com/articles/turkey-shoots-down-jet-near-syria-border-1448356509 (explaining that Turkish F-16s shot down a Russian military jet along the Syrian border sparking fury in Moscow that has threatened to undercut efforts to create a new international coalition to confront expanding Islamic State Terrorism).

[21] *See e.g.,* Neil MacFarquahar, *Warming Relations in Person, Putin and Erdogan Revive Pipeline Deal*, The New York Times, October 11, 2016, available at http://www.nytimes.com/2016/10/11/world/europe/turkey-russia-vladimir-putin-recep-tayyip-erdogan.html?_r=1.

nations on the prowl for tactical opportunities to advance short- and long-term goals that advance their mutual interest. Turkey, for instance, may see short-term benefits from this alliance because it may facilitate the Turkish military's capacity to block the transmission of cross-border support from Syrian and Iraqi Kurds to Turkey's often oppositional Turkish Kurdish population and thus improve its security. Turkey may have incentives to move down this path despite evidence that Syrian Kurds have attracted Western military and financial support because they are the most effective and reliable fighting force against ISIS. These events do not arise out of a vacuum.

Ever since 1910, during a war against rebels in remote Yemen, when a young officer of the Ottoman Empire, İsmet İnönü, played French and Italian operas to his soldiers, Turkey was primed to occupy a pivotal place in the world built on its own internal conflicts: an internal pull by elites drawn to the West in response to the decaying Ottoman Empire and a residual, deep-seated, and often hidden desire to return to its past as a shimmering Ottoman authoritarian state to which all or most of the world's Muslims look for leadership[22]. As is now well known, "Mustafa Kemal Atatürk, the secularist army officer who founded modern Turkey in 1923 sought to sever his land's ancient bonds to the Middle East"[23]. In the process, Turkey became a "rare example of a major Muslim country that is also a prosperous stable democracy"[24]. Or so we thought.

"Today that tradition is under attack as never before. Nearly a century after the Ottoman Empire gave way to today's Turkish republic, a tectonic shift is under way"[25]. Under the surly and increasingly iron-fisted rule of President Erdoğan, Turkey "is drifting away from its historic Western allies"[26] and looking "like just another troubled

---

[22] Trofimov, *supra* note____.
[23] *Id.*
[24] *Id.*
[25] *Id.*
[26] *Id.*

corner of the Middle East"[27]. Turkey is looking more and more like its Arab neighbors and "becoming infected with the same sickness-es—intolerance, autocracy and repression"[28]. Despite its position as a non-Arab state, Turkey has become plagued by one of the Arab world's most debilitating features: the advent of a culture of grievance that is defined more by what people oppose, than by what they aspire to, thus enabling the region's autocrats to adroitly channel public frus-tration toward external "enemies" and away from their own misrule[29]. Seduced by the possibilities of ruling without dissent, the failed coup, coupled with continued terrorist attacks[30], provides Erdoğan with an excuse to unleash an unprecedented crackdown[31]. But that is not enough for a man of Erdoğan's appetite. Instead, in a move that recalls the unlimited goals of the communist project that had an external and internal dimension as it sought to transform the world and demanded a radical transformation of society, culture and human beings[32], he now demands "constitutional changes[33] that would give him near-absolute authority and let him remain at the helm of this country of 80 mil-lion people until 2029"[34]. This maneuver, if successful, would permit him to extend his influence over the wider world. In reality, as Kemal

[27]   *Id.*

[28]   *Id.*

[29]   Scott Anderson, *Fractured Lands*, 1, 14, THE NEW YORK TIMES MAGAZINE, August 14, 2016.

[30]   *See e.g.,* Margaret Coker, *At Least 38 Dead, 150 Wounded in Istanbul,* THE WALL STREET JOURNAL, December 1, 2016 available at http://www.wsj.com/arti-cles/at-least-38-dead-150-wounded-in-istanbul-1481470024.

[31]   Trofimov, *supra* note___.

[32]   ALAIN BESANÇON, A CENTURY OF HORRORS: COMMUNISM, NAZISM, AND THE UNIQUENESS OF THE SHOAH (trans. By Ralph C. Hancock & Nathaniel H. Hancock) 46 (2007).

[33]   Emre Peker, *Turkey's Recep Tayyip Erdogan Seeks to Consolidate Power with Overhaul of Constitution,* THE WALL STREET JOURNAL, December 10, 2016, avail-able at http://www.wsj.com/articles/turkeys-recep-tayyip-erdogan-seeks-to-con-solidate-power-with-overhaul-of-constitution-1481384221 (the bill includes mea-sures that call for Turkey's president to run his own cabinet and acquire executive powers currently vested in the parliamentary government, enable government by decree and enable the current president to rule for two, five-year terms until 2029).

[34]   Trofimov, *supra* note___.

Kilicdarogul, the head of Turkey's largest opposition party, points out, Erdoğan's real objective is to take Turkey out of the Western bloc and turn Turkey into a Middle Eastern country that is shorn of secularism and rich in division along ethnic identity and beliefs[35]. If this prognosis is correct, Turkey has the potential to become just another Iraq, Syria or Libya[36], a Middle Eastern nation with global ambitions, staggering under the weight of plutocracy and nepotism that is braced by bloated bureaucracies[37].

These facts, taken together, signal that Turkey's relationship with the West and NATO is now in a state of flux that does not trend toward an optimistic outcome. Simultaneously, evidence on the ground suggests that Turkey's previously vibrant commitment to the rule of law has been fractured by the nation's response to the recent failed coup attempt[38]. Although the long-term consequences of the failed coup remain cloudy, the darkening trend is clear. Thus, it is foreseeable that Turkey's reputation will remain haunted as this proud nation descends into gloom and instability[39] birthed out of Erdoğan's limitless ambition reinforced by hubris. This situation is further compounded because the evidence shows that President Erdoğan suffers from delusions of grandeur that are deepened by mounting paranoia[40] as he seeks to return Turkey to its "rightful" role as the leader of the Islamic world. Corresponding with the ever-ramifying implications of this forecast, Turkey's tourism sector and much of its economy are already in free-fall[41]. As we have seen, this situation is compounded due to Turkey's security situ-

[35] *Id.*

[36] *Id.*

[37] Anderson, *supra* note___ at 13.

[38] *See* Bertrand *supra note*___ (noting that Erdoğan has drawn condemnation from the West for his decidedly undemocratic crackdown on those suspected of plotting or sympathizing with the coup).

[39] Harry G. Hutchison, *Turkish Coup: Democracy, Autocracy, Terror?*, AMERICAN CENTER FOR LAW AND JUSTICE July, 18, 2016, available at http://aclj.org/middle-east/the-turkish-coup-democracy-autocracy-and-the-rising-specter-of-terror [hereinafter, Hutchison, Turkish *Coup*].

[40] *Id.*

[41] *Id.*

ation – one destabilized by a wave of terrorism that reflects activity by Islamic state sympathizers and Kurdish nationalist opponents contributing to the decline in the value of Turkey's currency[42].

Given these facts, the world and the West, in particular, will discover that Turkey is a less-reliable ally and a less-predictable nation going forward. This is so because Erdoğan persists in implicating the West in Turkey's domestic politics[43] as he continues down a pathway that is littered with increasing strands of oppression. Because of the current state of flux in Turkey, the world and the West will discover that relations with the current Turkish government are likely to remain prickly. This signifies that the price of friendship with Turkey comes with a correlative risk of instability and unpredictability. Hence, one consequent remains clear: Turkey and Turkish policies are once again at the centre of any attempt to understand the Middle East and the geopolitics of the Persian Gulf. This indicates that Turkey ought to command acute attention from all observers who are interested in the future stability of the Middle East and the ongoing rivalry between the United States and Russia. In all likelihood, the Trump Administration will be required to devote more and more human capital to understand Turkey. Equally clear, such a reassessment will mean that Turkey may need to be treated as a former, as opposed to current, ally of the United States.

---

[42] *Id.*
[43] Ceylan Yeginsu and Daniel Victor, Erdoğan *Calls on U. S. to Arrest or Extradite Fethullah Gulen,* The New York Times, July 16, 2016 available at http://www.nytimes.com/live/turkey-coup-erdogan/erdogan-calls-on-u-s-to-arrest-or-extradite-fethullah-gulen/ (Erdoğan has accused Mr Gulen of being behind the coup attempt, a charge that Mr Gulen denies).

Editors'
Introduction:

The Centre for the Study of Law
& Public Policy at Oxford

Harry Hutchison, Andrew Ekonomou & Robert Ash

The past twenty-four months of world history bear poignant witness to a growing humanitarian disaster that envelops much of the Middle East and the Latin West as ISIS tries to maintain its grip on parts of Iraq and Syria and confirms its commitment to human savagery. This disaster has affected Turkey, which, in turn, has affected Western Europe. Indeed, some analysts believe that Syrian refugees fleeing to Turkey and thence to Europe were a contributing factor in Britain's vote to leave the European Union. Concurrent with such events, the West has concluded the negotiation of an Iran nuclear deal, an agreement that corresponds with unmistakable evidence of a resurgence in Russian support for its long-time ally[1], Syrian President Bashar al-Assad. Taking full advantage of this situation, President al-Assad, who is also allied with Iran, has reportedly inflamed the refugee crisis in order to tighten his grip on power[2]. Whilst bodies of toddlers wash up on Turkey's shores[3], whilst civilians flee Aleppo with alacrity whenever a truce is struck, and whilst evidence emerges showing that ISIS fighters continue to use the Turkish border as a transit point out

---

[1] See e.g., Chairman Royce, *U. S. Policy After Russia's Escalation in Syria*, Hearing before the Committee on Foreign Affairs, House of Representatives, 114th Congress, First Session, November 4, 2015, at 2 (stating that while President Obama characterizes Russia's moves as a sign of weakness, it is Assad who is growing stronger).

[2] Sam Dagher, Assad Inflames Refugee Crises, The Wall Street Journal, (Weekend), September 12-13, 2015.

[3] *See e.g.*, Lizzie Dearden, *Refugee crisis: Toddlers and children wash up dead on Turkish beaches after at least 39 drown in latest boat disaster*, The Independent, (30 January 2016), http://www.independent.co.uk/news/world/europe/refugee-crisis-toddlers-and-children-wash-up-dead-on-turkish-beaches-after-at-least-39-drown-in-a6843691.html

of the war-torn Middle East, the Turkish government, in an apparent effort to hedge its bets between Europe and the North Atlantic Treaty Organization (NATO), on one hand, and its Middle Eastern friends on the other, pauses to decide whether to fully invest the nation's political and ideological capital in the ongoing conflict with ISIS. At the same time, since this past summer's failed coup attempt, an event that has been followed by a string of bombings that have been punctuated by the assassination of the Russian ambassador[4], Turkey has taken a distinctly authoritarian turn, one that places Christians and other minorities at risk of being falsely charged and imprisoned without trial[5]. Turkey and Turkish policies are once again at the centre of any attempt to understand the Middle East. This prompts historians and others to recall the Ottoman Empire, which has apparently provided fodder to prompt delusions of grandeur among Turkey's current leadership. Consequently, strategic analysts are forced to revisit the contemporary and ancient history of the land that gave birth to the Ottoman Empire.

The Centre for the Study of Law & Public Policy at Oxford (the Centre), in concert with others, has taken up this daunting effort. The Centre, which houses several scholars who have served as Visiting Fellows at the University of Oxford, was established in Great Britain, in order to : (1) provide research and examine the history, legal principles, and public policies that underlie the international rule of law, international law, international relations, global economics, the global provision of healthcare, and related subjects; (2) make recommendations on how to improve each of the aforementioned areas and to educate the public regarding them; (3) organise and sponsor forums where subject matter experts on the foregoing topics

---

[4] Tim Arango and Rick Gladstone, *Russian Ambassador to Turkey Is Assassinated in Ankara*, The New York Times, (19 December 2016), available at http://www.nytimes.com/2016/12/19/world/europe/russia-ambassador-shot-ankara-turkey.html.
[5] 3 Jordan Sekulow, ACLJ.org, (14 December 2016) available at http://aclj.org/persecuted-church/american-pastor-andrew-brunson-wrongfully-imprisoned-in-turkey.

may gather to discuss ways to improve the laws and public policies applicable to each subject area; and (4) draft and produce books, notes, papers, pamphlets, and the like to capture the suggestions for improvement and to disseminate them for consideration by governments, academics, public interest groups, and others.

Responding to the events in the Middle East, the Centre hereby issues the papers presented during the Centre's inaugural Spring 2015 *Persecution, Peace, and Reconciliation Symposium* in this volume. This Symposium, which took place at Harris Manchester College of the University of Oxford, assembled a number of religious, policy, and legal experts to present various papers that considered the nation of Turkey: its history, its future, its insularity and its relationship with a number of countries that have important national interest in the near East. During a three-day period, the participants partook in a vigorous discussion that touched on Iran, Israel, Greece, Egypt, Cyprus, China, and the United States. Additional presentations focused on Turkey's relationship with Hamas as well as its fraught relationship with its non-Muslim population, the role of religion in Turkey as well as the politics of Turkey during the Holocaust. The Symposium brought together a diverse group of individuals representing more than eleven languages including a member of the Turkish Parliament, a member of the British House of Lords, a representative of the Ecumenical Patriarch of the Greek Orthodox Church, a legal and policy expert from the People's Republic of China, Visiting Fellows from the University of Oxford, individuals who have practiced law before the United States Supreme Court, the European Court of Human Rights and the International Criminal Court, and Oxford University graduate students in politics.

This volume contains seven articles which deal with Turkey. The first article authored by Dr Jay Sekulow is entitled *Turkey-Israel Relations*. Dr Sekulow, building on his experience as a member of the Summer Research Institute at Oxford, litigation experience as

Chief Counsel at the American Center for Law & Justice (ACLJ) and the European Centre for Law & Justice (ECLJ), highlights the fact that the relationship between Turkey and Israel is unique in the Muslim world. This world has become more fraught because, as Alan Dershowitz shows, the "greatest danger the world faces in the twenty-first century is an Iranian nuclear arsenal," and this danger may be intensified by virtue of the recently concluded Iran nuclear deal[6]. On the other hand, while most Muslim-majority nations have declined to recognise Israel, Turkey was the first Muslim-majority nation to do so. Dr Sekulow examines the secular roots of modern Turkey, the shifting sympathies of Turkish leaders under the guidance of a number of Islamist theorists, and the current status of the Turkey-Israel relationship under the direction of the leader of the Justice and Development Party (AKP), Recep Tayyip Erdoğan. Emerging as a continuation of the Welfare Party, the AKP's platform was rife with promises to re-orient toward the West, to respect a secular Republic, and to depart from political Islam in favour of a secular, conservative democracy. At the same time, many saw the issue of Turkish-Israeli relations as a benchmark for measuring the sincerity of the AKP's promise to instantiate a secular, Western-oriented government. At the present time, relations between Turkey and Israel show that Turkey's stance regarding Israel reflects a complex mix of religious ideology and political expediency that appears to include a burgeoning relationship with terrorist groups like Hamas. Hence, as this article suggests, the most optimistic forecasts are likely to suggest that this state-to-state relationship is likely to remain fragile.

The second paper in this volume is entitled *The Mavi Marmara Trial: Politicising the Turkish Justice System*. The paper offers a window into the increasingly politicised Turkish Justice System. Robert Ash, a senior lawyer with both the ACLJ and ECLJ, military expert, student of international affairs and a Founding Fellow of the Centre, clarifies

---

[6] Alan Dershowitz, The Case Against the Iran Deal: How Can We Stop Iran from Getting Nukes? 3 (2015).

the facts arising about of the 31 May 2010 clash between Israeli forces
and vessels of the Free Gaza Flotilla. The Mavi Marmara, a Comoros-
flagged vessel led by a Turkish Master with a Turkish crew, sought
to breach the Israeli naval blockade of the Gaza Strip. The ensuing
melee resulted in the deaths of nine passengers and serious injury to
other passengers as well as Israeli commandos. This event became
the opening act of a criminal inquiry that resulted in the attempt
by the Turkish government to try Israeli military officers for acts
that it would excuse with respect to its own public servants. Mr Ash
shows that the Mavi Marmara trial, representing the misapplication
of Turkish criminal and procedure law, is a political show trial that
neither comports with the minimal requirements for a fair trial nor
seeks to ascertain the truth and do justice. This trial, which violates the
Law of Armed Conflict, is part of a Turkish effort to impose Turkey's
view of applicable law on Israel. Beyond the trial's political motivation,
it makes a mockery of the rule of law and has turned the Turkish
judicial system into an object of ridicule.

The third paper considers the politics of Turkey during the
Holocaust. Authored by Stuart Roth, who is Senior Counsel with
both the ACLJ and the ECLJ, and a Senior Fellow of the Centre, the
paper, *The Politics of Turkey During the Holocaust*, takes as its point
of departure the systematic destruction of European Jewry during
the Holocaust. The methodological murder of six million Jews was
perpetrated not only by the Germans, but with the collaboration of
numerous countries that served as direct or indirect accomplices to
genocide. Turkey, by way of contrast with England, the United States,
and others, played a crucial role in rescuing Jews through the efforts of
its embassies and served as an uneasy escape route to Palestine due to
its geographic proximity. To be sure, Turkish efforts do not represent
a coherent organised government effort to rescue or repatriate Jews;
but, nonetheless, the humanitarian efforts of individual diplomats in
saving Jews needs to be acknowledged. Providing background on the

history of the Jews in the Ottoman Empire, Turkey's turn toward "Turkification" and the adverse effects of this effort on Jews, Turkey's invitation to Jewish scholars from Germany and Austria during World War II, and the effects of German anti-Semitism in Turkey, Mr Roth shows that Turkey's efforts, whilst not heroic, stand in stark contrast with American Anti-Semitism and Britain's policy aimed at appeasing the Arab population in Palestine. Despite Turkey's efforts, it is clear that Turkey could have done more.

The fourth paper in this volume is authored by David Benjamin, a lawyer who serves Of Counsel to the ACLJ. The paper, *Turkey's Support for Hamas: A Bridge Too Far*, shows that Turkey has become an operational base for Hamas. Despite Hamas' preference for an Arab country as its base, placing its base in Turkey provides a challenge to Turkey's relationship with both Israel and the United States. It may also weaken Turkey's credibility in confronting terror threats from the Islamic State of Iraq and al-Sham (ISIS) as well its ongoing confrontation with terror threats surfacing within its Kurdish population. Nonetheless, many commentators suggest that Turkey has a "model partnership" with the U.S. along with long-standing ties with the European Union. Turkey is also a long-standing member of NATO (since 1952). Still, if Turkey wants to remain a bridge between the Middle East and the West, it must acknowledge that allowing Hamas to operate a terror base on its soil is a "bridge too far".

Nathaniel Bennett, Research Associate of the Centre and Director of Government Affairs for the ACLJ, authored the fifth paper, which concentrates on the relationship between Turkey and the United States. The paper is entitled *Turkey and the United States : Friends or Foes?* Mr Bennett demonstrates that the United States has long viewed its alliance with Turkey as one of strategic importance both economically and symbolically. Turkey has served as a bridge between the East and West, but signs of strain—if not fracture—emerge as Turkey's leaders increasingly identify themselves as Islamic rather than secular. The seeds of conflict are spreading as Turkey deals with the deepening refugee crisis that has led the European community to essentially pay Turkey to maintain and sustain refugees who are a collateral consequence of the ongoing conflict in Syria. Such consequences, in combination with Turkey's undulating relationship with Israel, represent a stark challenge to U. S.-Turkey relations. Additional challenges to this relationship issue forth from Iran, the leading state sponsor of terror. This is so because Iran harbours ambitions of becoming the leading power in the Islamic world, a perspective that directly challenges the ambitions of President Erdogan that are made tangible by his thirst for power and his willingness to discount democratic norms. In addition, if Turkey's leadership implements its preference for Islamic authoritarianism rather than the rule of law, conflicts between Turkey and the U.S. are likely to remain front and centre for quite some time.

Marshall Goldman, Senior Research Associate of the Centre and Senior Associate Counsel at the ACLJ, has written the sixth paper in this volume, which is entitled *Turkey, Cyprus, and the Turkish Republic of Northern Cyprus*. He examines the vexed relationship between Turkey, Cyprus, and the Turkish Republic of Northern Cyprus. Turkey, Greece, and Cyprus have faced the challenges arising out of a civil war as both Turkey and Greece have vied for influence and control. Emerging out of the most recent conflict is the question of whether the Turkish Republic of Northern Cyprus has ever achieved the status of statehood within the parameters of international law. This question obviously implicates the fall of the Ottoman Empire following World War I and the severely contested Treaty of Sèvres of 1920. Because Turkey never ratified the Treaty of Sèvres, it was replaced in 1923 by the Treaty of Lausanne, which many Turks saw as a great victory that delineated the boundaries of the modern state of Turkey. Following World War II, the Cyprus question intensified because of Greece's effort to end British rule and unify the island with the Greek mainland. After many decades of conflict and in response to Greek attempts to incorporate Cyprus into Greece, Turkish Cypriot leaders issued a unilateral declaration of independence as they established the Turkish Republic of Northern Cyprus (TRNC). This declaration prompts persistent questions about the status of the TRNC within the bounds of international law.

The seventh and final paper, *L'Église Catholique et l'Anatolie (The Catholic Church and Anatolia)* is authored by Grègor Puppinck, Andreea Popescu & Christophe Foltzenlogel [hereinafter, Puppinck], all of whom are affiliated with the ECLJ. Grègor Puppinck is an internationally known author with expertise in the arena of religious liberty. Puppinck's article, *The Catholic Church and Anatolia*, explores the special relationship between the Catholic Church and Anatolia, which can be explained by the common and turbulent history of these two entities. Rome and Constantinople were two capitals of the Roman Empire. Nonetheless, Anatolia has gradually moved away from Rome although the Catholic Church has strengthened its authority from the tomb of St. Peter. Wars, religious quarrels and invasions have created a difficult and unstable relationship. However, efforts have been made to re-establish a closer union with the Orthodox churches, but no attempt has succeeded in completely healing the rifts. Relations between Catholic Rome and Anatolia remain under stress as Turkey continues to retain its undeniably important international role because of its location and power. Turkey's exercise of unbridled power has also led to much suffering for Catholics, who are still subject to local power without the possibility of a real "appeal to the Pope". Beyond the situation of Christians and Catholics in Anatolia, relations between Rome and Anatolia still largely determine the relationship between Turkey and Europe. The political process of re-Islamisation of Turkey and its current neo-Ottoman discourse tends to give fundamental importance to the religious dimension of the relationship between Turkey and Europe.

Turkey-Israel Relations

Jay Alan Sekulow*

Introduction

Turkish-Israeli relations are unique in the Muslim world. While most Muslim-majority nations have not recognised the State of Israel, Turkey has. In fact, despite its "No" vote in the United Nations General Assembly regarding the UNSCOP Plan, Turkey

*Dr Sekulow is a Founding Fellow of the the Centre for the Study of Law & Public Policy at Oxford. He has also been a Visiting Fellow at Harris Manchester College, University of Oxford, where he has lectured on Middle East Affairs and International Law. Dr Sekulow has served as a member of the Summer Research Institute at Oxford from 2013 to 2015. He is Chief Counsel at the American Center for Law & Justice (ACLJ), Washington, DC, and at the European Centre for Law & Justice (ECLJ), Strasbourg, France. Dr Sekulow received his Bachelor of Arts (B.A.) degree (*cum laude*) from Mercer University, Macon, Georgia; his Juris Doctor (J.D.) degree (*cum laude*) from Mercer Law School, where he served on the Mercer Law Review; and his Doctor of Philosophy (Ph.D.) degree from Regent University, with a dissertation on American Legal History. In his legal career, Dr Sekulow has argued 12 cases before the Supreme Court of the United States, several of which have become landmark cases in the area of religious liberty litigation. He is a Distinguished Professor of Law at Regent University School of Law where he teaches courses on Constitutional Law and Supreme Court History. He has also served as a faculty member for the Office of Legal Education at the United States Department of Justice. In addition, Dr Sekulow is a respected broadcaster who hosts a nationally syndicated radio broadcast that is carried by more than 950 radio stations. He also makes frequent guest appearances on nationally televised news programmes on FOX News, ABC, CBS, NBC, CNN, MSNBC, CNBC, and PBS. He is a prolific author of books, pamphlets, and law review articles and is the author of the recent #1 *New York Times* bestselling book, *Rise of ISIS: A Threat We Can't Ignore*.

was nonetheless the first Muslim-majority nation to recognise the newly established State of Israel. There have, in fact, been periods when the two nations worked closely together and had strong ties in pursuit of common interests. The relationship between the two countries strengthened as Turkey sought to retain strong ties with the West and emphasised the fact that Turkey was a secular, democratic republic. The relationship between Turkey and Israel has deteriorated significantly since Turkey's Islamist political parties have gained power and have denigrated Israel as Turkey sought to re-establish its leadership in the Sunni world. This paper discusses Turkey's historically amicable relations with Israel under Turkey's secular governments and how the Turkish relationship with Israel has changed due to the increasing Islamisation of the Turkish government, which, in recent years, has pushed Turkish-Israeli relations to an all-time low.

I. SECULAR BASIS OF MODERN TURKEY UNDER ATATÜRK

Modern Turkey has its roots in the once-powerful Ottoman Empire, an empire that experienced a long decline that led to its final collapse following World War I. The war hastened the Ottoman Empire's decline and resulted in the partition of the empire under the Treaty of Sèvres[1], a treaty of peace between the Ottoman government and the Allied Powers, signed on 10 August 1920[2]. The treaty was orchestrated by the Allied Powers who were concerned with the preservation of "their existing commercial and economic privileges in Turkey"[3]. As with all treaties following WWI, the terms of the Treaty of Sèvres were harsh: they imposed enormous reparation payments, divided the land of the once-vast Ottoman Empire, stripped the

---

[1] Treaty of Peace with Turkey, 10 Aug. 1920, GR. BRIT. T.S. No. 11 (1920) (Cmd. 964).

[2] A.E. Montgomery, *VIII. The Making of the Treaty of Sèvres of 10 August 1920*, 15 HIST. J. 775 (1972).

[3] *Id.* at 782.

Empire of its ability to govern its economy, and placed restrictive limits on the size and ability of the Ottoman military[4]. Especially galling for the Turks was the massive award of territory to the victors, including Greece[5]. The Treaty of Sèvres also included the ceding of the land of Palestine and acceptance of the Balfour Declaration—which ultimately led to the creation of the British Mandate for Palestine[6].

The last Ottoman sultan, Sultan Muhammad VI, accepted the Treaty of Sèvres, which, though painful and humiliating, left the Sultan with a rump empire[7]. Nonetheless, backed by popular dissent, Mustafa Kemal Atatürk, a young military leader inspired by European progress and secular ideas, gained power[8]. Atatürk led a nationalistic rebellion in a war for Turkish independence in which they defeated the Greeks, deposed the Sultan, and forced a conference at Lausanne to revise the terms of the Treaty of Sèvres[9], a treaty that never went into effect. The negotiations at Lausanne resulted in the Treaty of Lausanne, signed on 24 July 1923[10]. The revised treaty defined the borders of modern-day Turkey in return for Turkey's renunciation of its claim to all other land that comprised the former Ottoman Empire[11].

Even prior to the Lausanne peace conference, Atatürk had been the driving force behind the creation of the Great National Assembly in Ankara, a representative parliamentary body of which Atatürk was president[12]. Turkey was formally proclaimed a republic on 29 October

---

[4] Philip Marshall Brown, *From Sèvres to Lausanne*, 18 Am. J. Int'l L. 113, 113–14 (1924).

[5] *Id.* at 113.

[6] *See* Treaty of Peace with Turkey, *supra* note 1, at art. 95.

[7] Patrick Karl O'Brien, Oxford Atlas of World History 179 (2002).

[8] *Brief History of Republic of Turkey*, U. Mich., http://www.umich.edu/~turkish/links/reptr_brhist.html (last visited 19 Feb. 2015).

[9] *Id.*

[10] Brown, *supra* note 4, at 113.

[11] Treaty of Peace with Turkey, 24 July 1923, *in* II The Treaties of Peace 1919–1923 (1924), *available at* http://wwi.lib.byu.edu/index.php/Treaty_of_Lausanne.

[12] *Mustafa Kemal Atatürk*, Republic of Turkey MFA, http://www.mfa.gov.tr/ mus-

1923, and Atatürk became its first president[13]. Atatürk implemented swift and drastic measures to bring about the secularisation of Turkey. He abolished the caliphate in 1924, banned the Arabic language and removed Islam as the official State religion in 1928, instituted bans on traditional Islamic dress for both men and women, and modeled Turkey's legal system on European civil codes, even going so far as to create a parliament elected by universal male suffrage, which, in 1934, was extended to include women[14].

Atatürk remained Turkey's president until his death in 1938[15]. His successor, Ismet Inönü, "warily steered a neutral course through the first five years of World War II"[16]. Atatürk's political and social reforms, followed by Inönü's choice to side with the Allies in World War II, resulted in a post-WWII Turkey that was strongly aligned with the West[17]. This same shift, along with Turkey's rejection of Islamic values in the public square, had a large influence on Turkey's relations with the nascent State of Israel, created in 1948[18]. Following the conclusion of World War II, Turkey took further steps to align itself with the West, such as its participation in the 1945 conference that founded the United Nations[19]. A major step in realigning with the West was Turkey's decision to join NATO, an alliance established to contain the USSR[20].

---

tafa-kemal-ataturk.en.mfa (last visited 19 Feb. 2015).

[13] *Id.*

[14] *Brief History of Republic of Turkey, supra* note 8; *see also Mustafa Kemal Atatürk, supra* note 12.

[15] *Id.*

[16] *Brief History of Republic of Turkey, supra* note 8.

[17] *See* JOHN M. VANDERLIPPE, THE POLITICS OF TURKISH DEMOCRACY 1 (2012).

[18] *Kemal Atatürk (1881–1938),* BBC HISTORY, http://www.bbc.co.uk/history/historic_figures/ataturk_kemal.shtml (last visited 10 Mar. 2015).

[19] *Brief History of Republic of Turkey, supra* note 8.

[20] DAN ARBELL, CTR. FOR MIDDLE EAST POL'Y AT BROOKINGS, THE U.S.-TURKEY-ISRAEL TRIANGLE 4 (2014); *see also* David Kushner, *Before and Beyond The "Freedom Flotilla": Understanding Turkish–Israeli Relations,* 4 ISR. J. FOREIGN AFF. 21, 21 (2010).

At the same time, Turkey's relationship with Israel began on somewhat rocky ground when Turkey was one of thirteen States that voted against the United Nations Partition Plan for Palestine, a plan based on the UN Special Committee on Palestine's call for the partition of Mandatory Palestine and the establishment of a Jewish State alongside an Arab State[21]. Despite its opposition to the original plan, on 28 March 1949, Turkey became the first Muslim-majority nation to recognise the State of Israel[22]. Following this recognition, the two governments quickly established diplomatic ties[23]. Turkey and Israel shared many common regional interests, interests that they attempted to protect by establishing military and economic ties with one another[24]. Essentially, "[b]oth viewed themselves as pro-Western, secular, and democratic 'outsiders' in the region . . ."[25].

Turkey and the growing Israeli State had common interests, to be sure, but as early as 1956 their differences—and the political realities of the Middle East—began to put a strain on the relationship. For instance, Turkey was aligned with Iraq under the 1955 Baghdad Pact[26]. This alliance, an attempt to form a military alliance similar to NATO in order to thwart an expansionist USSR across the Middle East, ultimately resulted in the formation of the Central Treaty Organization (CENTO)[27]. In the fallout of the 1956 Sinai

---

[21] ISR. STATE ARCHIVES, *Introduction* to ISR. STATE ARCHIVES, ISRAEL-TURKEY RELATIONS, 1961–1967, [hereinafter ISRAEL-TURKEY RELATIONS, 1961–1967] *available at* http://archives.gov.il/archivegov_eng/publications/electronicpirsum/ Israel-turkey/israel-turkeyintroduction.htm.

[22] Kushner, *supra* note 20, at 21.

[23] ISRAEL-TURKEY RELATIONS, 1961–1967, *supra* note 21.

[24] Matthew S. Cohen & Charles D. Freilich, *Breakdown and Possible Restart: Turkish–Israeli Relations Under the AKP*, 8 ISR. J. FOREIGN AFF. 39, 40 (2014).

[25] *Id.*

[26] *Central Treaty Organization (CENTO)*, ENCYCLOPEDIA IRANICA, http://www.iranic aonline.org/articles/central-treaty-organization-cento-a-mutual-defense-and-economic -cooperation-pact-among-persia-turkey-and-pakistan-wi (last visited 10 Mar. 2015).

[27] *Id.*

Campaign[28], Turkish Prime Minister Adnan Menderes pressured the government to terminate relations with Israel, a move that he felt would show solidarity with Iraqi Prime Minister Nuri as-Said, who had publicly condemned the Israeli, French, and British invasion of Egypt[29]. Ultimately, the Turkish government compromised by downgrading its level of relations with Israel from "that of ministers to [that of] chargé d'affaires"[30].

Despite this reduced level of official relations between Israel and Turkey, changes in the region led Turkey to reconsider its approach. Egypt and Syria had formed the United Arab Republic in 1958, and the pro-Western Iraqi monarchy had been overthrown[31]. Thus, Turkey felt threatened. Israel's sense of isolation, coupled with Turkey's similar sense of isolation, once again led the two nations to establish more friendly relations. Secret meetings between Israeli Prime Minister David Ben-Gurion and Turkish Prime Minister Adnan Menderes resulted in a series of agreements to cooperate through diplomacy, economics, and the military[32]. These agreements, which lasted into the mid-1960s, comprised the Peripheral Alliance, also called the Periphery Pact because it linked Turkey, Israel, Iran, and Ethiopia, countries on the periphery of the Middle East[33].

Although the Peripheral Alliance benefitted both countries, it technically existed in secret[34]. The Turkish government had never fully normalised its relations with Israel following the Sinai Campaign; however, when a civilian government led by the former

---

[28] The Sinai Campaign of 1956 was Israel's move to root out "Palestinian guerrilla incursions from Egypt and to try to remove an Egyptian blockade of its port of Ei-lat". *1956: The Sinai Campaign*, BBC NEWS (6 May 2008), http://news.bbc.co.uk/2/hi/ middle_east/7377716.stm.

[29] ISRAEL-TURKEY RELATIONS, *supra* note 21.

[30] *Id*.; *see also* ARBELL, *supra* note 20, at 5.

[31] Kushner, *supra* note 20, at 22; *see also* ARBELL, *supra* note 20, at 5.

[32] Kushner, *supra* note 20, at 22; *see also* ARBELL, *supra* note 20, at 5.

[33] *Id*.; ISRAEL-TURKEY RELATIONS, *supra* note 21.

[34] ARBELL, *supra* note 20, at 5.

Prime Minister, Ismet Inönü, took power in 1961, Israel thought that relations could be restored[35]. Turkey, however, had other ideas. Turkish leaders made overtures that they intended to normalise relations but only at the "'right time'", a time that seemed to never come[36]. This hedging on the part of Turkey revealed an important reality about Turkey's view of its own relationship with Israel: "[D]espite its clear interest in developing and maintaining closer ties with Israel, Turkey simultaneously tried to keep Israel at arm's length because of Turkey's desire to be on good terms with the Arab bloc"[37].

Following the relative success of the Peripheral Alliance, success that accompanied the two nations' increasing economic cooperation, the "Cyprus question" began to negatively affect Turkish-Israeli relations. In a nutshell, the Cyprus question involves the conflict between the Greek Cypriot population's desire for "Enosis", full unification with Greece, and the Turkish Cypriot population's desire to form two separate states, dividing the island between the two communities[38]. Initially, Israel had taken sides with Turkey on the issue, but when Cyprus gained independence in 1960 and its president became an independent ruler, Israel had hoped to improve relations with Cyprus[39]. Although Israel had attempted to remain neutral after hostilities and a series of violent riots broke out on Cyprus—due to the Cypriot President having demanded a constitutional amendment that would have reduced the rights of the Turkish minority—Turkey responded harshly to a supportive message that Israel had sent to the Cypriot president, further weakening the relationship between Turkey and Israel[40].

---

[35] ISRAEL-TURKEY RELATIONS, 1961–1967, *supra* note 21.

[36] *Id.*

[37] ARBELL, *supra* note 20, at 5; *see also* ISRAEL-TURKEY RELATIONS, 1961–1967, *supra* note 21.

[38] *Factbox: Key Issues in Cyprus Dispute*, REUTERS (10 Nov. 2009), http://www. reuters.com/article/2009/11/10/us-cyprus-conflict-factbox-idUSTRE5A94EV20091 110.

[39] ISRAEL-TURKEY RELATIONS, 1961–1967, *supra* note 21.

[40] *Id.*

By the late 1960s, it had become apparent that Turkey was shifting its political sympathies toward the Arab world. The Turkish government voiced strong objections to the situation before, during, and after the Six-Day War of 1967, all the while claiming technical neutrality[41]. However, Turkish statements in opposition to Israel marked a shift in Turkey's position[42]. For instance, in reaction to Israel's capture of territory as a result of the Six-Day War, Turkish Prime Minister Demirel said, "'I am against annexing territory by force. If that door is opened, there will be no end to it'"[43]. At an emergency UN General Assembly session immediately following the Six-Day War, Turkey voted against the Soviet-proposed resolution that "demanded [Israel] withdraw its armed forces from the occupied territories and pay compensation to the Arab countries"[44]. However, Turkey worked with several other Muslim nations to draft a proposal that was ultimately adopted[45]. This resolution provided that Israel would not extend Israeli law's jurisdiction to East Jerusalem and would avoid doing so in the future[46].

The global oil crisis of the 1970s had a dramatic effect on Turkey's economy, leading it to pursue even closer relations with its Arab neighbors, to the further detriment of its relations with Israel[47]. Turkey strengthened its economic ties with Iraq and Libya, two Arab countries awash in oil[48]. At the same time, Turkey took several public actions that demonstrated its shift toward a more pro-Arab and anti-Israel stance. For instance, in 1975 Turkey recognised the Palestinian Liberation Organization (PLO) as the sole representative of the Palestinian people[49]. It also voted to adopt UN General Assembly

[41] *Id.*; ARBELL, *supra* note 20, at 6.
[42] *Id.*; *see also* Kushner, *supra* note 20, at 22.
[43] ISRAEL-TURKEY RELATIONS, 1961–1967, *supra* note 21.
[44] *Id.*
[45] *See id.*
[46] *Id.*
[47] *See* ARBELL, *supra* note 20, at 6.
[48] *Id.*; *see also* Kushner, *supra* note 20, at 22.
[49] ARBELL, *supra* note 20, at 6.

Resolution 3379 which equated Zionism with racism[50]. In 1979, Turkey allowed Yasir Arafat to open a PLO office in Ankara[51]. The most significant action came as a reaction to Israel's 1980 Jerusalem Act, which combined East and West Jerusalem into a unified capital[52]. Turkey responded to the Act by officially downgrading diplomatic relations with Israel "to the level of second secretary"[53]. It also leveraged the Jerusalem Act in its favour, using the incident to obtain financial assistance from concerned Arab nations[54].

Following a period of decline in Turkish-Israeli relations, there was a period of improvement and growth in relations between the countries from the late 1980s into the 1990s. Turkey finally formalised its diplomatic relations with Israel when it upgraded Israel's representation to the level of ambassador in 1991[55]. Israel was surprised by this development, but the upgrade followed on the heels of the 1991 Madrid Conference and reflected Turkey's desire to play a larger role in the peace talks[56].

Turkey's more friendly relationship with Israel during this period was largely driven by the growing role that the military played in Turkey's domestic politics[57]. Turkey hoped to take advantage of military cooperation with Israel in order to further its own regional aspirations[58]. Leading up to the 1990s, Turkey's relationship with its European allies and with the United States had grown increasingly strained because of issues with its Kurdish population, such that during the 1990s, Turkey found it "hard to obtain Western technology

[50] G.A. Res. 3379 (XXX), U.N. Doc. A/RES/3379 (XXX) (10 Nov. 1975), *revoked by* G.A. Res. 46/86, U.N. Doc. A/RES/46/86 (16 Dec. 1991).

[51] ARBELL, *supra* note 20, at 6.

[52] *Id.*; *see also* Kushner, *supra* note 20, at 22.

[53] *Id.*

[54] *Id.*

[55] Arbell, *supra* note 20, at 6; *see also* Kushner, *supra* note 20, at 23.

[56] Özlem Tür, *Turkey and Israel in the 2000s—From Cooperation to Conflict*, ISR. STUDIES, Fall 2012, at 45, 47.

[57] *Id.* at 47.

[58] *Id.*

and military equipment"[59]. Turkey's improved relations with Israel "was a pragmatic approach by which the military-bureaucratic elite could counter the challenges posed by Turkey's European allies"[60].

In addition to the military benefits Turkey received from an improved relationship with Israel, Turkey also improved its relations with Israel because of the economic benefits reaped by both parties[61]. In the interest of preserving their economic growth, officials in both nations avoided "public political support for one another on internationally controversial issues"[62]. Apparently, this toned-down approach paid off for both countries, as they conducted several high level visits throughout the 1990s. In February 1996, the two nations instituted a military cooperation agreement providing for joint military exercises, joint air force and naval training, and Israel's sale of missiles and jet planes to Turkey[63]. The agreement also placed a strong focus on fighting extremism and terrorism in the region[64].

During Turkish President Demirel's March 1996 visit to Israel, the two nations reached a Free Trade Agreement[65]. The agreement provided for "cooperation in areas such as investment, construction, manufacturing, environment", and more[66]. "This high-level cooperation withstood even the year-long term of office (1996–97) of the government headed by the Islamist leader Necmettin Erbakan, as well as ongoing pressure emanating from popular sympathies toward" the

---

[59] *Id.*

[60] *Id.*

[61] ARBELL, *supra* note 20, at 7; *see also* Kushner, *supra* note 20, at 23.

[62] Alan Makovsky, *Turkish-Israeli Ties in the Context of Israeli-Arab Tension*, THE WASH. INST. (10 Nov. 2000), http://www.washingtoninstitute.org/policy-analysis/view/turkish-israeli-ties-in-the-context-of-israeli-arab-tension.

[63] ARBELL, *supra* note 20, at 7; *see also* Kushner, *supra* note 20, at 23; Tür, *supra* note 56, at 48.

[64] *Id.*

[65] Soner Cagaptay & Tyler Evans, *The Unexpected Vitality of Turkish-Israeli Trade*, RES. NOTES: THE WASH. INST., June 2012, at 1.

[66] Tür, *supra* note 56, at 48.

Palestinians[67]. Turkey's renewed relationship with Israel also drew the ire of Arab nations. For instance, the Lebanese daily newspaper, *al-Safir*, wrote that "the alliance was directed against all Arabs, and that it exclusively served Israeli interests at the expense of Arab and Muslim interests"[68].

The relationship between Turkey and Israel grew stronger as the 1990s drew to a close, but in Turkey, political opposition to Israeli relations began to gain a foothold. When Necmettin Erbakan and the Refâh Partisi (Welfare Party) briefly gained office in 1996, Erbakan vowed to "eliminate all traces of this 'Jewish-based system' and reorient Turkey from the Jewish-led West (including the EU) towards the Muslim world"[69]. Thus, in the mid-to-late 1990s, Turkish relations with Israel became a sticking point in domestic Turkish politics— Turkey's military bureaucracy sought to strengthen relations, while Islamist political parties, like the Welfare Party, strove to weaken such relations[70].

Despite the growing domestic disagreement, Turkish Chief of General Staff Huseyin Karadayi visited Israel in 1997 and Israel reciprocated with visits to Ankara by Foreign Minister David Levy and Defence Minister Yitzhak Mordechai, a sign that Turkish-Israeli relations remained strong in the face of the Welfare Party's growing opposition[71]. By 2002, trade had more than doubled, from $449 million in 1996 to over $1.2 billion[72].

Several events during the period at the close of the 20th century had a negative effect on Turkish-Israeli relations. First, the capture of Kurdistan Workers' Party (PKK) leader Abdullah Ocalan and the effective defeat of the PKK itself removed a military threat that

---

[67] Kushner, *supra* note 20, at 23.

[68] Tür, *supra* note 56, at 48.

[69] *Id.* at 49.

[70] *Id.*

[71] *Id.*

[72] Cagaptay & Evans, *supra* note 65, at 1.

had driven Turkish foreign policy since the 1980s[73]. Second, the Adana Accords with Syria removed the threat to Turkey's southern border, thereby allowing Turkey to place less emphasis on the military necessities that had motivated it to repair relations with Israel[74]. In addition, Turkey's grant of candidate status before the EU led it to shift its goals toward reform and "the adoption of a more EU-style foreign policy orientation and instruments"[75].

The Justice and Development Party's (AKP) 2002 electoral victory—building on reform that had begun under the previous coalition government, which included the Islamist Fazilet (Virtue) Party—was the beginning of a significant decline in Turkish-Israeli relations[76]. The AKP was formed in August 2001 by a group of Islamist politicians including, Recep Tayyip Erdoğan, Abdullah Gül, and Bülent Arınç[77]. Many in the political sphere viewed the AKP as merely a continuation of the Erbakan-led Welfare Party[78]. The AKP gained a majority in the 2002 elections, forming Turkey's first majority government since the 1980s[79]. The AKP's platform included promises to re-orient toward the West, to respect a secular Republic, and to depart from political Islam in favour of a secular, conservative democracy[80]. At the time of the AKP's rise to power, many Turkish writers saw the issue of Turkish-Israeli relations as a benchmark for measuring the sincerity of the AKP's promise to institute a secular, Western-oriented government[81]. The AKP's subsequent moves to

---

[73] Tür, *supra* note 56, at 50.

[74] *Id.*

[75] *Id.*

[76] Cohen & Freilich, *supra* note 24, at 39.

[77] Hakan Yavuz, *Adalet ve Kalkinma Partisi (AKP)*, Oxford Encyclopedia Islamic World, http://www.oxfordislamicstudies.com/article/opr/t236/e0924?_hi=0&_pos=8 (last visited 10 Mar. 2015).

[78] Tür, *supra* note 56, at 51.

[79] *Id.*; *see also* Thomas Patrick Carroll, *Turkey's Justice and Development Party: A Model for Democratic Islam?*, Middle East Intelligence Bulletin, June/July 2004, http://www.meforum.org/meib/articles/0407_t1.htm.

[80] Tür, *supra* note 56, at 51.

[81] *Id.*

harm Turkish relations with Israel, discussed in detail below, can, therefore, be seen as evidence that the AKP's original promises of reform were less than totally honest.

Erdoğan in particular played a large role in orchestrating the creation of the AKP, a party that "emerged from the ashes of the mostly Islamist entities of [the] Welfare and Virtue [P]arties that were closed down by the Constitutional Court on charges of being a forum for and proponent of anti-secular activities"[82]. Erdoğan spent his early political career as part of the Welfare Party, making his breakthrough in 1994 when he was elected Mayor of Istanbul[83]. Although the Welfare Party achieved brief success when it joined in a coalition government in 1996, the party head, Necmettin Erbakan, "became Turkey's first defiantly Islamist prime minister"[84]. Erbakan was a vocal proponent of the idea that the political violence Turkey experienced in the 1970s was caused by Zionism alone[85]. This view—now referred to as political Islam—has endured within Turkish political parties despite the ban of the National Salvation Party (NSP) in 1981 and the Welfare Party in 1998[86].

Erbakan's policies led to what was called a "post-modern coup": he was ousted from office in 1997, and the military led investigations against several Islamic groups that had gained ground during Erbakan's government[87]. Erdoğan was affected by these investigations

---

[82] Yavuz, *supra* note 77.

[83] Mustafa Akyol, *The Making of Turkey's Prime Minister*, HURRIYET DAILY NEWS (31 Oct. 2010), http://www.hurriyetdailynews.com/default.aspx?page-id=438&n=the-making-of-tayyip-erdogan-2010-10-31.

[84] *Id.*

[85] Rifat N. Bali, *The Image of the Jew in the Rhetoric of Political Islam in Turkey*, CEMOTI (1999), http://www.cemoti.revues.org/590#quotation.

[86] Seth J. Frantzman, *Terra Incognita: Will Erdogan Ever Overreach?*, JERUSALEM POST (12 Mar. 2014), http://www.jpost.com/Opinion/Columnists/Terra-Incogni-ta-Will-Erdogan-ever-overreach-345195.

[87] *Turkish Generals Go on Trial Over 1997 'Post-Modern Coup'*, REUTERS (2 Sep. 2013), http://www.reuters.com/article/2013/09/02/us-turkey-army-coup-idUS-BRE98 10B220130902.

in 1998 when he received a ten-month prison sentence for a speech in which he criticised the dissolution of the Welfare Party[88], a result of Turkey's Constitutional Court banning the party[89]. Specifically, Erdoğan had quoted lines from a poem dealing with the Turkish War of Liberation: "'The mosques are our barracks, the domes our helmets, the minarets our bayonets and the faithful our soldiers'"[90]. In addition to the ten-month sentence, Erdoğan was ostensibly banned from politics for the rest of his life[91].

Despite his political ban, in 2001 Erdoğan and others formed the AKP. When the party won a majority in 2002, Erdoğan, as party head, could not become the prime minister because his 1998 political ban was still effective[92]. Abdullah Gül, another founding member of the AKP, became the prime minister, but in December 2002, the Supreme Election Board canceled the general election results because of voting irregularities[93]. The new election took place on 9 February 2003, but, in the meantime, the government changed the law to renew Erdoğan's eligibility for political office[94]. After Erdoğan won a parliamentary seat in the by-election, he was asked to form a new government[95]. Gül duly resigned his post as the AKP Prime Minister to make way for Erdoğan, and in 2003, less than five years after supposedly being banned from politics forever, Erdoğan became the Prime Minister of Turkey[96].

Erdoğan entered office with a foreign policy situation that allowed him to justify building close relationships with Muslim nations at the

---

[88] Frantzman, *supra* note 86.

[89] Yavuz, *supra* note 77.

[90] Akyol, *supra* note 83.

[91] Yavuz, *supra* note 77.

[92] Akyol, *supra* note 83.

[93] *Id.*

[94] *Turkish PM Quits for Erdogan*, CNN (11 Mar. 2003), http://edition.cnn.com/2003/ WORLD/europe/03/11/turkey.elections/.

[95] *Id.*

[96] *Id.*; *see also* Akyol, *supra* note 83.

expense of Turkey's relationship with Israel. For instance, the Iraq War "and the common threat perceptions of other regional powers such as Syria and Iran, brought Turkey closer to these countries"[97]. A specific event that increased Turkey's reputation in the Muslim world was its rejection of the 1 March 2003 Resolution that would have allowed the United States to open a northern front in the Iraq War[98]. Regional developments—such as the "Arab Spring" uprisings in Tunisia and Egypt—were opposed by Israel but well received by Turkey, yet another disconnect in the relationship between the two[99].

Even before the AKP's rise to power, Erdoğan and other party leaders made public statements against Israel and in favour of the Palestinian cause, a trend that would only grow as the AKP remained in power. For instance, after Ariel Sharon took power in Israel, Erdoğan was quoted as saying: "The Sharon government is in fact moving in the direction of state terrorism"[100]. Then-Prime Minister Bulent Ecevit called Israel's actions toward Palestine a "genocide", and another top AKP official, Bülent Arınç, compared Israeli Prime Minister Sharon to Adolf Hitler[101]. The timing of Erdoğan's statements about Israel and Palestine—directly before the Organisation of Islamic Cooperation elections where Turkey was vying for the presidency—strongly suggests that he was using the Palestinian issue to his political advantage[102].

These statements and many similar examples from the time after the AKP took power were a signal of the gradual decline in relations between Turkey and Israel that would occur during the first decade of the millennium. Some claimed that the AKP's harsher stance toward Israel was undertaken because a majority of Turkish citizens were

---

[97] Tür, *supra* note 56, at 51.

[98] *Id.* at 57.

[99] *Id.* at 59–60.

[100] *Id.* at 53.

[101] *Id.*

[102] *Id.*

sympathetic to the Palestinian cause[103]. The effect of such statements was that Turkey's relationship with Israel grew increasingly strained, while its relationship with Muslim countries in the region grew stronger[104]. By 2005, Turkish-Israeli relations had reached a new low, due in part to Erdoğan's refusal to meet with Israel's Deputy Prime Minister Olmert in July 2004[105]. On the same day that Erdoğan ignored his scheduled meeting with Olmert, he, instead, met with Syrian Prime Minister el-Otri[106].

In the face of such tension between the two countries, they also made efforts to repair relations. Multiple Turkish representatives, including Abdullah Gül, traveled to Israel in late 2004 and early 2005, and Turkish Chief of General Staff İlker Başbuğ[107] led a military dialogue meeting[108]. In 2005, Turkey signaled an earnest desire to mend relations, a shift that was shown in Erdoğan's May 2005 visit to Israel[109]. This attempt to mend relations was likely pragmatic, as the AKP desired to foster close relations among Middle East nations, not to mention the reality that it had also strained Turkey's relations with the US since coming to power and the surest way to improve those relations was to soften its stance toward Israel[110].

Yet, in 2006, Turkey became the first non-Arab country to officially meet with Hamas when a Hamas delegation led by Khaled Meshaal visited Ankara following Hamas' victory in the Palestinian

---

[103] *Id.*

[104] *Id.* at 54.

[105] *Id.*

[106] *Id.*

[107] İlker Başbuğ was arrested in 2012 "on charges of leading a terrorist organization aimed at toppling the democratically elected government". *Turkey's Former Chief of Staff* **İlker** *Başbuğ Released from Jail After Top Court Ruling*, HURRIYET DAILY NEWS (7 Mar. 2014), http://www.hurriyetdailynews.com/turkeys-former-chief-of-staff-ilker-basbug-released-from-jail-after-top-court-ruling.aspx?page-ID=238&nid= 63321.

[108] Tür, *supra* note 56, at 54.

[109] *Id.*

[110] *Id.* at 55.

parliamentary elections[111]. The Israeli Prime Minister, through a spokesman, stated that Turkey's reception of Hamas was "'a mistake that can deeply hurt [bilateral] relations'", and so it did[112]. With tense relations due to the Palestinian question still lingering, Turkey attempted to mediate Israel's dispute with Syria[113]. This mediation seemed to be successful throughout 2008, but when Israel initiated Operation Cast Lead at the close of 2008, relations took a nose dive from which they have not since recovered[114].

After receiving word that Israel had begun Operation Cast Lead, Erdoğan accused Israel of hypocrisy, saying that Israelis spoke of peace in one place while "killing and bombing children" in another[115]. At the January 2009 World Economic Forum in Davos, Erdoğan confronted President Shimon Peres, saying, "'When it comes to killing, you know well how to kill'"[116]. Turkey followed these comments by excluding Israel from their previously scheduled joint military exercises[117]. In this same period, a nationally syndicated Turkish TV series named *Ayrilik* depicted Israeli soldiers as blood-thirsty killers who enjoyed killing Palestinian civilians at random[118]. It was in this political climate that a Turkish NGO began making plans to join in the Free Gaza Movement, an attempt to break Israel's naval blockade of Gaza.

---

[111] *Id.*; *Hamas' Meshaal: We Received Support and Advice from Turkey*, HURRIYET DAILY NEWS (17 Feb. 2006), www.hurriyetdailynews.com/default.aspx?pageid=438 &n=hamas-meshaal-we-received-support-and-advice-from-turkey-2006-02-17.
[112] Tür, *supra* note 56, at 55.
[113] *Id.*
[114] *Id.* at 56.
[115] *Id.*
[116] *Id.* at 56; *see also* Katrin Bennhold, *Leaders of Turkey and Israel Clash at Davos Panel*, N.Y. TIMES (29 Jan. 2009), http://www.nytimes.com/2009/01/30/world/europe/30clash.html?_r=0.
[117] Tür, *supra* note 56, at 56.
[118] *Id.*; *see also* Donald MacIntyre, *Israel Vents Fury at Ally Turkey over 'Barbaric' TV Drama*, INDEP. (16 Oct. 2009), http://www.independent.co.uk/news/world/middle-east/israel-vents-fury-at-ally-turkey-over-barbaric-tv-drama-1803653.html.

II. The Mavi Marmara Incident

After Hamas gained control of Gaza in 2006, Israel instituted a naval blockade of Gaza to help restrict the flow of military and militarily useful goods into the Hamas-controlled region[119]. In response, several groups worked together to organise a flotilla that would attempt to break the naval blockade[120]. Among the main organisers was the Turkish charity, the Humanitarian Relief Foundation (IHH)[121].

On 30 May 2010, Israel attempted to avoid a confrontation with the flotilla by offering it dockage at an Israeli port so the goods being shipped could be inspected and transported to Gaza, but the flotilla refused[122]. The flotilla's refusal inexorably led to the Israelis' having to enforce the blockade by military means. When Israeli forces boarded the flotilla's six vessels on 31 May 2010, the only vessel whose passengers chose to fight was the Mavi Marmara, a vessel owned and controlled by IHH members[123]. The IHH activists "attacked Israeli soldiers with steel clubs and knives as the soldiers were being lowered onto the deck by helicopters"[124]. The Israeli soldiers were forced to return fire in self-defence, and nine activists were killed with several more wounded[125].

In response to the Mavi Marmara incident, Erdoğan accused Israel of lying about the IHH's possession of weapons, calling the raid "'inhumane state terrorism'"[126]. He made his, and Turkey's, position

---

[119] Joshua Mitnick, *Flotilla Assault Spurs Crisis*, Wall St. J. (1 June 2010), http://www.wsj.com/articles/SB10001424052748703703704575277632709673018.
[120] *Id.*
[121] *Id.*
[122] *Id.*
[123] Marc Champion & Margaret Coker, *Turkish Charity Group Sounds Defiant Note*, Wall St. J. (4 June 2010), http://www.wsj.com/articles/SB10001424052748704025304575284081264400448.
[124] Mitnick, *supra* note 119.
[125] *Id.*
[126] Sabrina Tavernise, *Raid Jeopardizes Turkey Relations*, N.Y. Times (31 May 2010),

clear when he also said, "'today is a turning point in history. Nothing will be the same again'"[127]. Further anti-Israel rhetoric was spoken by Turkish officials at an emergency UN Security Council meeting, a meeting that was called for by Turkey[128]. At the meeting, then-Foreign Minister Davutoğlu referred to Israel's actions as "'banditry and piracy . . . murder conducted by a state . . . and barbarism'"[129]. Turkey's actions in response to the incident included expulsion of the Israeli ambassador from Turkey[130], recalling its own ambassador from Israel, cancelling joint military exercises, halting cooperation in the energy field, and demanding that Israel publicly apologise, compensate the victims' families, and lift the blockade of Gaza[131].

RELATIONSHIP SINCE 2010

When the United Nations published the so-called Palmer Report after a year-long investigation into the Mavi Marmara incident, Turkey continued its acrimonious rhetoric. The UN report found that Israel's actions in forming the blockade were legal, albeit its use of force in the boarding question was "'excessive and unreasonable'"[132]. Then-Turkish President Gül called the ruling "'null and void'", while Erdoğan said "'it means nothing to us'"[133]. In other remarks about the UN report and the incident itself, Erdoğan stated that the Mavi Marmara incident was "cause for war but we decided to act in line with

http://www.nytimes.com/2010/06/01/world/middleeast/01turkey.html.

[127] Marc Champion, *Turkey Lashes out at Israel and Denounces 'Massacre'*, WALL ST. J., 2 June 2010, at A11.

[128] Carol Migdalovitz, *Israel's Blockade of Gaza, the* Mavi Marmara *Incident, and Its Aftermath*, CONG. RES. SERV. 5 (23 June 2010), https://www.fas.org/sgp/crs/mideast/R41275.pdf. *See also* Robert Weston Ash, *The Mavi Marmara Trial: Politicising the Turkish Justice System*, 1 J. CTR. FOR STUDY OF L. & PUB. POL'Y AT OXFORD 49 (2015).

[129] *Id.*

[130] *Israel and Turkey: Can It Get Worse?*, THE ECONOMIST (10 Sept. 2011), http://www.economist.com/ node/21528687.

[131] Migdalovitz, *supra* note 128, at 14.

[132] *Israel and Turkey: Can It Get Worse?*, *supra* note 130.

[133] *Id.*

Turkey's grandeur and showed patience"[134].

The Mavi Marmara incident was the culmination of the tension that had grown between Turkey and Israel regarding the Palestinian issue. As discussed previously, Erdoğan and the AKP took political advantage of popular Turkish support for the Palestinian people, but the AKP's support of Hamas and Hamas' continuing policy of violence toward Israel are indications that there are deep ideological ties between the two groups.

Hamas is not formally considered a terrorist organisation in Turkey although most of Turkey's Western allies consider it to be one[135]. Despite being a NATO member and an aspiring member of the European Union, questions about Turkey's allegiances have arisen for several reasons[136]. For one, Erdoğan has gone on record stating that Hamas is not a terrorist group and he has repeatedly vowed to visit Gaza[137]. Further, top AKP officials have met with top Hamas leadership since as early as 2006 for the purpose of developing the relationship between the two groups; this occurred at the same time that Turkey's relationship with Israel suffered[138]. In Ankara,

---

[134] Suzan Fraser, *Turkey: Gaza Flotilla Raid Was 'Cause for War'*, World Post (12 Sept. 2011), http://www.huffingtonpost.com/2011/09/12/turkey-gaza-flotilla-raid_n_958362.html.

[135] "Hamas is on the list of terrorist organizations of the United States, the European Union, Canada and several other countries, but not on that of the UN Security Council and it is not considered a terrorist organization in Turkey." Pinar Tremblay, *Is Turkey Hamas' New Headquarters?*, Al Monitor (25 Aug. 2014), http://www.al-monitor.com/pulse/originals/2014/08/turkey-palestine-israel-gaza-hamas-meshal-kidnapping.html. *But see* Alan Cowell, *European Court Reverses Designation of Hamas as a Terrorist Organization*, N.Y. Times (17 Dec. 2014), http://www.nytimes.com/2014/12/18/world/europe/hamas-palestinian-statehoodvote-european-parliament.html (reporting that a European Union court has reversed this designation for the bloc on 17 December 2014).

[136] Jonathan Schanzer, *Why Is Turkey Sheltering a Dangerous Hamas Operative?*, Foreign Pol'y (17 Sept. 2013), http://foreignpolicy.com/2013/09/17/thorn-in-the-side/.

[137] *Id.*

[138] Fadi Elhusseini, *Will Erdogan Visit Gaza?*, Wash. Inst. (28 June 2013), http://www.washingtoninstitute.org/policy-analysis/view/will-erdogan-visit-gaza.

Erdoğan has held highly publicised meetings with Hamas leader Khaled Meshaal and the Gaza administration's Prime Minister, Ismail Haniyeh[139].

Although President Erdoğan has never followed through on his plans to personally visit Gaza[140], through his meetings with top Hamas officials, Erdoğan and his government have attempted to further the Palestinian cause in Gaza. Usame Hamdan, a Hamas spokesperson, said that at the 2013 meetings, Erdoğan and the Hamas leadership discussed "the construction of Israeli settlements and Israel's 'imposition policies' aimed at the Palestinian economy"[141]. Another topic that was discussed at the meeting was Turkey's hope that Hamas could come to a reconciliation with the other main Palestinian representative group, Fatah[142]. Other top AKP officials attended the meetings, including then-Foreign Minister Ahmet Davutoğlu, a man who was appointed Prime Minister after Erdoğan assumed the presidency in 2014[143].

In addition to aiding Hamas on a national political level, including the donation of over $300 million of "foreign aid"[144], Turkey has also allowed many Hamas operatives to operate out of Turkey. Among the most notorious Hamas members to be given shelter in Turkey is Saleh al-Arouri, a man who is identified by Hamas as the founder of the Izz al-Din al-Qassam Brigades[145]. Arouri is generally seen as the head of Hamas operations originating in Turkey, and he is believed to have planned the Summer 2014 kidnapping of three Israeli teens,

[139] *Turkish PM Erdoğan Meets Hamas Leader Meshal and Gaza PM Haniyeh*, HURRIYET DAILY NEWS (18 June 2013), http://www.hurriyetdailynews.com/turkish-pm-erdogan-meets-hamas-leader-meshal-and-gaza-pm-haniyeh.aspx?pageID=238&nID=49066&NewsCatID=338.
[140] Elhusseini, *supra* note 138.
[141] *Turkish PM Erdoğan Meets Hamas Leader, supra* note 139.
[142] *Id.*
[143] *Id.*
[144] Schanzer, *supra* note 136.
[145] *Id.; Saleh Al-Aruri*, AL-QASSAM, http://www.qassam.ps/prisoner-37-Saleh_Al_Aruri.html (last visited 5 Jan. 2015).

the kidnapping that led to the 2014 Gaza War[146]. A 2014 news report quoted an anonymous Hamas member as confirming "that Turkey is indeed used as a base by Hamas operatives led by Salah al-Arouri, a Hamas leader based in Turkey who has amassed significant power within the terror group's infrastructure and directs his own wing from the NATO country"[147].

Beyond Arouri himself, Turkey has consistently hosted other Hamas operatives, including ten Hamas members who were released by Israel as part of the 2011 deal to free kidnapped Israeli soldier Gilad Shalit[148]. Many of these operatives were in prison following convictions for murder and kidnapping; yet, in Turkey, they "attend local universities, join Turkish organizations, and play a role in its politics, and also appear to travel freely into and out of the country"[149].

Further, an Israeli news source reported in February 2015 that: "Turkey has become a Hamas hotbed, and members of the organization's military wing are undergoing military training on Turkish soil, with the knowledge, support and assistance of the local authorities"[150]. The report claims that Hamas has set up a "West Bank and Jerusalem Headquarters" in Istanbul after it was expelled from Damascus in 2011[151]. This source asserts that Arouri recruits West Bank and Gaza Strip residents studying in Arab nations and then sends them to military training camps outside of Istanbul[152]. The

---

[146] Yoni Ben Menachem, *Hamas' New Base in Turkey*, Jerusalem Ctr. For Pub. Aff. (29 Dec. 2014), http://jcpa.org/hamas-new-base-turkey/.

[147] Aaron Klein, *Hamas Admits: 'We Have Headquarters in Turkey'*, WND (2 Dec. 2014), http://www.wnd.com/2014/12/hamas-admits-we-have-headquarters-in-turkey/.

[148] Jonathan Schanzer, *Lying Down With Dogs*, Foreign Pol'y (20 Aug. 2014), http://foreignpolicy.com/2014/08/20/lying-down-with-dogs/.

[149] *Id.*

[150] Alex Fishman, *Forced from Damascus, Hamas Establishing Itself in Turkey*, ynetnews.com (02 Feb. 2015), http://www.ynetnews.com/articles/0,7340,L4630331,00.html.

[151] *Id.*

[152] *Id.*

report claims that recruits are then sent to Syria to further enhance their military capabilities and then sent right back to the West Bank and the Gaza Strip to join Hamas operatives there[153].

In August 2015, Israeli news reported that Turkey has asked Arouri to leave the country[154]. While Hamas denied this claim[155], Turkish Foreign Ministry informed media that "Arouri is not in Turkey at the moment"[156]. Hamas further claimed that Arouri "'is carrying out his activities as usual and is travelling between a number of countries, including Turkey, Qatar and Lebanon'"[157]. The source also said, this "'does not mean that Turkey has expelled [Arouri]'"[158].

Interestingly, in December 2014, eight months prior to the news of Arouri's departure from Turkey to Qatar, Turkey had concluded a joint agreement with Qatar to establish a Supreme Strategic Committee[159]. This was among the first in a series of steps taken after Erdoğan's victory in Turkey's 2014 elections that demonstrates his intentions for Turkey's future. The Emir of Qatar said that one goal of the agreement was to focus on "the importance of restoring the rights of the Palestinian people"[160]. Jonathan Schanzer, an expert in Middle East history and the Vice President for Research at the Foundation for

---

[153] Id.

[154] Hamas Denies Israeli Claims of Official's Expulsion from Turkey, MEMO (7 Aug. 2015), https://www.middleeastmonitor.com/news/middle-east/20289-hamas-denies- israeli-claims-of-officials-expulsion-from-turkey.

[155] Id.

[156] Sevil Erkus, Turkey: Hamas Leader Arouri Not in Turkey, HURRIYAT DAILY NEWS (12 Aug. 2015), http://www.hurriyetdailynews.com/turkey-hamas-leader-arouri-not-in-turkey-.aspx?pageID=238&nID=86851&NewsCatID=510.

[157] Hamas Denies Israeli Claims of Official's Expulsion from Turkey, supra note 154.

[158] Id.

[159] Qatar, Turkey Take Bold Step for Strategic Cooperation, HURRIYET DAILY NEWS (19 Dec. 2014), http://www.hurriyetdailynews.com/qatar-turkey-take-bold-step-for-stra-tegic-cooperation.aspx?PageID=238&NID= 75852&NewsCatID=510.

[160] HH the Emir, Turkish President Sign Agreement to Establish Supreme Strategic Committee, QATAR NEWS AGENCY (19 Dec. 2014), http://welcomeqatar.com/en/emir-turkish-president-sign-agreement/.

Defense of Democracies, described the Supreme Strategic Committee with Qatar as Turkey's agreement to "jointly pursue aggressive foreign policies that the two countries have embraced separately for the better part of a decade", adding that "Hamas is undeniably a significant part of that joint agenda"[161].

On 27 December 2014, Hamas political bureau chief, Khaled Meshaal, appeared at an AKP assembly in Konya, Turkey[162]. Meshaal met with President Erdoğan in Ankara prior to the AKP assembly, but Prime Minister Ahmet Davutoğlu was present at the Konya rally[163]. Meshaal gave a short speech that was frequently interrupted by the chants of Palestinian flag-waving AKP supporters who cried, "'Allahu akbar'" (God is great), and, "'Down with Israel'"[164]. In his speech, Meshaal praised the people of Turkey "for having Davutoğlu and President Recep Tayyip Erdoğan"[165]. Meshaal was also quoted as saying, "A strong Turkey means a strong Jerusalem and a strong Palestine. . . . Inshallah [God willing], we will liberate Jerusalem together. A strong Turkey is a source of power for all Muslims"[166].

For his part, Prime Minister Davutoğlu also gave a speech in which he said, "God is witness . . . . we will make this red flag [the Turkish national flag] a symbol of the innocent. This red flag will fly side-by-side with the flags of Palestine, free Syria and all other

---

[161] Jonathan Schanzer & David Andrew Weinberg, *The Turkey-Hamas Nexus*, The Nat'l Interest (16 Jan. 2015), http://nationalinterest.org/feature/the-turkey-hamas-nexus-12044?page=2.

[162] Pinar Tremblay, *Meshaal's Visit to Turkey Catches Media Off Guard*, Al-Monitor (28 Dec. 2014), http://www.al-monitor.com/pulse/originals/2014/12/turkey-gaza-top-hamas-officials-unannounced-visit.html.

[163] *Hamas Leader Mashaal Endorses Turkish Leaders in Surprise Speech*, Hurriyet Daily News (27 Dec. 2014), http://www.hurriyetdailynews.com/hamas-leader-mashaal-endorses-turkish-leaders-in-surprise-speech.aspx?PageID=238&NID=76166&NewsCatID=352.

[164] *Id.*; *see also* Tremblay, *supra* note 162.

[165] *Hamas Leader Mashaal Endorses Turkish Leaders*, *supra* note 163.

[166] Tremblay, *supra* note 162.

innocents' flags anywhere in the world"[167]. Davutoğlu also stated that "Turkey will do whatever needs to be done to protect Jerusalem and the al-Aqsa Mosque"[168].

Then, on 6 January 2015, reports emerged that the Qatari government had deported Hamas leader Khaled Meshaal after allowing him to stay in the country for the past three years[169]. The Israeli Foreign Ministry congratulated the Qatari government on the decision and implored the Turkish government to "follow suit"[170]. However, most commentators expected Meshaal to simply relocate to Turkey, based on President Erdoğan's past relationship with Meshaal[171]. Hamas officials denied the claims that Meshaal had been deported[172]. A Hamas official named Ezzat al-Rishq was quoted as saying, "'There is no truth to what some media outlets have published over the departure of my brother Khaled Meshaal from Doha'"[173]. Senior Middle East analysts for the Jerusalem Center of Public Affairs reported that Meshaal has not left Qatar[174].

---

[167] *Meshaal: Democratic Turkey Means a Strong Palestine*, MA'AN NEWS AGENCY (30 Dec. 2014), http://www.maannews.net/eng/ViewDetails.aspx?ID=750074; *see also* Kellan Howell, *Hamas Leader: Turkey Is a 'Source of Power for All Muslims'*, WASH. TIMES (27 Dec. 2014), http://www.washingtontimes.com/news/2014/dec/27/hamas-leader-meshaal-turkey-is-a-source-of-power-f/.

[168] Burak Bekdil, *Why Hamas Feels So At Home In Turkey*, MIDDLE EAST FORUM (1 Jan. 2015), http://www.meforum.org/4956/why-hamas-leader-khaled-mashaal-feels-so-at-home.

[169] Elhanan Miller, *Hamas Leader Mashaal Said Deported from Qatar*, TIMES OF ISRAEL (6 Jan. 2015), http://www.timesofisrael.com/hamas-leader-mashaal-said-deported-from-qatar/.

[170] *Id.*

[171] *Id.*; *see also Report: Hamas' Mashaal Expelled from Qatar, Heading for Turkey*, TODAY'S ZAMAN (6 Jan. 2015), http://www.todayszaman.com/diplomacy_report-hamas-mashaal-expelled-from-qatar-heading-for-turkey_369063.html.

[172] Robert Tait, *Fate of Exiled Hamas Leader Unclear After Reported Expulsion to Turkey*, TELEGRAPH (6 Jan. 2015), http://www.telegraph.co.uk/news/worldnews/middleeast/israel/11328804/PICandPUB-Fate-of-exiled-Hamas-leader-unclear-after-reported-expulsion-to-Turkey.html.

[173] *Id.*

[174] Paul Alster, *Suspicions of Turkey, Hamas Alliance Stoke Fears in Israel*, FOX NEWS (4 Mar. 2015), http://www.foxnews.com/world/2015/03/04/turkey-red-carpet-for-hamas-stokes-fears-in-israel/.

The most noteworthy recent development occurred on 12 January 2015, when Palestinian Authority (PA) President Mahmoud Abbas made an official visit to the presidential palace in Ankara where he met with President Erdoğan[175]. The meeting marked the first time that the Turkish president welcomed Abbas according to the official protocols for receiving a Head of State[176]. The two officials took pictures in front of an array of Turkish soldiers in historical military uniform, sixteen different uniforms to represent the sixteen empires of Turkish history that "are also symbolized in the sixteen stars of the official seal of the Turkish presidency that has been given a new prominence since Erdoğan moved from the office of the prime minister after August's presidential elections"[177].

At their private meeting, Erdoğan and Abbas discussed "the repercussions of the failure of the UN Security Council (UNSC) to adopt a draft resolution setting a deadline to end Israel's occupation of Palestinian territories, issues related to Palestinian statehood and the reconstruction of war-torn Gaza following the Israeli offensive last year"[178]. They were also expected to discuss the ties between the two governments and the amount of aid given to Palestine by the Turkish government[179]. In Turkey's 2015 budget, over $200 million have been allocated to help rebuild the Gaza Strip[180]. In addition, the Turkish State-run Turkish International Cooperation and Development Agency (TİKA) began a campaign to build 1,000 homes in Gaza as a part of the rebuilding campaign[181].

---

[175] *Abbas Welcomed at Turkish Presidential Palace by Erdoğan – And 16 Warriors*, GUARDIAN (12 Jan. 2015), http://www.theguardian.com/world/2015/jan/12/abbas-erdogan-16-warriors-turkish-presidential-palace.

[176] Sena Alkan, *Abbas Meets Erdogan as Leaders Show Unity to End Israeli Occupation*, DAILY SABAH (13 Jan. 2015), http://www.dailysabah.com/politics/2015/01/13/abbas-meets-erdogan-as-leaders-show-unity-to-end-israeli-occupation.

[177] *Abbas Welcomed at Turkish Presidential Palace by Erdoğan, supra* note 175.

[178] Alkan, *supra* note 176.

[179] *Id.*

[180] *Id.*

[181] *Id.*

These recent events demonstrate that Turkey and the AKP appear to be doubling-down on their policy of backing the Palestinian cause in spite of the harm that this approach causes to Turkish-Israeli relations. Notably, Erdoğan's formal reception of Abbas as a Head of State came after Erdoğan's victory in Turkey's presidential election[182]. With his move to the office of president, Erdoğan extended his and the AKP's "12-year grip on power" in Turkey[183]. In his victory speech, Erdoğan said that his rise to the presidency signaled the closing of doors to one era and the "first step to a new phase"[184]. If the history of Erdoğan's time in power, not to mention his first actions as president, is a lesson, then this "new phase" will continue the recent trend of decline in Turkish-Israeli relations and rise in Turkish-Palestinian relations.

CONCLUSION

The historical development of relations between Turkey and Israel, including the recent changes wrought by the AKP, show that Turkey's stance regarding Israel is driven by a mix of religious ideology and political expediency. In the early relationship between the two countries, although they experienced periods of stress, they managed to forge a strong relationship based on the mutual military and economic benefits of their relations. However, the rise of Islamist political parties in Turkey, including the NSP and the Welfare and Virtue Parties, directly harmed Turkey's relations with Israel while simultaneously strengthening Turkey's ties with Arab nations and terrorist groups like Hamas. The current party in power, the AKP, is a continuation of Islamist parties that were previously banned, and the AKP's initial promises of reform were misleading, perhaps to reduce

---

[182] Joe Parkinson & Emre Peker, *Turkey Election: Erdogan Wins Landmark Victory*, WALL ST. J. (11 Aug. 2014), http://www.wsj.com/articles/turks-cast-votes-in-presidential-election-with-erdogan-primed-for-win-1407658125.
[183] *Id.*
[184] *Id.*

the chances of its being removed from power by the Turkish military, a strong defender of Turkey as a secular State. Instead, the AKP has welcomed Hamas with open arms, has donated hundreds of millions of dollars to their cause, and has made a habit of condemning Israel on the geopolitical stage. With Erdoğan's 2014 presidential election victory, he has gained a chance to tighten both his and the AKP's grip on Turkish politics, an outcome that makes the future of Turkish-Israeli relations even more tenuous.

THE MAVI MARMARA TRIAL:

POLITICISING THE TURKISH JUSTICE SYSTEM

ROBERT WESTON ASH*

* * * * *

"He who justifies the wicked,
and he who condemns the righteous,
Both of them alike are an abomination to the Lord"[1].

*Mr Ash is a Founding Fellow of the Centre for the Study of Law & Public Policy at Oxford. He is also Senior Counsel at the American Center for Law & Justice (ACLJ), Virginia Beach, Virginia, and at the European Centre for Law & Justice (ECLJ), Strasbourg, France. Mr Ash received his Bachelor of Science (B.S.) degree from the United States Military Academy at West Point, New York; his Master of International Public Policy (M.I.P.P.) degree from the School of Advanced International Studies (SAIS) of the Johns Hopkins University, Washington, DC; and his Juris Doctor (J.D.) degree (*cum laude*) from the Regent University School of Law, Virginia Beach, Virginia. In 2014, Mr Ash was a Visiting Fellow of Harris Manchester College, University of Oxford. In 2014, he also participated in a Post-Doctoral Programme in Middle East Studies at Exeter College, University of Oxford, under the tutelage of Professor Farhang Jahanpour and Dr Gareth Winrow. During his Army career, Mr Ash was a George and Carol Olmsted Scholar, studying at the University of Zurich, in Zurich, Switzerland. He also served as a Congressional Fellow for one year in the office of Senator John McCain of Arizona. Mr Ash currently heads the national security practice of the ACLJ. Mr Ash is also a co-author of the recent #1 *New York Times* bestselling book, *Rise of ISIS, A Threat We Can't Ignore*.

[1] Proverbs 17:15 (NASB)

"Right is right, even if everyone is against it, and wrong is wrong, even if everyone is for it"[2].

INTRODUCTION

On or about 6 November 2012, the 7th High Criminal Court in Istanbul began a trial against four senior Israeli military officers[3]. The four Israelis were on trial for alleged offences committed by Israeli forces during and after the 31 May 2010 clash on the high seas between Israeli commandos and passengers on board the Mavi Marmara, a Comoros-flagged vessel, seeking to breach the Israeli naval blockade of the Gaza Strip. Because the ship's Turkish Master refused either to change course away from the Gaza Strip when directed to do so by the Israeli Navy or to accept the Israeli offer to deliver the vessel's humanitarian goods to Gaza over land, Israeli military forces ultimately boarded the ship to enforce the blockade[4]. Israeli forces boarding the ship were met with deadly force from a significant number of the ship's passengers[5]. The ensuing melee resulted in the

---

[2] *Quotes About Justice*, http://www.goodreads.com/quotes/tag/justice?page=2 (quoting William Penn).

[3] The four senior Israeli officers are: Gabi Ashkenazi, Eliezer Marom, Amos Yadlin, and Avishai Levi. *Trial of Israeli Generals Over Mavi Marmara Raid Begins*, TODAY'S ZAMAN (6 Nov. 2012), http://www. todayszaman.com/diplomacy_trial-of-israeli-generals-over-mavi-marmara-raid-begins_297274.html.

[4] San Remo Manual on International Law Applicable to Armed Conflicts at Sea, arts. 98, 100, 12 June 1994, [hereinafter San Remo Manual], *available at* https://www. icrc.org/ihl/INTRO/560.

[5] TURKISH NAT'L COMM'N OF INQUIRY, REPORT ON THE ISRAELI ATTACK ON THE HUMANITARIAN AID CONVOY TO GAZA ON 31 MAY 2010, 93 (Feb. 2011) [hereinafter TURKISH REPORT], *available at* http://www.mfa.gov.tr/data/Turkish%20Report%20 Final%20-%20UN%20Copy.pdf ("Israeli soldiers descended into a group of passengers *resisting with make-shift weapons*" (emphasis added)); U.N. Human Rights Council, Report on the International Fact-finding Mission to Investigate Violations of International Law, Including International Humanitarian and Human Rights Law, Resulting From the Israeli Attacks on the Flotilla of Ships Carrying Humanitarian Assistance, U.N. Doc. A/HRC/15/21, at 23 (27 Sept. 2010) [hereinafter UNHRC Report] (passengers had fashioned weapons out of wood and chains and had been provided with gas masks), 26 (they were armed with sticks, metal rods, knives, and handheld catapults), 37 (they were armed with sticks and knives); REPORT OF

deaths of nine passengers[6] and serious injury to other passengers as well as to Israeli commandos[7]. Both prior to the commencement of the Mavi Marmara trial and since the trial began in November 2012, there have been a number of significant legal and procedural irregularities involving the trial, all of which establish that the trial is nothing more than a political show trial motivated by Turkish politics rather than by any claimed fidelity to the principles of justice and the rule of law[8].

THE SECRETARY-GENERAL'S PANEL OF INQUIRY ON THE 31 MAY 2010 FLOTILLA INCIDENT (Sept. 2011) [hereinafter PALMER REPORT] at ¶¶ 50 (weapons found on Mavi Marmara included flares, rods, axes, knives, tear gas, gas masks, protective vests, and night vision goggles), 55 (reporting that Israeli soldiers had been attacked with clubs, iron rods, slingshots, and knives), 123–24 (reporting that passengers fashioned and used metal bars, slingshots, chains, and knives).

[6] Eight of the nine killed were Turkish nationals, and one was an American citizen of Turkish descent. See PALMER REPORT, supra note 5, ¶ 34. A tenth passenger, also a Turk, recently died of injuries sustained in the 31 May 2010 clash. Mavi Marmara Death Toll Rises to 10, AL JAZEERA (25 May 2014), http://www.Aljazeera.com/humanrights/2014/05/mavi-marmara-death-toll-rises-102014525145911267813.html.

[7] PALMER REPORT, supra note 5, ¶ 56; TÜRKEL COMM'N, THE PUBLIC COMMISSION TO EXAMINE THE MARITIME INCIDENT OF 31 MAY 2010, REPORT PT. 1 ¶¶ 142, 149–57 (Jan. 2010) [hereinafter TÜRKEL REPORT], available at http://www.turkel-committee.gov.il/files/wordocs/8808report-eng.pdf.

[8] The Mavi Marmara trial appears to be another in a long line of political trials in Turkey. See, e.g., Turkey Must Abandon 'Show Trial' Against Gezi Park Protest Organizers, AMNESTY INTERNATIONAL (12 June 2014), https://www.amnesty.org/en/articles/news/2014/06/turkey-must-abandon-show-trial-against-gezi-park-protest-organizers/ (condemning politically motivated show trial of group of peaceful activists); Turkey Ergenekon Case: Ex-army Chief Basbug Gets Life, BBC (5 Aug. 2013), http://www.bbc.com/news/world-europe-23571739 (accusing current Turkish government of trying to silence its secularist opponents by arresting and trying hundreds of military officers); Owen Bowcott, Kurdish and Turkish Lawyers on Trial for Representing Imprisoned Leader, THE GUARDIAN (9 Jan. 2013), http://www. theguardian.com/law/guardian-law-blog/2013/jan/09/kurdish-turkish-lawyers-trial (reporting on mass trial of lawyers for defending Kurdish leader Abdullah Ocalan); Dexter Filkins, Show Trials on the Bosphorus, THE NEW YORKER (13 Aug. 2013), http://www.newyorker.com/news/daily-comment/show-trials-on-the-bosphorus (discussing the prosecution of Turkey's military and political leaders in the so-called "Ergenekon case" and noting the following about one of the accused: "The evidence against Şirin was not merely thin; it was preposterous, as though it had been assembled by a group of schoolchildren—or by a prosecutor who never imagined that an independent observer would examine it".).

The issues surrounding the Mavi Marmara clash and subsequent trial will be discussed in four sections, followed by the conclusion. Section I provides a quick review of pertinent facts about the clash between Israeli forces and vessels of the Free Gaza Flotilla, with emphasis on what transpired on the Comoros-flagged Mavi Marmara. Section II discusses which law applied to the naval clash and the legal implications that flow from the differing conclusions made by Israel and Turkey. Section III discusses the numerous misapplications of international law, Turkish criminal law, and Turkish criminal procedure in trying the Israeli military officers for acts that Turkish law would excuse with respect to its own public servants, thereby establishing the political nature of the ongoing trial in Istanbul. Section IV discusses the Mavi Marmara Master's criminal recklessness in seeking to breach the Israeli naval blockade as well as the Turkish Prosecutor's notable lack of interest in prosecuting such criminal activity, once again suggesting a political motivation to go after Israelis while giving a pass to the one individual on the Mavi Marmara who had the responsibility, the authority, and the opportunity to avoid subjecting his passengers, ship, and crew to the danger of death and serious bodily injury. Given the theatrics surrounding the trial and the Prosecutor's and the Court's obvious failure to follow their own law and procedures, this paper concludes that the Mavi Marmara trial is a political show trial that neither comports with the minimal requirements for a fair trial nor seeks to ascertain the truth and do justice with respect to the Mavi Marmara matter.

I. FACTUAL SUMMARY

For a number of years, there has been an ongoing armed conflict between the State of Israel and Hamas and other Palestinian Islamist groups located in, and firing rockets and mortars into Israel from, the Gaza Strip[9]. Because of the ongoing attacks directed at its people

---

[9] *See New Gaza War 'Only a Question of Time,'* BBC (23 Dec. 2010), http://www. bbc.com/news/world-middle-east-12064775; Tim Butcher, *Hamas Ends Ceasefire*

and territory from Gaza, Israel has opted to exercise its inherent right under international law to defend itself and its citizens[10]. Exercising Israel's inherent right to self-defence requires that Israeli forces comply with the Law of Armed Conflict (LOAC)[11]. Establishing a naval blockade during an armed conflict to interdict delivery of war materiel to one's adversaries is permitted under international law[12]. Once Israel had established its naval blockade, Israel not only had the right but also the duty to inspect cargoes bound for enemy-controlled territory, including the right to take ships into a nearby port for such inspection[13]. The so-called "Free Gaza Flotilla" (which included the Mavi Marmara plus five other vessels) was composed of self-described human rights activists who disputed the legality of the Israeli blockade and who made no secret of their intent to breach the Israeli blockade and sail to Gaza[14]. Israel warned the Turkish government (and other governments whose nationals were participating in the flotilla) in advance that Israel would enforce its blockade[15]. Nevertheless, in

---

with Israel, TELEGRAPH (18 Dec. 2008), http://www.telegraph.co.uk/news/ worldnews/middleeast/palestinianauthority/3834450/Hamas-ends-ceasefire-with-Israel.html; *The Hamas Terror War Against Israel*, ISR. MINISTRY OF FOREIGN AFF. (Mar. 2011), http://www.mfa.gov.il/mfa/foreignpolicy/terrorism/palestinian/pages/ missile%20fire%20from%20gaza%20on%20israeli%20civilian%20targets%20 aug%202007.aspx.

[10] U.N. CHARTER art. 51.

[11] *See, e.g.*, PALMER REPORT, *supra* note 5, ¶¶ 47(f), 59(e). Note that the Law of Armed Conflict (LOAC) is also referred to as the Law of War and International Humanitarian Law (IHL).

[12] San Remo Manual, *supra* note 4, arts. 93–104.

[13] *Id.* arts. 97, 98.

[14] Michal Zippori, *Convoy of Ships Heads to Gaza in Attempt to Break Blockade*, CNN (27 May 2010), http://edition.cnn.com/2010/WORLD/meast/05/27/gaza.aid. convoy/index.html?iref=allsearch ("'The objective of the boats is to break Israel's siege on Gaza, to break Israel's blockade on Gaza,'. . . said Greta Berlin, co-founder of Free Gaza movement"); *see also* Paul McGeough, *Humanitarian Flotilla Heads to Israel*, SYDNEY MORNING HERALD (24 May 2010), http://www.smh.com.au/multi media/world/humanitarian-flotilla-heads-to-israel/20100523-w3wt.html (containing video footage of a passenger who states her purpose is to "breach Israel's Naval blockade of Gaza").

[15] *See* TÜRKEL REPORT, *supra* note 7, ¶ 118; *Gaza Aid Fleet Undeterred as Israel Steps Up Warnings*, WAZA (27 May 2010), https://wazaonline.com/en/archive/ga-

an attempt to avoid a confrontation with the Flotilla, Israel publicly offered to allow the Flotilla's humanitarian cargo to be unloaded at the Israeli port of Ashdod for subsequent delivery to the Gaza Strip over land under the auspices of UN personnel[16]. The Israeli offer was summarily rejected by Flotilla participants[17].

The Flotilla set sail for Gaza on or about 30 May 2010[18]. On 31 May 2010, as the Flotilla continued to approach waters affected by the blockade, the Israeli Navy queried the ships by radio as to their destination and warned them that they were approaching restricted waters[19]. The ships responded that they were bound for Gaza and refused either to alter course away from Gaza or to divert to the port of Ashdod[20]. Following the ships' refusal to comply with Israeli Navy instructions concerning the blockade, Israeli military personnel ultimately boarded the vessels to enforce the blockade[21]. On five of the six vessels, there was no armed resistance to the boarding, and no serious casualties occurred on either side[22]. On the sixth ship, the Comoros-registered vessel, Mavi Marmara, a group of passengers took up arms—metal rods, knives, chains, and other weapons—and physically attacked the Israeli commandos attempting to board the ship[23]. The Israelis boarding the Mavi Marmara had not expected

---

za-aid-fleet-undeterred-as-israel-steps-up-warnings.

[16] Isabel Kershner, *Defying Blockade, Cargo and Passenger Vessels Head for Gaza*, N.Y. TIMES, (27 May 2010), *available at* http://www.nytimes.com/2010/05/28/world/
middleeast/28mideast.html?fta=y.

[17] *Id.*; *see also* TÜRKEL REPORT, *supra* note 7, ¶ 124.

[18] *TIMELINE–Main Events in the Gaza Flotilla Affair*, REUTERS (7 June 2010), http://in.reuters.com/article/2010/06/07/idINIndia-49106720100607 [hereinafter *TIMELINE*].

[19] *Id.*; TÜRKEL REPORT, *supra* note 7, ¶¶ 123–25; *see also* Israel Defense Forces, *Unedited Radio Transmission Between Gaza Flotilla and Israeli Navy*, YOUTUBE (4 June 2010), http://www.youtube.com/watch?v=9dE2StbDL_Q.

[20] *TIMELINE*, *supra* note 18; TÜRKEL REPORT, *supra* note 7, ¶ 124.

[21] *TIMELINE*, *supra* note 18.

[22] *Id.*; TÜRKEL REPORT, *supra* note 7, ¶¶ 147–51.

[23] Isabel Kershner, *Deadly Israeli Raid Draws Condemnation*, N.Y. TIMES (31 May 2010), http://www.nytimes.com/2010/06/01/world/middleeast/01flotilla.html

such resistance and, hence, had been armed primarily with non-lethal paintball guns[24]. Only when Israeli assault personnel had begun to sustain life-threatening injuries inflicted by armed passengers did they resort to lethal weaponry in self-defence[25]. Further, some of the passengers on board the Mavi Marmara had publicly stated, prior to sailing, that they had hoped to become martyrs (i.e., shaheed)[26]. Such statements clearly indicated that at least some passengers aboard the Mavi Marmara were planning to engage in activities that they considered likely to result in their deaths. In the melee that ensued on the Mavi Marmara during the resisted boarding operation, nine of the 581 passengers aboard the ship were killed[27]. Nine Israeli military

[hereinafter Kershner, *Deadly*]; *see also* TÜRKEL REPORT, *supra* note 7, ¶¶ 127–40.

[24] Dan Williams, *Paintballs to Pistols, Israel Admits Ship Blunders*, REUTERS (1 Jun. 2010), http://www.reuters.com/article/idUSLDE650280; *see also* TÜRKEL RE-PORT, *supra* note 7, ¶¶ 121, 127–140, 214, 227.

[25] Kershner, *Deadly*, *supra* note 23; *see also* TÜRKEL REPORT, *supra* note 7, ¶¶ 127–40.

[26] Anath Hartmann, *Activists Aboard Gaza-bound Flotilla Wanted to be 'Martyrs,'* WASH. TIMES BLOG (3 June 2010), http://www.washingtontimes.com/blog/water cooler/2010/jun/3/activists-aboard-gaza-bound-flotilla-wanted-be-mar/. This news story includes a video of a passenger stating, "When I went on the first convoy, I wanted to be a shaheed [martyr]. I wasn't that lucky. Second time, I wanted to be a shaheed. Didn't work. Third time, lucky, [with the help of God] I will be a sha-heed." *Id.*; *see also* Richard Spencer, *Gaza Flotilla Attack: Turkish Activists Killed in Raid 'Wanted to Be Martyrs,'* TELEGRAPH (2 June 2010), http://www.telegraph. co.uk/news/worldnews/europe/turkey/7798493/Gaza-flotilla-attack-Turkish-activ-ists-killed-in-raid-wanted-to-be-martyrs.html. *Seeking martyrdom* is hardly a con-vincing indication of peaceful intent on the part of such passengers.

[27] *Factbox: Details of Activists Aboard Gaza Flotilla*, REUTERS (1 June 2010), http:// www.reuters.com/article/2010/06/01/us-israel-flotilla-passengers-idUKTRE650 4L020100601; *see also* TÜRKEL REPORT, *supra* note 7, ¶ 155. A tenth passenger recently died of injuries sustained in the 31 May 2010 clash. *See Mavi Marmara Death Toll Rises to 10*, AL JAZEERA (25 May 2014), http://www.aljazeera.com/human rights/2014/05/mavi-marmara-death-toll-rises-10-2014525145911267813.html. De-spite the obvious fact that all such deaths are regrettable, in this matter, they were also wholly avoidable. Israel had offered Flotilla participants a good faith alterna-tive to deliver their humanitarian goods to the Gaza Strip, i.e., by unloading them at the Israeli port of Ashdod and allowing them to be delivered over land under the auspices of UN personnel. *See, e.g.*, PALMER REPORT, *supra* note 5, ¶ 100; TÜRKEL REPORT, *supra* note 7, ¶¶ 3, 110. Unfortunately, the offer was refused, and the Flo-tilla attempted to breach the blockade instead, thereby triggering the need for the boarding operation.

personnel were injured, some seriously, by passengers on board the Mavi Marmara who attacked them[28]. Once the Mavi Marmara had been brought under Israeli control, injured Israeli commandos and ship's passengers were triaged by medical personnel and given medical treatment priority based on the seriousness of their respective injuries, irrespective of their nationality[29]. Once all Flotilla vessels were under Israeli control, they were sailed to Israel[30].

Despite the violence that occurred during the attempted breach of the blockade, once the Flotilla vessels reached the Israeli port of Ashdod, Israel nonetheless unloaded the humanitarian cargo and attempted to deliver it to the Gaza Strip[31]. The Turkish group that had organised the Flotilla, the Foundation for Human Rights and Freedoms and Humanitarian Relief (commonly referred to by the initials, IHH), is a group known (by the Turkish government and others) to have ties to Islamist terrorist groups opposed to Israel[32]. Those ties include ties to Hamas (a Palestinian group whose sworn goal is to destroy Israel[33]). A significant number of IHH members

---

[28] TÜRKEL REPORT, *supra* note 7, ¶ 157.

[29] PALMER REPORT, *supra* note 5, ¶ 144; TÜRKEL REPORT, *supra* note 7, ¶¶ 141, 142.

[30] *See, e.g.*, TURKISH REPORT, *supra* note 5, at 39; TÜRKEL REPORT, *supra* note 7, ¶ 152.

[31] Bill Varner, *UN to Deliver Aid Flotilla's Cargo to Gaza Strip Under Accord With Israel*, BLOOMBERG (15 June 2010), http://www.bloomberg.com/news/2010-06-15/un-to-deliver-aid-flotilla-s-cargo-to-gaza-strip-under-accord-with-israel.html. Gaza authorities refused to accept the goods. Harriet Sherwood, *Hamas Refuses Flotilla Aid Delivered By Israel*, THE GUARDIAN (3 June 2010), http://www.the guardian.com/world/2010/jun/03/hamas-flotilla-aid-israel.

[32] *Turkish Charity Behind Flotilla Had 'Ties to Terrorism and Jihad,'* FOX NEWS (2 June 2010), http://www.foxnews.com/world/2010/06/02/french-judge-says-turkish-charity-gaza-flotilla-terror-ties/ (quoting Jean-Luis Bruguiere, the former French lead anti-terrorism investigating judge, regarding IHH's "clear, long-standing ties to terrorism and Jihad").

[33] *See, e.g.*, Hamas Charter pmbl., 18 Aug. 1988, *available at* http://avalon.law.yale. edu/20th_century/hamas.asp ("Israel will exist and will continue to exist until Islam will obliterate it . . .". (quoting Hassan al-Banna)). Moreover, the current Turkish government has allowed Hamas to establish an office in Istanbul, and Hamas leaders have been invited guests at the ruling party's convention, *Turkey Provides Hamas with New Headquarters*, ISRAEL TODAY (27 Nov. 2014), http://www.israeltoday.

were aboard the Mavi Marmara when it attempted to breach the blockade[34]. The IHH members had brought onto the ship with them, inter alia, gas masks and protective vests[35], unusual items when planning for and anticipating a peaceful humanitarian voyage. Accordingly, it is evident that at least some of the passengers aboard the Mavi Marmara were not simply "peaceful human rights activists" but rather active supporters and allies of the terrorist group Hamas, who fashioned weapons and were prepared to resist by force any attempted Israeli boarding[36]. Further, the Flotilla had been bound for the Gaza Strip, a territory controlled and dominated by Hamas, a group recognised as an international terrorist organisation by the United States, Canada, and others.[37]

Once the Flotilla vessels had been brought into the Israeli port of Ashdod, Flotilla participants were turned over to, and processed by, Israeli police officials[38]. Since all Flotilla participants were

---

co.il/NewsItem/tabid/178/nid/25579/Default.aspx, a further indication that the current Turkish government has taken sides and is not objective in pursuing the trial against Israeli military leaders.

[34] UNHRC Report, *supra* note 5, ¶ 99; PALMER REPORT, *supra* note 5, ¶¶ 86, 91; TÜRKEL REPORT, *supra* note 7, ¶ 127.

[35] PALMER REPORT, *supra* note 5, ¶ 50; TÜRKEL REPORT, *supra* note 7, ¶¶ 179, 206–07, 278.

[36] PALMER REPORT, *supra* note 5, ¶¶ 93, 96, 119; TÜRKEL REPORT, *supra* note 7, ¶ 176 & n.733.

[37] *See, e.g.*, OFF. OF THE COORDINATOR FOR COUNTERTERRORISM, U.S. DEP'T OF STATE, COUNTRY REPORTS ON TERRORISM 2008 *passim* (2009), *available at* http:// www. state.gov/documents/organization/122599.pdf (detailing the United States' categorisation of Hamas as a terror organisation); Regulations Establishing a List of Entities, SI/2008-143 (Can.), *available at* http://laws-lois.justice.gc.ca/eng/ regulations/SI-2008-143/FullText.html (listing Canada's classification of Hamas as an entity that "has knowingly carried out, attempted to carry out, participated in or facilitated a terrorist activity or is knowingly acting on behalf of, at the direction of or in association with such an entity"); Council Common Position (EC) No. 67/2009 of 27 Jan. 2009, pmbl., arts. 1–4, annex, 2009 O.J. (L 23) 37, 41, *available at* http:// eur-lex.europa.eu/LexUriServ/LexUriServ.do?uri=OJ:L:2009:023:0037:0042:EN:PDF (noting the European Union's classification of Hamas as an entity that employs terrorism as a tactic).

[38] TÜRKEL REPORT, *supra* note 7, ¶ 152 (noting that upon arrival in Ashdod, responsibility passed from the Israeli armed forces to the counter-terrorism force of the

aboard vessels that had sought to breach a properly established and announced naval blockade in violation of the LOAC[39], they were dealt with by Israeli authorities as lawbreakers[40]. Nonetheless, consistent with requirements of international law, non-Israeli Flotilla passengers were permitted visits by diplomats from their respective countries[41], and, despite Israel's absolute right to try Flotilla participants for violating the LOAC, Israel opted instead to forego such trials and to deport all foreign passengers from Israeli soil[42]. Accordingly, Israeli police officials placed the passengers in temporary confinement until they could be expelled from Israel. All foreign Flotilla participants were, in fact, deported from Israel within a matter of days[43].

Following their deportation from Israel, some of the Flotilla passengers sought to bring legal action in Turkey against Israel for what had occurred on the Mavi Marama and other Flotilla vessels. Since the vessel on which the Turkish nationals had been killed was a Comoros-flagged vessel[44], Comoran courts had primary jurisdiction over what transpired aboard that ship with respect to the passengers and crew, not Turkish courts[45]. Further, although not one of the four accused Israeli officers had been present on the Mavi Marmara at any

Israeli Border Police).

[39] *See, e.g.,* San Remo Manual, *supra* note 4, art. 98 ("Merchant vessels believed on reasonable grounds to be breaching a blockade may be captured. Merchant vessels which, after prior warning, clearly resist may be attacked".).

[40] *See* TÜRKEL REPORT, *supra* note 7, ¶ 152.

[41] *See id.* ¶ 153.

[42] *See id.* ¶ 154.

[43] *Id.*

[44] *See, e.g.,* TURKISH REPORT, *supra* note 5, at 15; UNHRC Report, *supra* note 5, ¶ 81 & n.64; PALMER REPORT, *supra* note 5, ¶ 83.

[45] *See, e.g., Indictment Seeks Life for Israeli Commanders for Mavi Marmara Raid,* WEEKLY ZAMAN (26 May 2012), http://www.weeklyzaman.com/en/newsDetail_open PrintPage.action?newsId=5756. The fact that the Union of Comoros declined to conduct an investigation of the 31 May incident that took place aboard one of its flagged ships does not mean that Turkey had jurisdiction to do so. *See, e.g.,* TURKISH REPORT, *supra* note 5, at 52 n.213 (citing the S.S. Lotus Case (Fr. v. Turk.), 1927 P.C.I.J., as establishing the *exclusive jurisdiction of the flag State* (emphasis added)). Having made that argument, Turkey has nonetheless asserted jurisdiction over what occurred on the non-Turkish-flagged vessel Mavi Marmara on the high seas.

time during which the events complained of by passengers took place, the Turkish prosecutor nonetheless prepared—and a Turkish court approved—a criminal indictment accusing the four Israeli military officers of personal responsibility for alleged "crimes" they clearly did not commit and, indeed, could not have committed, since they were neither present aboard the ship when the alleged crimes took place nor were they in charge of the civilian police officers who processed and controlled the passengers and crew once they arrived at Ashdod.

Among the alleged crimes charged in the indictment are the following: "willful killing; torture or inhuman treatment; willfully causing great suffering or serious injury to body or health; arbitrary detention and arrest; violation of the freedom of expression; qualified robbery; illegal seizure of personal items; [and] illegal capture of a sea vehicle"[46]. Moreover, despite the four accuseds' absence from the scene of the alleged crimes, the indictment called for sentences against them *exceeding* 18,000 years imprisonment[47]. Such sentences are totally outlandish and reveal the sensational, political nature of the trial. Yet, equally, if not more, remarkable, is the fact that Turkish prosecutors have failed to indict the Turkish Master of the Mavi Marmara for his criminal dereliction of duty as ship's Master and for his criminally reckless actions, actions that recklessly rejected two alternatives *known to him at the time* that would have altogether avoided the possibility of a military confrontation with Israeli armed forces as well as actions that recklessly and inexorably led to the deaths of nine passengers on

[46] *F.A.Q.*, IHH, http://www.ihh.org.tr/en/main/pages/sik-sorulan-sorular-ve-cevap-lari/303 (last visited 14 May 2015).

[47] Rick Gladstone, *Turkey May Indict Senior Israeli Officers Over Deadly Gaza Flotilla Raid*, N.Y. TIMES (23 May 2012), http://www.nytimes.com/2012/05/24/world/middleeast/turkey-may-indict-israeli-generals-over-flotilla-raid.html. Seeking sentences of so many years strongly implies that the Turkish prosecutor has charged the four Israeli officers criminally for all alleged offences against all complainants, including non-Turks aboard the ship. If that is true, the prosecutor (with the court's concurrence) has improperly assumed jurisdiction over offences which should have been dealt with exclusively by the Union of the Comoros, since the Mavi Marmara was a Comoros-flagged ship when the alleged crimes occurred on board the ship.

board his ship, injuries to many others, and a serious diplomatic rift between Turkey and Israel, States that had hitherto enjoyed good diplomatic relations[48].

II. THE LAW OF ARMED CONFLICT VS. PEACETIME MARITIME LAW: WHICH LAW GOVERNED THE 31 MAY 2010 CLASH ON THE HIGH SEAS & WHO MAY DETERMINE THE ANSWER?

One of the fundamental, ongoing disagreements regarding the 31 May 2010 clash between the Israeli armed forces and the so-called Free Gaza Flotilla concerns what "law" governed the situation on that fateful day—the Law of Armed Conflict (LOAC) or peacetime maritime law. The Israeli government, based on its ongoing armed conflict with Hamas and other Palestinian terrorist groups in the Gaza Strip, had determined that the LOAC governed[49], whereas Flotilla participants claimed that peacetime maritime law applied[50]. Turkish authorities agreed with the view of the Flotilla participants[51]. Following the clash, both the Israeli and Turkish governments formed commissions[52] to investigate the incident and, not surprisingly, each

---

[48] *See* Part IV, *infra*, for more thorough discussion.

[49] PALMER REPORT, *supra* note 5, ¶ 46; TÜRKEL REPORT, *supra* note 7, ¶ 31.

[50] PALMER REPORT, *supra* note 5, ¶ 105 & n.337.

[51] *See generally* TURKISH REPORT, *supra* note 5.

[52] *See id.*; TÜRKEL REPORT, *supra* note 7. It is interesting that Turkey created a Commission to assess what transpired aboard the Mavi Marmara, since the Mavi Marmara was not a Turkish-flagged vessel at the time and, hence, jurisdiction over what transpired aboard the vessel belonged to the Union of the Comoros. *See supra* note 44. Because Turkish nationals were killed and injured, Turkey could lawfully assert jurisdiction based on the passive personality principle in international law vis-à-vis its own nationals, which recognises a State's jurisdiction over those who injure its nationals. *See, e.g.*, RESTATEMENT (THIRD) OF THE FOREIGN RELATIONS LAW OF THE UNITED STATES § 402 comment g (1987). Foreign nationals injured during the incident, however, would fall outside normal Turkish jurisdiction, since the incident occurred outside Turkey on a foreign-flagged vessel. Yet, Turkey's right to choose which international law principles to apply obligates it to recognise that Israel enjoys the same right to choose applicable international law principles, as well. Hence, Israel can rely on principles of the LOAC in defence of its actions, since Israel had determined that the LOAC applied and acted accordingly.

commission reached a different conclusion[53].

Both Israel and Turkey are sovereign States which routinely make sovereign determinations concerning which law to apply in various circumstances. Concerning the so-called Free Gaza Flotilla and its claimed humanitarian mission, both States came to radically different conclusions. Those differing conclusions are significant because they have affected (and continue to affect) how each side has reacted (and continues to react) to the clash at sea as well as to what legal consequences flowed therefrom. If, as Israel concluded, the LOAC applied, then Israel acted lawfully in establishing and enforcing the blockade. In fact, under the LOAC, Israel was duty-bound to enforce a lawfully constituted blockade against all neutral ships[54], including ships on self-proclaimed, humanitarian missions. Hence, when the Master of the Mavi Marmara refused to comply with repeated Israeli instructions to either change course away from the Gaza Strip or divert to the Israeli port of Ashdod to unload its humanitarian cargo, that fateful decision compelled Israel to act and inexorably led to the Israeli use of force to enforce the blockade (as was its duty under the LOAC[55]), which, in turn, led to the deaths and other injuries sustained by passengers aboard his ship when some passengers resorted to deadly force in resisting the Israeli boarding.

If, however, as Turkey has claimed, peacetime maritime law

---

[53] Interestingly, the Union of the Comoros initiated no investigation despite the fact that the Mavi Marmara was a Comoros-flagged vessel and, hence, a Comoros national for purposes of investigating any criminal liability that occurred on board the ship in the days surrounding the incident. *See supra* note 44. Further, it was a Turkish law firm actively involved in the Istanbul trial that encouraged Comoros to file a complaint with the International Criminal Court (ICC) over what had transpired aboard the Mavi Marmara on 31 May 2010. This conduct once again suggests how political the entire incident is. *See Referral of the "Union of the Comoros" With Respect to the 31 May 2010 Israeli Raid on the Humanitarian Aid Flotilla Bound for the Gaza Strip*, ICC, http://www.icc-cpi.int/iccdocs/otp/Referral-from-Comoros.pdf (last visited 14 May 2015) [hereinafter *Comoros Referral*].

[54] San Remo Manual, *supra* note 4, arts. 95, 98, 100.

[55] *Id.*

applied, then Israel overstepped its authority and acted unlawfully under international law. Yet, given the ship's Comoran nationality, it is the Union of the Comoros (Comoros) which possessed sole authority to press such a claim, not Turkey. Moreover, *even if one were to conclude that Israel had been wrong in applying the LOAC*, the Israeli decision (*even if wrong*) did not relieve the Master of the Mavi Marmara from his well-established legal duty under customary international law to ensure the safety of his ship, crew, passengers, and cargo. The Master was fully aware *at the time* that the Israelis had established a naval blockade, that the Israelis believed that their blockade was lawful, that the Israelis had stated their intention to enforce it, *and* that the Israelis had offered a peaceful alternative to deliver the Flotilla's humanitarian goods to Gaza[56]. Accordingly, the Master had it within his hands to wholly avoid any confrontation with the Israelis. Despite two alternatives offered by Israel which would have avoided a confrontation altogether—i.e., to change course away from Gaza *or* to divert to the port of Ashdod to unload his cargo for subsequent delivery to Gaza over land—the Master knowingly, deliberately, and recklessly assumed the risk of attempting to breach the blockade and thereby placed his passengers, ship, and crew in grave danger. The Master's assumption of the risk placed his ship and passengers in so much danger, in fact, that nine of his passengers were ultimately killed and other passengers were severely injured because of his reckless decisions.

Two investigations of the clash were also initiated by the UN— one by the UN Secretary-General[57] and one by the UN Human Rights Council[58]. The resulting UN commissions also reached opposite conclusions as to which law applied and the legal implications that flowed therefrom[59]. As a result, there is no consensus at either the

---

[56] The implications of such knowledge and the legal duty that flows therefrom are discussed more thoroughly in Section IV, *infra*.

[57] PALMER REPORT, *supra* note 5.

[58] UNHRC Report, *supra* note 5.

[59] PALMER REPORT, *supra* note 5; UNHRC Report, *supra* note 5.

State or international levels regarding which law applied at the time of the clash. As sovereign States, each State made its own determination, as was its right, and, based on the principle of the sovereign equality of States, neither State can legitimately force its decision on the other[60]. Having said that, *one must acknowledge that the ongoing Turkish trial is, in fact, an attempt by Turkey to impose its conclusion of criminal wrongdoing on Israel by trying the four Israeli officers in a Turkish court,* despite the fact that both the Israeli Türkel and the UN Palmer Commissions concluded that the Israeli naval blockade was lawful under international law[61], that the Israelis had a duty to enforce it against all neutral ships[62], and that the Mavi Marmara was wrong to have sought to breach the blockade and to resist Israeli enforcement of it[63]. Further, trying Israeli officers before a Turkish court is also significantly presumptuous on Turkey's part, given that the Mavi Marmara was not a Turkish-flagged vessel at the time of the clash[64]. Any legal injury to the ship, its passengers, crew, and cargo was a legal injury to Comoros, not Turkey, given the ship's nationality.

One must also recognise that certain legal principles apply in the Israeli-Hamas context. Although the UN Charter clearly forbids "aggressive war"[65], Article 51 of the Charter explicitly recognises a State's inherent right of self-defence: "Nothing in the present Charter shall impair the inherent right of individual or collective self-defence if an armed attack occurs against a Member of the United

---

[60] *See, e.g.*, U.N. Charter art. 2.1. (noting that the UN "is based on the principle of the sovereign equality of all its Members".).

[61] *See, e.g.*, PALMER REPORT, *supra* note 5, ¶ 75; TÜRKEL REPORT, *supra* note 7, ¶¶ 26, 58.

[62] San Remo Manual, *supra* note 4, art. 100.

[63] *See, e.g.*, PALMER REPORT, *supra* note 5, ¶ 158.

[64] *See supra* note 44.

[65] *See, e.g.*, U.N. Charter art. 2.4 ("All Members shall refrain in their international relations from the threat or use of force against the territorial integrity or political independence of any state, or in any other manner inconsistent with the Purposes of the United Nations".). In these circumstances, it is the Palestinian groups like Hamas in the Gaza Strip that are engaging in aggressive war. As such, they are the ones to be condemned and prosecuted for war crimes.

Nations . . . ."[66] Customary international law also recognises the right of self-defence against non-State actors[67]. Moreover, when acting in self-defence, international law "does not require a defender to limit itself to actions that merely repel an attack; *a State may use force in self-defense to remove a continuing threat to future security*"[68]. Thus, a State has full authority to act unilaterally or collectively in its self-defence. That includes, when appropriate, establishing and enforcing a naval blockade[69].

It is essential to note that Article 51 of the UN Charter does not create the right of self-defence; it is an inherent right of all States under customary international law.

> Article 51 neither creates, nor abolishes, a right of self-defense. Nor, for that matter, does it purport to define one. In fact, by its own terms it appears to be nothing more than a rule of construction—making clear that nothing else in the Charter purports to eliminate the right of self-defense in the face of armed attack . . .[70].

While the UN Charter and customary international law both recognise the inherent right of self-defence, the responsibility for determining when self-defence is appropriate lies, as it always has, with

---

[66] U.N. Charter art. 51 (noting that such self-defence is conditioned in the Charter as follows: self-defence is recognised as legitimate under the Charter "until the Security Council has taken measures necessary to maintain international peace and security. Measures taken by Members in the exercise of this right of self-defence shall be immediately reported to the Security Council and shall not in any way affect the authority and responsibility of the Security Council under the present Charter to take at any time such action as it deems necessary in order to maintain or restore international peace and security.").

[67] *See, e.g.*, Armed Activities on the Territory of the Congo (Dem. Rep. Congo. v. Uganda), 2005 I.C.J. ¶ 11 (17 Dec.) (separate opinion of Judge Simma), *available at* http://www.icj-cij.org/docket/files/116/10467.pdf.

[68] SEAN D. MURPHY, PRINCIPLES OF INTERNATIONAL LAW 447 (2006) (emphasis added).

[69] *See, e.g.*, San Remo Manual, *supra* note 4, arts. 10, 67(a), (f), 93–100.

[70] David B. Rivkin Jr. et al., *Preemption and Law in the Twenty-First Century*, 5 CHI. J. INT'L L. 467, 476 (2005).

the government of each State. Under the UN Charter, however, the UN Security Council is specifically charged with the responsibility to lift the burden of individual national self-defence and to take appropriate steps internationally to restore international peace and security[71]. Having said that, it must be readily admitted that the muscular Security Council originally envisioned in the UN Charter has never materialised, and, hence, the Security Council has failed repeatedly in fulfilling its responsibilities in such circumstances. As such, threatened States are almost always required to make their own decisions and bear their own burdens when threatened. Such is the current case with Israel; it must defend itself against repeated Palestinian terrorist, rocket, and mortar attacks from the Gaza Strip[72]. Accordingly, the LOAC permits the use of a naval blockade to stanch the flow of war materiel to Israel's enemies in the Gaza Strip[73].

As a sovereign State, Israel has the inherent authority and right to determine when it must take steps in its national self-defence. Given the frequent attacks against Israeli territory originating from the Hamas-controlled Gaza Strip, Israel acted consistent with the principles of the LOAC in establishing its naval blockade of Gaza to interdict military, and militarily-useful, supplies bound for its enemies. Israel notified the proper maritime authorities about the blockade, putting neutral States and their flagged ships on notice[74]. Although Turkish authorities may believe that the Israeli naval blockade is not lawful, that does not give Turkish-flagged ships or ships flagged by

---

[71] Geoffrey Corn & Dennis Gyllensporre, *International Legality, the Use of Military Force, and Burdens of Persuasion: Self-Defense, the Initiation of Hostilities, and the Impact of the Choice Between Two Evils on the Perception of International Legitimacy*, 30 PACE L. REV. 484, 507 (2010) (noting that the Security Council maintains the authority to critique the state's judgement and to "take actions to reverse an unjustified assertion of the inherent right of self-defence").

[72] *See, e.g.*, PALMER REPORT, *supra* note 5, ¶¶ 46 (noting that thousands of rockets and mortar shells have been fired at Israel from the Gaza Strip) & 71 (same).

[73] San Remo Manual, *supra* note 4, arts. 10, 48, 67(a), (f), 93–100.

[74] *See, e.g.*, PALMER REPORT, *supra* note 5, ¶¶ 46, 75; *see also* San Remo Manual, *supra* note 4, art. 93.

other States with Turkish Masters and crews (like the Comoros-flagged Mavi Marmara at the time of the clash) any authority to take the law into their own hands and attempt to breach such a blockade. Neutral ships attempting to breach such a naval blockade do so at their own risk[75]. The Masters of such ships bear full legal responsibility for the reckless decisions they make in such circumstances. With respect to the 31 May 2010 clash, the Turkish Master assumed the risk and lost. *But for* the Master's failure to timely alter course away from Gaza or accept the good faith Israeli offer to unload the goods at the port of Ashdod and send them to Gaza under UN supervision via land routes, there would have been no need for Israeli forces to board the vessel, and no injuries to persons on either side would have occurred.

In summary, *because the Master of the Mavi Marmara rejected Israel's good faith offer to deliver the humanitarian goods over land to Gaza and precipitated the Israeli military response by attempting to breach a lawfully established and announced blockade, he bears primary responsibility for what transpired as a result of his unlawful and reckless conduct,* not Israeli commanders or soldiers who, pursuant to the LOAC, had an internationally-recognised, legal duty to respond to the attempted breach and enforce the blockade[76]. *The Master of the Mavi Marmara held the key to a fully peaceful resolution of the crisis regarding his ship, yet he knowingly and deliberately decided to reject the peaceful alternatives offered by Israel and thereby assumed the risk of injury to life and limb occasioned by the forced boarding of his vessel by Israeli armed forces to enforce the blockade.* For his criminal dereliction of duty as Master of the Mavi Marmara which resulted in the deaths of, and serious bodily injuries to, his passengers, he should be investigated, indicted, and brought before a court of justice to answer for his knowing and willful criminal recklessness.

---

[75] *See, e.g.*, San Remo Manual, *supra* note 4, art. 98.
[76] *Id.* art. 100.

III. TURKISH JUDICIAL OFFICIALS ARE OPENLY & NOTORIOUSLY MISAPPLYING TURKISH CRIMINAL LAW & CRIMINAL PROCEDURE IN THE MAVI MARMARA MATTER FOR POLITICAL ENDS

Turkish criminal courts are bound by both the Turkish Penal Code[77] (Penal Code) and the Turkish Criminal Procedure Code[78] (Criminal Procedure Code). Together, these Codes are intended to govern what occurs in the Turkish criminal justice process. In accordance with the Penal Code, the Turkish criminal process takes place in two phases: the *investigation phase* and the *prosecutorial phase*. According to the Criminal Procedure Code, when a public prosecutor is made aware of a report "creat[ing] an impression that a crime has been committed", he must immediately investigate the factual truth of that report to make a decision as to whether to bring public charges[79]. As part of the investigative process, the prosecutor *may* issue a subpoena to the suspect or accused to appear for an interview or interrogation[80]. Further, when a subpoena is issued, the Criminal Procedure Code requires that "[a] copy of the subpoena *shall be handed* to the suspect or accused"[81]. Where it is impossible to serve the subpoena, the reason must be documented for the record[82]. If, at the end of the investigation phase, the prosecutor concludes that he has obtained enough evidence to constitute sufficient suspicion that a

---

[77] VAHIT BIÇAK & EDWARD GRIEVES, TÜRK CEZA KANUNU [TURKISH PENAL CODE] (2007) [hereinafter Penal Code].

[78] CEZA MUHAKEMESI KANUNU [TURKISH CRIMINAL PROCEDURE CODE] 2009 [hereinafter Criminal Procedure Code], *available at* http://www.legislationline.org/ documents/id/17788.pdf.

[79] *Id.* art. 160(1).

[80] *Id.* art. 146(1). An interview is the "[q]uestioning of the suspect by the law enforcement authorities or by the public prosecutor about the crime, which is under investigation." *Id.* art. 2(g). An interrogation is "[a] hearing of the suspect or the accused by the judge or the court about the crime, which is under investigation or prosecution." *Id.* art. 2(h).

[81] *Id.* art. 146(3) (emphasis added).

[82] *Id.* art. 146(6).

crime has been committed, he shall prepare an indictment[83].

To begin the prosecutorial phase, the prosecutor must prepare and file an indictment[84]. The indictment must be addressed to the court with appropriate subject matter jurisdiction and venue, and it must present, *inter alia*, the identity of the suspect, the identity of the victims, the crimes charged and the related articles from the Criminal Code, the evidence of the crime, the factual events that constitute the crime, *a conclusion stating the issues that are both favourable and unfavourable to the suspect,* and a clear statement of the punishment sought[85]. The court must examine the indictment within fifteen days[86]. If the court finds the indictment to be insufficient, it may return it to the prosecutor for correction[87]. However, if the court approves the indictment, the prosecutorial phase begins, and the court must set a trial date and send out summonses for those required to be at the main hearing of the trial[88]. The court is required to send out a copy of the indictment together with a summons to the accused[89]. If it is not possible to serve a summons on the accused, the public prosecutor may

---

[83] *Id.* art. 170(1).

[84] *Id.* art. 170.

[85] *Id.* art. 170(3) (emphasis added). One of the issues favourable to the four accused Israelis is the fact that Israeli *political authorities* had determined that the LOAC was the applicable law. Hence, the Turkish prosecutor should have considered that fact when preparing the indictment, since, under the LOAC, naval blockades are not only lawful, but they must be enforced impartially, i.e., all neutral ships must be treated alike. As such, Israeli soldiers were obeying lawful orders of their superiors when they were sent to board the Mavi Marmara to enforce the blockade, something that Turkish law recognises as releasing a public officer from criminal liability and something that Turkish courts would doubtless recognise as appropriate if Turkish soldiers had been ordered to perform a similar act (such as to enforce a naval blockade of war materials bound for the PKK). *See* Penal Code arts. 6(1)(c) (defining "public officer") & 24(2) ("A person who carries out an order given by an authorized body as part of his duty, and the execution of his duty is compulsory[,] he shall not be held culpable for such act".).

[86] *Id.* art. 174(1).

[87] *Id.*

[88] *Id.* art. 175.

[89] *Id.* art. 176.

seek the issue of an apprehension order or an arrest warrant[90].

Before the trial, the accused is permitted to request the ability to collect evidence and present it at trial[91]. As a general rule, it is necessary for the accused to be present at the main hearing of the trial[92]. After the court establishes the identity of the accused, explains the charges against him, and informs him of his rights, it then proceeds to interrogate[93] the accused[94]. The judge will ask the accused questions related to his personal and economic status, but the accused is not required to give any account about the crime charged[95]. At the conclusion of the interrogation, the prosecutor begins the presentation of evidence[96]. The accused may also present witnesses and evidence at the appropriate time[97]. At the conclusion of the main hearing, the court then determines and pronounces a judgment[98]. The court must read the judgment *to the individual who was accused* and inform him of his rights[99].

The Penal Code outlines, *inter alia*, what actions are considered criminal if committed *in Turkey*. Article 8 of the Penal Code establishes the general territorial jurisdiction of Turkish law. Article 8(1) reads that "Turkish law shall apply to all criminal offenses

---

[90] *Id.* arts. 98(1) & 100(1). Note, however, that, although such a document would have no authority except in Turkey, Turkey might seek to enforce its national warrant via INTERPOL.

[91] *Id.* art. 177.

[92] *Id.* arts. 191 & 193. *See also* nn.109–14, 137–47 and accompanying text, *infra*.

[93] It is important to note that an interrogation is distinct from an interview. An interrogation is "[a] hearing of the suspect or the accused by the judge or the court about the crime, which is under investigation or prosecution." *Id.* art. 2(h). An interview is the "[q]uestioning of the suspect by the law enforcement authorities or by the public prosecutor about the crime, which is under investigation." *Id.* art. 2(g).

[94] *Id.* art. 191. Note that such actions presume the accused's presence before the court.

[95] *Id.* art. 147.

[96] *Id.* art. 206.

[97] *Id.* arts. 177–179.

[98] *Id.* art. 223.

[99] *Id.* art. 231. Once again, the presumption is that the accused is present before the court.

committed in Turkey"[100]. Article 8(2)(b) extends the presumption of Turkish territorial jurisdiction to "on the open sea . . . *and* in, or by using, Turkish sea . . . vessels"[101]. Hence, a criminal act perpetrated on the high seas *in a Turkish ship* would qualify as having been committed "in Turkey" for purposes of criminal jurisdiction[102]. Article 12 of the Penal Code generally deals with offences committed by non-Turkish citizens. In subsections (1) and (2) of Article 12, the non-citizen criminal offender "shall be subject to penalty under Turkish law" if he "*is present in Turkey*"[103]. Article 20(1) of the Penal Code mandates that "[c]riminal responsibility is personal. *No one shall be deemed culpable for the conduct of another*"[104]. Further, in accordance with Article 21 of the Penal Code, "[t]he existence of a criminal offence depends upon the presence of intent"[105]. Intent is further defined as "knowingly and willingly conducting the elements in the legal definition of an offence"[106].

Article 13 of the Penal Code deals with "Miscellaneous Offences" and appears to be a universal jurisdiction provision for dealing with very serious crimes such as genocide, other crimes against humanity, and torture. Article 13 reads, in pertinent part: "Turkish law shall apply to the following *offences committed in a foreign country whether or not committed by a citizen or non-citizen of Turkey*: [followed by a list of crimes]"[107]. Given the list of crimes reportedly set forth in the indictment[108], it is possible that the Turkish prosecutor has charged the Israeli officers with violations of Penal Code Articles 77 (Other

---

[100] Penal Code art. 8(1) (emphasis added).

[101] *Id.* art. 8(2)(b).

[102] Note, however, that the Mavi Marmara was a Comoros-flagged vessel at the time of the clash. *See supra* note 44. Accordingly, Turkish *territorial jurisdiction* did not extend to the Mavi Marmara.

[103] Penal Code art. 12(1), (2) (emphasis added).

[104] *Id.* art. 20(1) (emphasis added).

[105] *Id.* art. 21.

[106] *Id.*

[107] *Id.* art. 13 (emphasis added).

[108] *See supra* note 46 and accompanying text.

Offences Against Humanity), 94 (Torture), and 223(3) (Seizure of a Sea Vessel)[109].

In order to enforce these Codes, the Criminal Procedure Code articulates the proper procedure that must be undertaken to prosecute an accused. According to the Penal Code, a person may not be punished "for any act which did not constitute a criminal offence *under the law in force* at the time it was committed"[110]. Further, the general rule concerning an accused's presence at trial is that "[t]he main hearing *shall not be conducted* about the *accused who fails to appear*"[111]. Hence, the general rule prohibits in absentia trials. There are two exceptions to the general rule. *First*, a trial may be held in the absence of the accused when "the crime requires as punishment a judicial fine or confiscation,"[112] i.e., it is a relatively minor crime not allowing imprisonment. That is clearly not the case in the Mavi Marmara trial—there, the Turkish prosecutor is seeking jail sentences totaling *more than 18,000 years* for the four accused Israeli officers[113]. *Second*, "[t]he main trial may be concluded in the absence of the accused, even if he has not been interrogated as to the merits of the case, *if the collected evidence is sufficient to give a judgment other than conviction*,"[114] i.e., when the evidence indicates that no conviction is warranted. The phrase, "even if he has not been interrogated as to the merits of the case", demonstrates the general requirement under the Criminal Procedure Code that *the accused must be interrogated about the case before he can be tried*. An interrogation is a "hearing of the suspect or the accused by the judge or the court about the crime, which is under investigation or prosecution"[115].

---

[109] *See supra* note 46.
[110] Penal Code art. 7(1) (emphasis added). Once again, this appears to be a significant factor in the LOAC versus peacetime maritime law debate.
[111] Criminal Procedure Code art. 193(1) (emphasis added).
[112] *Id.* art. 195(1).
[113] Gladstone, *supra* note 47.
[114] Criminal Procedure Code art. 193(2) (emphasis added).
[115] *Id.* art. 2(h).

The Criminal Procedure Code does outline special adjudication procedures for persons, dubbed as either "defaulters" or "fugitives", who do not appear when summoned or subpoenaed by a court. Yet, neither procedure allows for a trial *in absentia* which *ends in conviction*. The Criminal Procedure Code defines a "defaulter" as an "accused, whose whereabouts are not known, or *who is outside of the country and cannot be brought in*, or it is not appropriate to bring him before the competent court"[116]. No main hearing may be opened against a defaulter, although the court may take steps to "obtain[] or protect[] evidence"[117]. A "fugitive", on the other hand, is an "individual who hides himself within the country in order to invalidate a pending prosecution against him, or is in a foreign country and for this reason the court cannot reach him"[118]. Hence, a fugitive is a person over whom the court already had jurisdiction but who actively seeks to evade his trial, either by hiding from authorities within Turkey or by leaving the country. As such, the trial of a fugitive may proceed. Yet, *even then, if a fugitive has not already been interrogated by a judge*, a judgment of conviction may not be rendered[119]. As such, whether an accused is designated as a defaulter or as a fugitive, *absent a valid interrogation*, no conviction may lawfully be rendered.

Analysis of the Prosecutor's and the Court's Actions Against the Israeli Accuseds in Light of the Requirements Set Forth in the Penal Code & Criminal Procedure Code

There are numerous, significant, obvious deviations from the Penal Code and the Criminal Procedure Code in the prosecution of the four Israeli officers, deviations which clearly establish that the

---

[116] *Id.* art. 244(1) (emphasis added).

[117] "There shall be no main hearing opened against a defaulter; the court shall conduct necessary interactions with the aim of obtaining or protecting evidence". *Id.* art. 244(2).

[118] *Id.* art. 247(1).

[119] "The prosecution may be conducted against the fugitive accused. However, if he has not been priorly interrogated by a judge, a judgment concerning his conviction *shall not* be rendered". *Id.* art. 247(3) (emphasis added).

trial is a political show trial. One of the most obvious is a violation of Article 20(1) of the Penal Code, which states that "[c]riminal responsibility is personal. *No one shall be deemed culpable for the conduct of another*"[120]. Not one of the four accused Israeli officers was on board the Mavi Marmara (or any other vessel in the flotilla) when any of the alleged criminal acts took place. Hence, not one of them discharged a weapon at anyone or otherwise injured anyone on the ship, but they are nonetheless being tried in a Turkish court for alleged crimes committed by others. It is *uncontested* that Israeli political authorities had determined that the LOAC governed what transpired concerning the boarding of the Mavi Marmara[121]. Under the LOAC, once a blockade has been established, it *must be enforced* impartially against all neutral ships[122]. Further, the armed forces of the enforcing State have authority to use military force to enforce the blockade against a renegade ship, when necessary[123]. The Mavi Marmara was just such a renegade ship on 31 May 2010, whose Master refused to change course as directed and openly stated that he planned to breach the blockade[124]. Trying Israeli officers who were not even present for alleged crimes committed aboard the Mavi Marmara violates the Penal Code and is a perversion not only of justice, in general, but of the Turkish justice system, in particular, and clearly reveals the political nature of the trial. Further, once the ship had been brought into port, responsibility for the passengers and crew devolved upon police officials[125] over whom the accused military officers had no lawful authority. Yet, some of the alleged "crimes" of which the officers are accused took place after the passengers and crew had been placed under civilian police control, once again in clear and obvious violation

---

[120] *Id.* art. 20(1) (emphasis added).

[121] *See, e.g.*, PALMER REPORT, *supra* note 5, ¶ 73; TÜRKEL REPORT, *supra* note 7, ¶ 16. *See also* San Remo Manual, *supra* note 4, arts. 98, 100.

[122] San Remo Manual, *supra* note 4, arts. 95, 100.

[123] *Id.* art. 98.

[124] *Gaza Flotilla Raid: No Israel Charges Over Mavi Marmara*, BBC (6 Nov. 2014), http://www.bbc.com/news/world-middle-east-29934002.

[125] TÜRKEL REPORT, *supra* note 7, ¶ 152.

of Article 20(1) of the Penal Code.

Coupled with the requirement that "[c]riminal responsibility [be] personal" is the requirement that "[t]he existence of a criminal offence depends upon the presence of intent"[126]. In other words, without the requisite intent, there is no criminal offence. In that regard, it is also *uncontested* that Israeli military leaders had neither anticipated nor planned for a situation where Israeli forces would encounter serious violent resistance when boarding Flotilla vessels to enforce the blockade[127], as even the UN Human Rights Council's Report explicitly found and confirmed[128]. Accordingly, Israeli forces had expected and trained for a relatively peaceful boarding[129] and, hence, the boarding party had been armed primarily with non-life-threatening weapons, like paintball guns[130]. The decisions by senior Israeli military officers to use non-lethal weapons as the primary weapons of the commandos indicate that the Israelis lacked the requisite evil intent necessary to be culpable of the crimes alleged. They had expected (albeit wrongly) to board the vessels peacefully[131]. Hence, killing and serious injuries were not expected, much less explicitly sought, thereby wholly rebutting any presence in the accused Israeli officers of the evil intent required for

---

[126] *Id.* ¶ 21.

[127] *See, e.g.,* TÜRKEL REPORT, *supra* note 7, ¶ 119 (noting that the level of violent resistance was "clearly underestimated").

[128] UNHRC Report, *supra* note 5, ¶ 165, n.78. It is significant that Israeli forces encountered a level of resistance that was wholly unexpected. That, added to the confusion during the boarding, could have led to errors in judgement and outright mistakes when soldiers had to make instantaneous decisions in a highly chaotic situation. Yet, errors in judgement and mistakes lack the requisite evil intent and are not crimes. Further, the Report details the Rules of Engagement (ROE), which clearly indicated that the Israeli boarders were to use the minimum force they deemed necessary at the time, once again a strong indicator that the accused soldiers lacked the requisite evil intent to have committed any of the alleged crimes.

[129] *See, e.g.,* TÜRKEL REPORT, *supra* note 7, ¶ 121. Note especially sub-para. b (regarding non-lethal weapons) and sub-para. c (regarding Rules of Engagement).

[130] *See id.*

[131] The Israeli military admitted after the event that its presumption of peacefulness had been incorrect. *Deaths as Israeli Forces Storm Gaza Aid Ship*, BBC (31 May 2010), http://www.bbc.com/news/10195838.

the offences charged. Moreover, the fact that the Israelis had offered flotilla participants a good faith, peaceful alternative for delivering the humanitarian goods to Gaza over land further subverts any allegation of evil intent on the Israelis' part[132]; instead, the Israelis had sought a peaceful resolution of the matter from the outset. Additionally, once the Israeli commandos had been met with lethal force, to wit, "clubs, knives and steel pipes"[133], they had the right to use lethal force in self-defence[134]. The indictment's reported claim that the resisting Mavi Marmara passengers had been armed solely with "flagpoles, spoons and forks"[135] is absurd on its face and so easily refuted[136] that inclusion of such an allegation in the indictment, if the press reports are correct,

---

[132] Varner, *supra* note 31.

[133] Daniel Dombey & Tobias Buck, *Turkey Draws up Indictment of Israeli Soldiers*, FINANCIAL TIMES (23 May 2012), http://www.ft.com/cms/s/0/9cad8bdc-a4f2-11e1-b421-00144feabdc0.html#axzz3SyXg7llB; *see also IDF Forces Met with Pre-planned Violence when Attempting to Board Flotilla*, ISR. MINISTRY OF FOREIGN AFF., (31 May 2010), http://www.mfa.gov.il/MFA/PressRoom/2010/Pages/Israel_Navy _warns_flotilla_31-May-2010.aspx.

[134] *Turkey Indictment Targets Israel*, GULF NEWS (25 May 2012), http://gulfnews. com /turkey-indictment-targets-israel-1.1027466.

[135] Dombey, *supra* note 133; *see also Indictment Seeks Life For Israeli Command-ers for Mavi Marmara Raid*, *supra* note 45. The Weekly Zaman article explicitly claims that passengers possessed "sticks, spoons and forks" and that they had no weapons:

> Self-defense [for the Israeli boarders] is out of question in spraying and killing people possessing sticks, spoons and forks with [ammuni-tion from] heavy weapons and automatic rifles on the grounds that they attacked them. For self-defense [to be legitimate] there should be a concrete [threatening] act and this act should be illegal. No attacks by victims or complainant occurred during the incident that would require Israeli soldiers to use heavy weapons. *The fact that complainants and victims possessed no weapons was confirmed by international reports and inspections of the ship.*

Id. (emphasis added).

[136] *See, e.g.*, UNHRC Report, *supra* note 5, ¶¶ 101 (noting that passengers were fashioning weapons) & 116 (noting use of "sticks, metal rods, and knives" to re-sist the Israeli commandos); PALMER REPORT, *supra* note 5, ¶¶ 50 (noting flares, rods, axes, knives, tear gas, gas masks, protective masks, and night vision goggles were found on board the Mavi Marmara), 55 (soldiers were attacked with clubs, iron rods, slingshots, and knives) & 124 (soldiers were met with iron bars, staves, chains, slingshots, and knives).

would be a public embarrassment to the entire Turkish judicial system, but especially to the prosecutor who drafted such absurd language and to the judges who approved it. Further, it is *uncontested* that the ship's Master was aware that some of the passengers aboard his ship had been fashioning weapons in anticipation of an Israeli boarding[137]. Accordingly, any claim that the Israelis had been met by unarmed passengers is utter nonsense and simply provides additional evidence that the trial is grounded and motivated by politics, rather than a search for the truth.

Moreover, because the general rule concerning an accused's presence at trial is that "[t]he main hearing *shall not be conducted* about the *accused who fails to appear*"[138], in absentia trials are generally forbidden. The Criminal Procedure Code gives two exceptions: (1) where "the crime requires as punishment a judicial fine or confiscation,"[139] i.e., it is a relatively minor crime not requiring imprisonment, which is clearly not the case in the Mavi Marmara trial, and (2) where "the collected evidence is sufficient to give a judgment other than conviction,"[140] i.e., when the evidence indicates that no conviction is warranted, a conclusion with which the prosecutor and the court would disagree in this matter. The phrase, "even if he has not been interrogated as to the merits of the case" in Criminal Procedure Code Article 193(2), demonstrates the general requirement under the Criminal Procedure Code that *the accused must be interrogated about the case before he can be tried*[141]. Despite the clear limits on conducting in absentia trials, the Mavi Marmara trial is proceeding apace in spite of the absence of the accuseds. This indicates that the prosecutor and the court are willing to disregard explicit, written limits on their authority to act when such limits are politically inconvenient to the ends they seek to achieve. That is part and parcel of a political show trial. The

---

[137] *See, e.g.,* UNHRC Report, *supra* note 5, ¶ 101.
[138] Criminal Procedure Code art. 193(1) (emphasis added).
[139] *Id.* art. 195(1).
[140] *Id.* art. 193(2) (emphasis added).
[141] *Id.*

following example reveals this more fully.

Another obvious violation concerns the court's designation of the accused Israeli officers as "fugitives". The obvious designation under the Criminal Procedure Code for the accused Israeli officers should have been "defaulters", since they are accuses "who [are] outside the country and *cannot be brought in*"[142]. As Israeli nationals not present in Turkey and as persons owing no allegiance or legal duty to Turkey, Turkey had (and has) no lawful authority to compel the accused Israeli officers to appear at a Turkish judicial hearing for an interrogation or any other purpose. "Fugitive" is not the appropriate category for the Israeli accuseds for a number of reasons. *First*, the Criminal Procedure Code defines a "fugitive", in part, as an "individual who hides himself *within the country* in order to invalidate a pending prosecution against him"[143]. Hence, a fugitive is an individual who is otherwise within the jurisdiction of Turkish courts but who is actively evading his attendance at court. *Second*, the part of the definition, "or is in a foreign country and for this reason the court cannot reach him"[144], might seem, at first glance, to apply to persons like the Israeli military officers, but the means Turkish law possesses to encourage a fugitive's presence in court belies that interpretation. Article 247 of the Criminal Procedure Code (which deals solely with fugitives) notes that, should an accused not appear as required, "[t]he court shall render a decision on advertising the invitation in a newspaper, *which shall be posted at the door of the accused's domicile*"[145]. The court could only do so if the accused had a domicile in Turkey, which foreign accuseds like the Israeli military officers would not. *Third*, if the accused does not respond in fifteen days to the invitation *in the newspaper*, the court would then designate him as a fugitive and could inflict on him the measures set forth in Article 248 of the Criminal Procedure Code, to

---

[142] Criminal Procedure Code art. 244(1) (emphasis added).
[143] Criminal Procedure Code art. 247(1) (emphasis added).
[144] *Id.*
[145] *Id.* art. 247(1)(a) (emphasis added).

wit, seizing the accused's belongings in Turkey as well as seizing his "rights and credits"[146]. Hence, *fugitives* are presumed to have assets in Turkey, which suggests that they are either Turkish nationals or foreigners resident in Turkey. There is no analogous provision to try to compel defaulters to appear before a Turkish court. As such, defaulters have no such ties to Turkey. Hence, the Israeli officers meet the definition of defaulters under the Criminal Procedure Code. Accordingly, no main hearing should *lawfully* have been opened against the Israeli military officers[147]. Nonetheless, in the Mavi Marmara "trial", the Turkish court acquiesced in the legal stretch and designated the Israeli accuseds as "fugitives", doubtless to allow the main hearing to proceed (which would not be permitted under the Criminal Procedure Code for defaulters[148]). Yet, making such a legal stretch violates the rule of law and indicates, once again, the political nature and motivation of the Mavi Marmara "trial". It also indicates that judicial officials are fully complicit in the politicisation of the Turkish justice system in this matter.

Despite the prohibition on *in absentia* trials, the main hearing of the trial nevertheless commenced on 6 November 2012 in Istanbul. It began without the presence of any of the accuseds and despite the fact that no interrogations of any of the accuseds had been conducted. According to the indictment, approximately 500 witnesses were expected to be heard[149]. Yet, there was another obvious legal impediment to starting the trial on 6 November. It has been reported that "[t]he 'accused' ha[d] not been served, summoned, notified or informed in any way that they [we]re going to be charged, or what the charges against them [were]"[150], all in clear violation of Turkish

---

[146] *Id.* arts. 247 (1)(b) & 248.

[147] *Id.* art. 244(2).

[148] *Compare* Criminal Procedure Code art. 244(2) *with* art. 247(3).

[149] Ece Toksabay, *Turkey Begins Trial of Israeli Military Over Gaza Ship Killings*, REUTERS (6 Nov. 2012), http://www.reuters.com/article/2012/11/06/us-turkey-israel-trial-idUSBRE8A50KO20121106.

[150] Gul Tuysuz, *Trial Opens in Turkey Against Israeli Military Officers in 2010 Ship Raid*, CNN (6 Nov. 2012), http://www.cnn.com/2012/11/06/world/meast/tur-

criminal law and procedure[151]. Conveying such information to an accused is a basic requirement in any legitimate justice system. Having failed to do so is incredible—and inexcusable. Such open, notorious, and obvious violations of Turkish criminal law and procedure establish the notorious, political nature of the ongoing "trial" and can only mean that judicial officials involved in this matter are more concerned with getting the show trial underway than they are in following the rule of law in the pursuit of truth and justice, thereby tainting the entire Turkish system of justice.

As a final point, Article 24(2) of the Penal Code reads as follows: "A person who carries out an order given by an authorized body as part of his duty, and the execution of this duty is compulsory[,] shall not be held culpable for such act"[152]. Pursuant to this article, persons are not to be held culpable for mandatory acts they have been ordered to carry out. In fact, the article states that they *"shall not* be held culpable"* for such acts.[153] This would surely apply to members of the

key-israeli-officers-trial/ (quoting an email to CNN from Israeli Foreign Ministry spokesman Yigal Palmor); *see also Turkey Tries Israeli Officers, Seeks 18,000-Year Sentences for Mavi Marmara Deaths*, TIMES OF ISRAEL (6 Nov. 2012), http:// www. timesofisrael.com/turkey-tries-israeli-commanders-in-absentia-seeks-18000-year-sentence/ ("The so-called accused were not even informed or served or notified that they were going to be charged, which makes th[e trial] one big puppet show".); Toksabay, *supra* note 149 ("This is not a trial, this is a show trial with a kangaroo court. This is a trial taken right out of a Kafka novel, a grotesque political show that has nothing to do with law and justice".). *See also An Istanbul Court Holds a Show Trial of Israelis Accused of Responsibility for the Deaths of Nine Turkish Operatives Aboard the Mavi Marmara*, MEIR AMIT INTELLIGENCE & TERRORISM CTR. (13 Nov. 2012), http://www.terrorism-info.org.il/en/article/20422, ¶¶ 2 (claiming deliberations were postponed after three days to 21 February 2013 "because of legal flaws") & 6 (citing report by Turkish journalist Efkan Bulaç on the Ulkede-haber website, November 7, 2012, that the accused Israelis had not received formal summonses prior to the commencement of the trial).

[151] Criminal Procedure Code arts. 175(2) (requiring the issuing of summonses to those to appear at main hearing) & 176(1) (requiring that the "indictment and sum-mons shall be notified to the accused all together".).

[152] Penal Code art. 24(2).

[153] *Id.* (emphasis added). Although Article 24(3) reads, in effect, that an unlawful order should not be carried out at any time, enforcing a properly announced and es-tablished naval blockade is not an unlawful order under the LOAC. In fact, enforc-

armed forces of a country executing an operation in defence of that country as determined by the appropriate national political authorities. Defence policy in Israel is made at the Parliamentary level, *inter alia*, by the Prime Minister and the Minister of Defence of Israel. When Israeli political authorities determine that an armed conflict exists, Israeli armed forces must then conduct themselves in accordance with the LOAC. Moreover, when Israeli government officials determine that the armed forces of Israel are needed to defend the country by enforcing a naval blockade established pursuant to the LOAC, then such soldiers (from the highest echelons to the lowest) are duty-bound to obey such an order, i.e., it is "compulsory". As such, based on the principle of comity among sovereigns, Turkey is obligated to grant to Israeli public servants the same respect and legal leeway that it grants to its own public servants. Accordingly, the accused Israeli officers should never have been charged since they were carrying out the compulsory orders of their government. Once again, deciding to try Israeli officers for acts for which Turkish military officers would not be tried or held legally culpable clearly reveals the political nature of the ongoing "trial" in Istanbul.

IV. THE TURKISH PROSECUTOR'S FAILURE TO INDICT THE MAVI MARMARA'S MASTER FOR CRIMINALLY RECKLESS CONDUCT IN PRECIPITATING THE EVENTS THAT RESULTED IN THE DEATHS OF NINE PASSENGERS ABOARD HIS SHIP REVEALS THE POLITICAL MOTIVATION OF THE ONGOING TRIAL

On 31 May 2010, the date of the clash between the Israeli armed forces and the so-called Free Gaza Flotilla, the Mavi Marmara was a Comoros-flagged ship[154]. As such, the Union of Comoros could have—*and should have*—intervened to prevent the unlawful actions of

---

ing such a blockade is itself *required* by the LOAC. *See, e.g.*, San Remo Manual, *supra* note 4, art.100.

[154] *See supra* note 44.

the ship's Master and crew, since the Mavi Marmara was a Comoros national under international law. It is the responsibility of Comoros to ensure that its flagged vessels abide by international law[155]. Yet, in addition to failing to prevent the Master's unlawful conduct on that date, Comoros has taken no subsequent legal action against the Master of the ship, despite his having violated his obligations under international law by knowingly placing his ship, crew, passengers, and cargo at grave risk when he attempted to breach a properly announced and defended naval blockade in a recognised zone of armed conflict.

It is well-established as customary international law that the captain of a ship is the Master of the vessel[156]. Accordingly, the Master bears ultimate responsibility for the safety of the vessel and all persons aboard it: *"The master is charged with the safety of the ship and cargo; in his hands are the lives of passengers and crew"*[157]. The Master of the Mavi Marmara on the day of the clash on the high seas was a Turkish national over whom Turkish courts have jurisdiction by virtue of his nationality[158] and over whom Comoran courts have jurisdiction by virtue of his serving as Master of a Comoros-flagged vessel.

---

[155] Jeremy Firestone & James Corbett, *Combating Terrorism in the Environmental Trenches: Responding to Terrorism: Maritime Transportation: A Third Way for Port and Environmental Security*, 9 WID. L. SYMP. J. 419, 437 (2003).

[156] EDGAR GOLD, COMMAND: PRIVILEGE OR PERIL? THE SHIPMASTER'S LEGAL RIGHTS AND RESPONSIBILITIES 7 (Background paper prepared for the 12th International Command Seminar, London 2003), *available at* http://www.ifsma.org/fairtreatment/documents/commandGold.pdf (discussing that the master's legal authority and responsibility have "been confirmed by numerous legal decisions in many states over a long period of time, despite the fact that it has never been set out in any international instrument. In other words, the master's authority and responsibility is something that is *accepted in terms of customary law on a global basis*". (emphasis added)).

[157] HERBERT HOLMAN, A HANDY BOOK FOR SHIPOWNERS & MASTERS 1 (William H. Maisey 6th ed. 1906) (1896) (emphasis added). *See also* CHRISTOPHER HILL, MARITIME LAW 495 (5th ed. 1995) ("[The master] is also the commander of men, his crew, and he occupies a position of special trust, a fiduciary relationship with his owners. He is absolutely responsible for the safety of the ship and remains in command regardless of whether or not his ship is in charge of a pilot at any given time".)

[158] TURKISH REPORT, *supra* note 5, at 122.

Regarding the 31 May attempt to breach the Israeli naval blockade of the Gaza Strip, the Master of the Mavi Marmara was aware of the following facts at the time he made the fateful decision to breach the Israeli naval blockade:

(1) That the Israeli navy had established a naval blockade of the Gaza Strip[159];

(2) That the blockade had been properly announced to mariners[160];

(3) That the Israeli navy considered the blockade to be a lawful blockade[161];

(4) That the Israeli navy intended to enforce the blockade against the Flotilla of vessels of which the Mavi Marmara was a part[162];

(5) That the Israeli navy had given multiple warnings to Flotilla

---

[159] *Id.* at 64; UNHRC Report, *supra* note 5, ¶ 108; Türkel Report, *supra* note 7, ¶ 123. There is also a very telling comment in the UNHRC Report that mentioned the reluctance of commercial shipping companies to allow their vessels to be chartered by the planned flotilla. UNHRC Report, *supra* note 5, ¶ 81 (noting that Flotilla supporters had to purchase their own vessels in light of the reluctance of commercial firms to lease their ships to the Flotilla). Although the reason for such reluctance is not explicitly stated in the UNHRC Report, it is well-known that commercial shipping companies are reluctant to put their ships in harm's way, and challenging an announced naval blockade in a zone of armed conflict would clearly constitute such a danger. The Master of the Mavi Marmara would have known that, but he sought to breach the blockade anyway, once again establishing how reckless his actions truly were.

[160] Turkish Report, *supra* note 5, at 64; Palmer Report, *supra* note 5, ¶ 75; Türkel Report, *supra* note 7, ¶¶ 26 & 58.

[161] Turkish Report, *supra* note 5, at 64; Türkel Report, *supra* note 7, ¶ 123.

[162] UNHRC Report, *supra* note 5, ¶ 108; Türkel Report, *supra* note 7, ¶ 123; Palmer Report, *supra* note 5, ¶ 105 & n.337 (citing Turkish Report, Annex 5/1/i, at 1 ("I told them [the Israelis] again that we were in international waters and our route was directed towards Israel [Gaza] and that they could not ask us to change our route".), Annex 5/5/x, at 2 ("I proceeded to communicate to the Israeli Navy over VHF radio on behalf of the Freedom Flotilla, stating . . . that we were unarmed civilians aboard six vessels carrying only humanitarian aid headed for the Gaza Strip".).

vessels about the blockade and its intent to enforce it[163];

(6) That the Israeli navy had directed the vessels to change course away from the Gaza Strip multiple times prior to attempting to board the Mavi Marmara[164];

(7) That, during the voyage towards the Gaza Strip, persons on board the Mavi Marmara had been fashioning weapons to resist any Israeli attempt to board the ship[165];

(8) That there were passengers aboard the ship who had expressed their hope to achieve martyrdom[166]; and

(9) That Israel had offered a peaceful alternative for delivering the humanitarian goods to the Gaza Strip over land under UN auspices and control[167].

Despite all that he knew, the Master knowingly and deliberately decided to reject the Israeli demand either to alter course away from the Gaza Strip or to change course to the Israeli port of Ashdod pursuant to the Israeli offer to deliver the humanitarian cargo to Gaza over land. *The captain's knowing and deliberate decision to reject the Israeli Navy's demands set in motion the series of events that directly led to the boarding of his ship by Israeli commandos and ultimately to the deaths of nine of the ship's passengers who resisted the Israeli boarding with*

---

[163] Palmer Report, *supra* note 5, ¶¶ 106, 111; Türkel Report, *supra* note 7, ¶ 123.

[164] Palmer Report, *supra* note 5, ¶ 106; Türkel Report, *supra* note 7, ¶ 123.

[165] UNHRC Report, *supra* note 5, ¶¶ 99–101; Palmer Report, *supra* note 5, ¶ 123 & n.384 (noting passengers' preparing for violent resistance "well in advance"); Türkel Report, *supra* note 7, ¶ 167 (noting that the Captain of the Mavi Marmara was aware that some passengers were fashioning metal clubs to resist any attempt to board the ship).

[166] Türkel Report, *supra* note 7, ¶ 168 (noting that six of the nine passengers killed had expressed a desire to become martyrs); Hartmann, *supra* note 26. This news story includes a video of a passenger stating, "When I went on the first convoy, I wanted to be a shaheed [martyr]. I wasn't that lucky. Second time, I wanted to be a shaheed. Didn't work. Third time, lucky, [with the help of God] I will be a shaheed". *Id.*; *see also* Spencer, *supra* note 26.

[167] Palmer Report, *supra* note 5, ¶ 100; Türkel Report, *supra* note 7, ¶ 123.

deadly force, an outcome that was clearly foreseeable given the Master's knowledge that some passengers aboard his ship had been fashioning weapons to resist any attempt to board the vessel. Given what he knew at the time, the Master's decision constitutes criminal recklessness. *But for* the Master's decision to reject both Israel's demand that he alter course away from the Gaza Strip as well as Israel's good faith offer of a peaceful alternative to deliver the humanitarian goods to Gaza over land, Israeli commandos would not have had to board the vessel to enforce the blockade, passengers on the vessel would not have attacked the Israelis with lethal force, the Israelis would not have had to resort to lethal force in self-defence, and no one aboard the Mavi Marmara would have been killed or injured. Remarkably, *despite the foregoing,* neither Turkish nor Comoran prosecutors have sought to indict and try the Master of the Mavi Marmara for his criminal recklessness in knowingly putting his ship, its passengers and crew, and its cargo in a situation where there was not only a serious *possibility* of death, injury, and/or damage, but where *actual* death and serious bodily injury did, in fact, occur.

In light of the foregoing, the ship's Master was criminally culpable for the deaths and serious injuries that occurred as a result of his criminally reckless decision to reject the peaceful alternative offered by the Israeli government and to continue to sail his vessel towards the Gaza Strip, knowing that the Israeli navy had repeatedly stated its intent to enforce the blockade against all ships seeking to breach it, including his ship. Moreover, *given that the Master was aware that passengers on his ship had been fashioning weapons to resist attempts to board the ship, he was fully on notice of the danger of death or serious bodily injury to which he was subjecting his passengers by continuing to sail toward the Gaza Strip.*

The Turkish Penal Code contains articles to deal with such criminal recklessness. It appears that the Turkish Master violated a number of criminal provisions in the Penal Code. He appears, for example, to have violated Article 179(2) of the Penal Code, which reads, in pertinent part: "Any person who directs and controls a . . . sea . . . transportation vehicle such as to risk the life, health or property of others shall be sentenced to a penalty of imprisonment for a term up to two years"[168]. The Master of the Mavi Marmara did exactly that by knowingly and deliberately sailing his ship into a recognised zone of armed conflict despite international maritime notices of the existence of the naval blockade and despite multiple warnings by Israeli naval forces that they would enforce the blockade[169]. It also appears that the Master violated Article 180(1): "Any person who endangers the life, health or property of another by recklessness during sea . . . transportation shall be sentenced to a penalty of imprisonment for a term of three months to three years"[170]. Once again, the Master was on clear notice of the danger, and he sailed on despite the multiple warnings he had received. Further, because the Master knowingly and willingly accepted the risk of death and severe bodily injury to his passengers and crew by disregarding the international maritime warning as well as Israel's warnings to alter course away from Gaza and Israel's good faith offer to deliver the ship's humanitarian cargo to Gaza by land, he appears to have violated Article 85 of the Penal Code: "Any person who causes the death of another by reckless conduct shall be sentenced to a penalty of imprisonment for a term of two to six years"[171]. Article 85 continues: "If the act results in the death of more than one person, or the injury of more than one person together with death of one or more persons, the offender shall be sentenced to a penalty of imprisonment for a term of two to fifteen years"[172]. The Master's knowing and willful reckless acts resulted in the deaths of nine persons and the injury of many others. Yet, no known indictment has been offered to a court for consideration.

---

[168] Penal Code art. 179(2).
[169] *See supra* notes 159 & 160.
[170] Penal Code art. 180(1).
[171] *Id.* art. 85(1).
[172] *Id.* art. 85(2).

The Master (and the IHH members who sought the armed confrontation with the Israeli armed forces) may also be criminally liable for violating Article 306(1), which reads in pertinent part as follows: "Any person who, without authorisation . . . engages in . . . hostile activities against a foreign state in a manner which exposes the Turkish state to the risk of war, shall be sentenced to a penalty of imprisonment for a term of five to twelve years"[173]. Then Turkish Prime Minister Erdoğan described the 31 May clash on the high seas as "a cause for war"[174]. Yet, once again, *but for* the Master's refusal to comply with Israeli instructions to choose one of the two alternatives that would have avoided a confrontation, there would have been no confrontation. It is the Turkish Master of the Mavi Marmara whose criminally reckless acts created the "risk of war". Article 306(3) continues: "If the act is such as to merely impair political relations with the foreign state or to expose the Turkish state or Turkish citizen to the risk of retaliation, the offender shall be sentenced to a penalty of imprisonment for a term of two to eight years"[175]. There is no doubt that diplomatic relations between Israel and Turkey have been significantly impaired since the Mavi Marmara and other Flotilla vessels attempted to breach the Israeli blockade[176].

A ship's Master has the duty to protect his ship, passengers, crew, and cargo[177]. Part and parcel of the Master's duty is to identify and evaluate known and potential dangers and to avoid them, if at all possible. The Master of the Mavi Marmara disregarded his clear legal duty and, instead of protecting his passengers and crew by avoiding danger, exposed them to clear and foreseeable *but wholly avoidable* danger. He did so knowingly and willingly. Such actions constitute

---

[173] *Id.* art. 306(1).
[174] *See, e.g., Erdoğan: Mavi Marmara Raid Was 'Cause for War'*, TODAY'S ZAMAN (12 Sept. 2011), http://www.todayszaman.com/diplomacy_erdogan-mavi-marmara-raid-was-cause-for-war_256509.html.
[175] Penal Code art. 306(3).
[176] *See supra* note 174.
[177] *See supra* notes 156 & 157.

criminal recklessness on the part of a ship's Master. Hence, *but for the Master's criminally reckless conduct, no Israeli boarding of the Mavi Marmara would have been necessary, and no clash would have occurred.* Nevertheless, it appears that no Turkish prosecutor has sought an indictment against the Master, despite his clear role in the deaths of eight Turkish passengers and one Turkish-American passenger, not to mention injuries to numerous other passengers and to the Israeli commandos carrying out their legal duty to enforce the blockade. *The Master of the Mavi Marmara had it solely within his power and authority to have altogether avoided the confrontation with the Israeli forces.* Instead of doing so, he knowingly and deliberately chose to risk the confrontation, thereby endangering the ship, its passengers and crew, and its cargo. That is the definition of criminal recklessness for the Master of a ship[178]. Moreover, the Master's knowing and deliberate acceptance of the risk inexorably led to the events that resulted in the deaths of nine passengers and in bodily injury to many more. Accordingly, the Master of the Mavi Marmara, *who by virtue of his position as such bore sole responsibility for the safety and welfare of his passengers,* failed dramatically in carrying out his duties to protect them. He was, therefore, personally responsible for what occurred due to his criminal recklessness in failing to properly execute his duties as ship's Master to protect his ship, passengers, crew, and cargo.

The Turkish prosecutor's failure to charge the Master of the Mavi Marmara, a Turkish national, for his role in the deaths of nine Turkish passengers and the serious bodily injury to many others that occurred on his ship due to his refusal to comply with the directions of the Israeli navy concerning a properly declared naval blockade once again reveals that Turkish authorities are more interested in politics than in justice and the rule of law. The Master of the Mavi Marmara, *like the Master of every ship of every nationality,* must comply with applicable international maritime law, whether in peace or in war. When a military blockade has been established and announced,

[178] *See id.*

the LOAC becomes *lex specialis* with respect to the blockade, and its requirements take precedence over peacetime maritime rules for all ships in the area of the blockade—irrespective of whether the ship's Master personally believed the blockade to be lawful or not. The Master knew that he was sailing his ship into harm's way and, hence, should have affirmatively acted to avoid the danger, especially since there were two obvious ways to do so, *known to him at the time*. He did neither. Instead, he knowingly and willfully continued on the course to breach the blockade, thereby placing his ship, passengers, crew, and cargo at risk in direct violation of his responsibilities as ship's Master. Accordingly, he is criminally culpable and should be tried for his criminal recklessness that resulted in the deaths of nine of the passengers under his care as well as the bodily injury to countless others for whose safety he bore sole responsibility as ship's Master.

CONCLUSION

The ongoing trial in Istanbul of four Israeli military officers is nothing more than a political show trial. The trial disregards the fact that Israeli political authorities had determined, based on the attacks emanating from the Gaza Strip, that a state of armed conflict exists between Israel and Hamas and its Islamist allies in Gaza; that Israel has an absolute right to defend itself and its people from such attacks; that the applicable law in periods of armed conflict is the LOAC; and that establishing a naval blockade to stanch the flow of militarily useful materiel to one's enemies is lawful. The Turkish trial also disregards Israel's obligation under the LOAC to enforce a blockade it establishes against all neutral ships, including those claiming to be on humanitarian missions. The 31 May 2010 clash between Israeli armed forces and the so-called Free Gaza Flotilla occurred—*not because Israel desired it*—but because Flotilla vessels knowingly and willfully refused to avail themselves of either of the two peaceful alternatives known to them—i.e., either to change course away from the Gaza Strip or to divert course into the port of Ashdod to unload their humanitarian cargo for subsequent delivery to Gaza over land under UN auspices—and because Israel was duty-bound under the LOAC to impartially enforce its blockade.

Further, despite Israel's attempt to avoid the confrontation altogether by making its good faith offer to deliver the humanitarian goods to Gaza over land, Turkish authorities are trying, via the ongoing trial, to force on Israel *their view* of what the applicable law was on 31 May 2010—to wit, peacetime maritime law. Turkey has no authority to force its view on another sovereign state. Moreover, the vessel Mavi Marmara was not a Turkish-flagged vessel on 31 May 2010. As such, Turkey lacks general jurisdiction over what occurred on that vessel on that date—that jurisdiction belongs to the flag state, the Union of the Comoros. Nonetheless, Turkey has asserted jurisdiction anyway. Yet, even assuming *arguendo* that Turkish courts have authority to assert jurisdiction, how the prosecutor and the judges are conducting the trial indicates without question that the trial is political theatre rather than a search for the truth and the achievement of justice. Turkish judicial authorities were so anxious to get the trial underway that the trial began *before* any of the accused Israeli officers had been served with summonses or copies of the indictment. Turkish judicial authorities were so anxious to get the trial underway that they improperly designated the Israeli officers as "fugitives" because designating them properly under Turkish law (i.e., as "defaulters") would have meant that no main hearing could be commenced without their presence. Turkish judicial authorities were so anxious to get the trial underway that the judges approved an indictment holding the Israeli officers personally responsible for alleged crimes they could not have committed. Finally, Turkish officials were so anxious to try Israelis that they declined to investigate and indict the one person who had both the authority and the opportunity to have avoided the confrontation altogether, the Turkish Master of the Mavi Marmara (a person over whom Turkish courts clearly have jurisdiction by virtue of his nationality as well as his presence in Turkey). It was the Master's knowing and willful dereliction of his duty as ship's Master to ensure the safety of his ship, passengers, crew, and cargo that inexorably led to the deaths and injuries of the passengers aboard his vessel. Instead of trying the one person whose actions directly precipitated the events that led to the deaths and injuries aboard the Mavi Marmara, Turkish authorities have instead decided to prosecute Israeli officers who were duty-bound by the LOAC to enforce the blockade against vessels seeking to breach it. In the final analysis, the ongoing political show trial in Istanbul constitutes a huge stain on the Turkish judicial system, makes a mockery of the rule of law, and has turned the Turkish judicial system into an object of ridicule before the world.

THE POLITICS OF TURKEY DURING THE HOLOCAUST

STUART J. ROTH*

INTRODUCTION

The systematic destruction of European Jewry during the Holocaust stands as the darkest moment in modern civilisation. The methodological murder of over six million Jews was perpetrated by not only the Germans, but with the collaboration of a long list of countries that were either directly or indirectly accomplices to genocide[1].

*Mr Roth is a Senior Fellow of the Centre for the Study of Law & Public Policy at Oxford. He is also Senior Counsel with both the American Center for Law & Justice (ACLJ), Washington, D.C., and the European Centre for Law & Justice (ECLJ), Strasbourg, France. He received his Bachelor of Science degree *cum laude* from Florida State University, and his *Juris Doctor* degree from the Walter F. George School of Law at Mercer University. Mr Roth has collaborated with ACLJ Chief Counsel Jay Sekulow on twelve United States Supreme Court cases, including the landmark decisions in *Mergens* and *Lamb's Chapel*, that have altered the landscape of religious liberties litigation. Mr Roth's international law practice focuses on constitutional law, human rights, religious liberties and democratic freedoms worldwide, which includes cases before the European Court of Human Rights and the International Criminal Court.

[1] *Collaboration*, USHMM.ORG, http://www.ushmm.org/wlc/en/article.php?Module Id=10005466 (last visited 1 June 2015). For example, after Germany's conquest of France, the French zealously implemented the Nazis' racist policies against the Jews. *See The Holocaust: The French Vichy Regime*, JEWISHVIRTUALLIBRARY. ORG, http://www.jewishvirtuallibrary.org/jsource/Holocaust/VichyRegime.html (last visited 1 June 2015).

At the time the Holocaust began in 1933[2], there were approximately 75,000 Jews living in Turkey[3]; and at the onset of the war, there were between 20,000-50,000 Turkish Jews living in European countries[4]. As a neutral country during WWII, Turkey was able to play a crucial role in rescuing Jews through the efforts of its embassies, and to serve as an escape route to Palestine due to its geographic proximity[5]. Nevertheless, Turkey has been properly criticised by observers for both creating too many economic, legal, and administrative obstacles to the repatriation of Turkish Jews and impeding refugee transit[6]. However, Turkey's foreign policy, which centred on its self-interest in remaining nonaligned, was forced to maneuver around a multifaceted set of competing interests, both domestic and international. Clearly, there was not a coherent, organised governmental effort to rescue or repatriate Jews[7], but the humanitarian efforts of individual diplomats in saving Jews have appropriately been credited[8].

[2] 30 January 1933, the date Adolph Hitler became Chancellor of Germany, is generally accepted as the start of the Holocaust. *See The Holocaust: An Introductory History, available at* http://www.jewishvirtuallibrary.org/jsource/Holocaust/history. html (last visited 21 Jan. 2015).

[3] CORRY GUTTSTADT, TURKEY, THE JEWS, AND THE HOLOCAUST 1, 24 (2009).

[4] Guttstadt places the number of Turkish Jews between 20,000–25,000 but notes that others estimate between 30,000–50,000. It is difficult to pinpoint the number of Jews of Turkish descent living in Europe and reports vary due to differences in census-taking processes. *Id.* at 135.

[5] DALIA OFER, ESCAPING THE HOLOCAUST 163–64 (1990); ARNOLD REISMAN, SHOAH: TURKEY, THE US AND THE UK 181 (2009); STANFORD J. SHAW, TURKEY AND THE HOLOCAUST 256 (1993) [hereinafter TURKEY AND THE HOLOCAUST].

[6] GUTTSTADT, *supra* note 3, at 242–43, 310–13.

[7] Guttstadt has criticised Turkey's efforts in this regard. GUTTSTADT, *supra* note 3, at 309–13. Her perspective is that the efforts of Turkish diplomats to save the Jews have also been greatly exaggerated. *Id.* at 149–51. Bahar also agrees. I. IZZET BAHAR, TURKEY AND THE RESCUE OF EUROPEAN JEWS 2361–412 (2013) (5 Dec. 2014 Kindle Edition). *See also* GUNTHER JIKELI & JOELLE ALLOUCHE-BENAYOUN, PERCEPTIONS OF THE HOLOCAUST IN EUROPEAN AND ISLAMIC COMMUNITIES 62–63 (2013).

[8] ARNOLD REISMAN, AN AMBASSADOR AND A MENSCH 227–29 (2010) [hereinafter AN AMBASSADOR AND A MENSCH]; *Turks Saved Jews from Nazi Holocaust*, RAOUL WALLENBERG FOUNDATION (25 Oct. 2008), http://www.raoulwallenberg.net/ highlights/turks-saved-jews-nazi/; *Prime Minister Erdogan Tells ADL That "Anti-Semitism Has No Place in Turkey"*, ALD.ORG, http://archive.adl.org/presrele/ asint_13 /4730_13.html#.VINq1ouNT9v (last visited 1 June 2015); *Unexpected*

Turkey's policies during the Holocaust must be examined in light of the contemporary challenges of deteriorating domestic economic conditions, European anti-Semitism[9], threat of invasion, and balancing the hostile foreign policies of Britain and the United States towards Jewish refugees. In this context, Turkey steered a path of a cautious and independent country caught in the crosshairs of war[10], and this was reflected at times in its apathy concerning the Jews. This paper will examine the implications of Turkey's political doctrine and its impact on both Turkish and European Jews during the Holocaust.

I. BACKGROUND: THE HISTORY OF JEWS IN THE OTTOMAN EMPIRE

Ottoman Empire Welcomes Persecuted Jews from Europe

There has been a Jewish presence in Turkey ever since the 4th century B.C. The Jewish historian, Josephus Flavius, noted that Aristotle encountered Jews in the region and archeologists have found temple ruins dating from as early as 220 BC[11]. In the 1400s, when Sephardic Jews[12] were expelled from Spain during the blood libel[13] attacks of the

---

Saviours: The Role of Turkey in Assisting Victims During the Holocaust, Dep't of Pub. Info. Non-Governmental Orgs (31 Jan. 2011), http://www.un.org/wcm/webdav/site/dpingorelations/shared/Documents/PDF%20Documents/Draft%20Programme.31%20Jan%20Holocaust%20doc.pdf.

[9] Roots of Hate: Anti-Semitism in Europe before the Holocaust 1–10 (2003), *available at* http://assets.cambridge.org/97805217/73089/excerpt/9780521773089_excerpt.pdf. Even before the outbreak of WWII, anti-Semitic laws had been implemented in Germany, Bulgaria, Hungary, Poland, Romania, Slovakia, and France.

[10] Youssef Aboul-Enein & Basil Aboul-Enein, The Secret War for the Middle East: The Influence of Axis and Allied Intelligence Operations During World War II 118, 120, 125 (2013); Selim Deringil, Turkish Foreign Policy During the Second World War 49 (1989).

[11] *Turkey*, jewishvirtuallibrary.org, http://www.jewishvirtuallibrary.org/jsource/vjw/Turkey.html (last visited 1 June 2015).

[12] Sephardic Jews refer to Jews from Spain and Portugal. *See Foundation for the Advancement of Sephardic Studies and Culture*, sephardicstudies.org, http://www.sephardicstudies.org/intro.html (last visited 1 June 2015).

[13] Blood libel refers to allegations that Jews drank the blood of Christian children during Passover. *See Blood Libel*, zionism-israel.com, http://www.zionism-israel.

inquisition, the Ottoman Empire and Sultan Bayazid II reached out and welcomed Jews to settle in their land, where the Jews flourished and integrated into the community[14]. The oppression of the Jews continued, as did their migration to the Ottoman Empire. Jews fled Serbia, Bulgaria, and the Ukraine in the late 1600s, and then Christian persecution in Eastern Europe and Greece during the 19th century[15].

As Jews were being victimised in Germany during the 15th century, influential Rabbi Safarti encouraged them to emigrate, proclaiming, "Here everyman dwells at peace under his own vine and fig tree . . . . The way to the Holy Land lies open to you through Turkey"[16]. The 16th and early 17th centuries were referred to as the Golden Age of Ottoman Jewry, and its bourgeoning Jewish population exceeded those in Christian Europe"[17]. Even more, the Ottoman Jews made up the most affluent Jewish community in the world[18]. Over the centuries, Jews were able to assimilate into society and served numerous régimes as court physicians, lawyers and educators; as innovators, they introduced modern technology such as the printing press[19]. They were also notably involved in lawmaking affairs and Ottoman diplomacy. That being the case, Jews enjoyed the favour of the government. For example, while responding to accusations of blood libel in 1840, Sultan Abdulmeci defended his Jewish citizens, saying, "and for the love we bear to our subjects, we cannot permit the Jewish nation, whose innocence for

---

com/dic/blood_libel.htm (last visited 1 June 2015).

[14] *Jews in the Ottoman Empire and Turkey*, PROJECTALADIN.ORG, http://www.projetaladin.org/holocaust/en/muslims-and-jews/muslims-and-jews-in-history/jews-in-the-ottoman-empire-and-turkey.html (last visited 1 June 2015). *See also Turkey, supra* note 11.

[15] STANFORD J. SHAW, THE JEWS OF THE OTTOMAN EMPIRE AND THE TURKISH REPUBLIC 2, 3–9, 237 (1991) [hereinafter THE JEWS OF THE OTTOMAN EMPIRE]. *See also Turkey, supra* note 11.

[16] *Turkey, supra* note 11. *See* full text of Safarti letter at *Letter of Rabbi Isaac Zafarti,* TURKISHJEWS.COM, http://www.turkishjews.com/history/letter.asp (last visited 21 Jan. 2015) (site references BERNARD LEWIS, THE JEWS OF ISLAM 135–36 (1984)).

[17] THE JEWS OF THE OTTOMAN EMPIRE, *supra* note 15, at 36–40.

[18] *Id.* at 36.

[19] *Jews in the Ottoman Empire and Turkey, supra* note 14.

the crime alleged against them is evident, to be worried and tormented as a consequence of accusations, which have not the least foundation in truth"[20].

On the other hand, there were long periods of decline for the Ottoman Jews in the 17th and 18th century[21]. This resulted in part from a void in effective leadership amongst the ruling class in the Empire; but economic, social and political reforms reinvigorated the community in the 19th and 20th century[22]. During the latter periods of the Ottoman Empire, laws were enacted that served to benefit the economically thriving Jewish population[23], prompting the Alliance Israelite Universelle in Paris to report, "there are but few countries, even among those which are considered the most enlightened and the most civilized, where Jews enjoy a more complete equality than Turkey"[24]. The culmination of WWI and the Treaty of Sèvres[25] brought an end to the Ottoman Empire; and in the aftermath of the Turkish War of Liberation[26], Turkey passed legislation that disfavoured Jews and other minorities[27]. Faced with a new social and political climate, many Turkish Jews decided to emigrate to escape the uncertainties inherent in this fledgling new nation[28]. The Republic of Turkey was born in 1923,

[20] *Id.*

[21] BAHAR, *supra* note 7, at 913–29.

[22] THE JEWS OF THE OTTOMAN EMPIRE, *supra* note 15, at 109–11,147–50.

[23] *Id.* at 155–57, 206–09.

[24] *Id.* at 210.

[25] *The National War of Independence,* HISTORYOFTURKEY.COM, http://www.history-ofturkey.com/independence/ (last visited 1 June 2015). Turkey fought with Germany on the losing side of WWI, and the Ottoman Empire was subsequently dissolved and divided up between France, Italy, Britain, and Greece at the Treaty of Sèvres. The Allies occupied parts of Istanbul and much of what is now modern Turkey, while the Turks were left with territory in the Anatolia region.

[26] *Id.* The Turkish people did not recognise the Treaty of Sèvres and the War of Liberation ensued, culminating in creation of the Republic of Turkey, with borders established by the Treaty of Lausanne.

[27] HANS-LUKAS KEISER, TURKEY BEYOND NATIONALISM 43–44 (I.B. Tauris & Co. Ltd. 2006, 2013).

[28] THE JEWS OF THE OTTOMAN EMPIRE, *supra* note 15, at 232–33, 237–43. After WWI, there were approximately 150,000 Jews in Turkey, but approximately 70,000 left by 1929. *See* GUTTSTADT, *supra* note 3, at 24.

the same year a young Adolf Hitler was arrested when he attempted to overthrow the Bavarian government[29].

II. THE POLITICS OF "TURKIFICATION" AND THE JEWS

Turkish Nationalistic Movement Causes Jews to Emigrate

The early republic was in the process of revolutionizing both politically and economically. The government took on modernising its roads, schools, and language by removing many components of its Ottoman history[30]. *Turkification* was a policy aimed at "creating a homogeneous nation-state on the ruins of the multi-ethnic Ottoman Empire"[31], and encountered immediate difficulties in a country of such rich and diverse populations. Most importantly, national identity was the principal concept; and although the nation boasted of democratic principles of equality, in practice there was a pressure on minorities to suppress their cultural identities and religious customs[32]. The impact on Jewish life was substantial. For instance, Jews were required to pray using the Turkish language in synagogues, adopt Turkish surnames, speak Turkish in public, eliminate religious community organisations and change the curriculum in religious schools[33]. Additionally, the government distinguished between Muslim and minority non-Muslim citizens, and used these criteria to define who was really a "Turk" and worthy to be trusted in re-building the economy[34].

As a consequence, the outgrowth of Turkification yielded a series of laws and restrictions that favoured the Islamic population at the ex-

---

[29] *Nazi Germany Timeline*, HIST. ON THE NET, http://www.historyonthenet.com/chronology/timelinenazigermany.htm (last updated 7 Aug. 2014).

[30] GUTTSTADT, *supra* note 3, at 2.

[31] *Id.* at 4.

[32] RIFAT N. BALI, MODEL CITIZENS OF THE STATE: THE JEWS OF TURKEY DURING THE MULTI-PARTY PERIOD 3–4 (2012).

[33] *Id.* at 3.

[34] *Id.* at 8–9.

pense of ethnic minorities such as Greeks, Jews, and Armenians[35]. But despite these new measures, the Jews were often referred to as a "model minority"[36]. The father of modern Turkey, Mustafa Kemal (Atatürk), remarked, "There are several loyal population groups that have tied their fate to that of the ruling group, the Turks; the Jews are first among them"[37]. Indeed, these feelings were reciprocated, as Atatürk was "deeply revered and loved by many Jews and was the subject of many poems and songs"[38].

But the surge in nationalism would lead to legislation regarding citizenship, nationality, and residency, which would have far reaching implications on whether Jews who emigrated to Europe could repatriate during the Holocaust[39]. These policies were the subject of much controversy, as they violated numerous provisions of the Treaty of Lausanne that protected religious minorities[40]. As a corollary of Turkification, the nation also experienced the proliferation of anti-Semitic publications caricaturing Jews as greedy, traitors, and disloyal if they had not participated in the War of Liberation[41]. Hence, the political climate and discriminatory polices negatively affected Jews and facilitated

---

[35] *Id.* at 10; BAHAR, *supra* note 7, at 738–805.

[36] GUTTSTADT, *supra* note 3, at 6.

[37] BALI, *supra* note 32, at 6.

[38] GUTTSTADT, *supra* note 3, at 7 (referencing in a footnote, HENRI NAHUM, JUIFS DE SMYRNE XIXE-XXE SIÈCLE 184ff (Paris:Aubier,1997)).

[39] *E.g.*, Laws on Expatriation 1514 and 1745 affected Jews most significantly because they prevented the issuance of passports to non-Muslims who left the country. Law 1312, Article 12, prevented people who lost citizenship from returning to Turkey. Law 1041 of 1927 revoked the citizenship of individuals who did not fight in the War of Liberation. GUTTSTADT, *supra* note 3, at 48–51.

[40] BAHAR, *supra* note 7, at 1024–68; THE JEWS OF THE OTTOMAN EMPIRE, *supra* note 15, at 245–56. The Treaty of Lausanne brought an end to the War of Liberation. *See also* Articles 37–45 of the Treaty that required religious minorities' equal treatment under the law. For complete text of Treaty, *see Lausanne Treaty*, HRI.ORG, http://www.hri.org/docs/lausanne/ (last visited 1 June 2015). For example, laws that discriminated, such as the Law of Civil Servants, mandated that only Turks hold certain positions. Foreign businesses had to trim their workforce of non-Muslims to meet government hiring quotas of Muslims and certification requirements for certain professions excluded non-Muslims. GUTTSTADT, *supra* note 3, at 9–14.

[41] BAHAR, *supra* note 7, at 928–81; GUTTSTADT, *supra* note 3, at 56-58.

resettlement to Europe, with France receiving the majority of Turkish immigrants[42].

III. THE HOLOCAUST BEGINS: THE NAZI PARTY RISES TO POWER IN GERMANY

Turkey Invites Jewish Scholars and Intellectuals from Germany and Austria

In 1933, Adolph Hitler and the Nazi party rose to power and immediately implemented a series of laws with the sole purpose of disenfranchising the Jews of Germany[43]. Daniel Jonah Goldhagen, in his book "Hitler's Willing Executioners", outlined Hitler's initial objectives:

1. To turn the Jews into "socially dead" beings—beings that were violently dominated, natally alienated, and generally dishonored—and, once they were, to treat them as such.

2. To remove the Jews as thoroughly and permanently from social and, as far as possible, from physical contact with the German people and thereby to neutralize them as a factor in German life[44].

As a consequence of these laws, Jews started fleeing Germany, and educators, professionals, and civil servants were terminated from their positions with the government and academic institutions[45]. At the invitation of Turkey, employment opportunities were offered to hundreds of Jewish intellectuals, scientists, and other professionals, who brought

---

[42] GUTTSTADT, *supra* note 3, at 25; BAHAR, *supra* note 7, at 2150–72.

[43] For example, Jews were prohibited from owning land, being newspaper editors, serving in the military, and practicing law and medicine; they were forced to register wealth, property and business; and denied access to national health insurance, etc. See complete timeline and restrictions implemented by Nazis at *Holocaust Timeline*, THE HISTORY

PLACE, http://www.historyplace.com/worldwar2/holocaust/timeline.html (last visited 1 June 2015).

[44] DANIEL JONAH GOLDHAGEN, HITLER'S WILLING EXECUTIONERS 135–36 (1997).

[45] *Id.* at 83.

their families from Germany and Austria to start new lives[46]. Further-more, many of these refugees were some of the most accomplished scholars and brilliant minds in Europe. With the help of the Turkish government, they found excellent positions at the universities in Istan-bul and Ankara, where they became instrumental in Turkey's efforts to upgrade its education system and economic infrastructure[47].

However, this was still a transitional chapter for Turkey and there was no shortage of severe economic hardships for a nation in the process of Turkifying the economy by favouring a workforce of Muslim Turks over minorities[48]. That being the case, the reaction of its citizens to such a large influx of Jewish refugees generated an undercurrent of anti-Semitism, which was encouraged by the local German com-munity[49]. Many of these Jewish professors replaced Turks and were sometimes paid up to five times as much in salary; and while living in the finest neighborhoods, they also received favourable tax benefits and government housing[50]. Yet, some critics dismiss Turkey's benevolence as being self-serving, and motivated solely to advance a struggling nation needing intellectual weight and credibility[51]. Further, it has been noted,

[46] GUTTSTADT, *supra* note 3, at 84–89. Eighty-two German professors started teach-ing at Istanbul University in the winter semester 1933-34; ironically, at the same time in the United States, Ivy League schools and teaching hospitals, like the Ger-mans, had a "Jew-Free" hiring policy for faculty. *See* REISMAN, *supra* note 5, at 20. Furthermore, President Roosevelt believed there were too many Jews at Harvard, and, as a Board member, recommended quotas. Rafael Medoff, *What FDR Said About Jews in Private*, L.A. TIMES (7 Apr. 2013), http://articles.latimes.com/2013/apr/07/opinion/la-oe-medoff-roosevelt-holocaust-20130407.

[47] TURKEY AND THE HOLOCAUST, *supra* note 5, at 4–9; BAHAR, *supra* note 7, at 7249–50. *See* REISMAN, *supra* note 5, at 353–73.

[48] SELIM DERINGIL, TURKISH FOREIGN POLICY DURING THE SECOND WORLD WAR 23–25 (1989); GUTTSTADT, *supra* note 3, at 65.

[49] THE JEWS OF THE OTTOMAN EMPIRE, *supra* note 15, at 252–53; GUTTSTADT, *supra* note 3, at 96–98.

[50] TURKEY AND THE HOLOCAUST, *supra* note 5, at 9–12; GUTTSTADT, *supra* note 3, at 90.

[51] Guttstadt believes the government's motivation was "utilitarian rather than hu-manitarian" in nature, GUTTSTADT, *supra* note 3, at 88–89, and Bahar agrees, BAHAR, *supra* note 7, at 1506–25. Interestingly, Turkish scholars spent a week in June, 2014, studying at the Yad Vashem International School for Holocaust Studies. Aron

correctly so, that Turkey's outreach to Jewish refugees was limited to individuals with outstanding credentials, as opposed to ordinary individuals seeking asylum[52]. By the same token, it has been suggested that Turkey's interest was principally on recruiting intellectuals from Europe and it was merely a coincidence that many of the scholars were indeed Jewish[53].

Germany Revokes Citizenship of Jews, Leaving Them "Stateless"

In September 1935, Germany passed another round of anti-Jewish legislation known as the Nuremberg Laws. One of these ordinances, the Reich Citizenship Law, revoked the citizenship of Jews in Germany and went to great lengths to define who was a Jew in the broadest possible terms in order to cast a wide net[54]. In order to further humiliate, isolate, and identify its Jewish population, additional regulations went into effect making it mandatory that all Jews visibly wear a large yellow Star of David with the word "Jude" on their clothing[55].

After Germany stripped the citizenship of its Jews, emigration increased exponentially to other European countries that were deemed safe at the time only to eventually come under Nazi occupation. As Germany invaded and conquered one country after another, the Nuremberg Laws were applied with full force in each occupied territo-

---

Donzis, *Turkish Academics Attend Yad Vashem Seminar*, THE TIMES OF ISRAEL (26 June 2014, 10:27 PM), http://www.timesofisrael.com/turkish-academics-partici-pate-in-yad-vashemseminar/.

[52] TURKEY AND THE HOLOCAUST, *supra* note 5, at 66; GUTTSTADT, *supra* note 3, at 88–89; BAHAR, *supra* note 7, at 1640–56.

[53] BAHAR, *supra* note 7, at 1855.

[54] The Nuremberg and Reich citizenship laws were aimed at isolating Jews from society. See laws in detail at *The Nürnberg Laws*, HOLOCAUST RES. PROJECT, http://www.holocaustresearchproject.org/holoprelude/nurlaws.html (last visited 1 June 2015); *The Nuremberg Laws: Background & Overview*, JEWISH VIRTUAL LIBRARY, http://www.jewishvirtuallibrary.org/jsource/Holocaust/nurlaws.html (last visited 14 Jan. 2015).

[55] GOLDHAGEN, *supra* note 44, at 138.

ry[56]. Consequently, Jews throughout Europe would eventually lose their citizenship rendering them "stateless", thereby leaving them without any government protection from Nazi persecution[57]. Moreover, the compulsory yellow Star of David badge easily identified them for export to concentration camps. Thus, Turkish Jews who immigrated to Europe were now at risk for deportation to death camps, and subject to anti-Jewish measures being employed by the Nazis.

IV. THE INFLUENCE OF GERMAN ANTI-SEMITISM AND NATIONALISM IN TURKEY

Germans Living Throughout Turkey Spread Nazi Propaganda

As Germany continued its march towards war and domination of Europe, the number of Jewish refugees to Turkey increased[58]. Furthermore, the German community in Turkey was influential, and took advantage of the large influx of Jews by using Nazi literature to generate anti-Semitism through distribution of books and publications[59]. Not to be left out, the German Embassy in Istanbul was responsible for rally-

---

[56] For example, Nuremberg laws were also applied in France, Slovakia, Hungary, Romania, Poland, and other Axis and occupied countries, see timeline at *Holocaust Timeline*, THE HISTORY PLACE, http://www.historyplace.com/worldwar2/holocaust/timeline.html (last visited 1 June 2015).

[57] GUTTSTADT, *supra* note 3, at 144.

[58] TURKEY AND THE HOLOCAUST, *supra* note 5, at 23. Jews were escaping discrimination not only in Germany, but in countries under its influence, such as Poland, Hungary, and Romania.

[59] GUTTSTADT, *supra* note 3, at 42. By 1939, there were approximately 2,000 Germans and 1,000 Austrians living in Turkey. Major German corporations, such as Bayer Pharmaceuticals and Daimler Benz, had offices in Istanbul. Turkish papers would engage in racist caricatures questioning the loyalty of *Jews*; *e.g.*, the *Türkishe Post and Cumhurtyet*. *Id.* at 41. The anti-Semitic *Protocols of the Elders of Zion* was published in the Turkish language. *Id.* at 56, 60. Further, the most notorious source for Nazi-propaganda was the publication *Anadolu*, which created so much unrest that the government shut it down, demonstrating Turkey's efforts to not have its society destabilised by German hate speech and racism. TURKEY AND THE HOLOCAUST, *supra* note 5, at 14.

ing not only local German residents, but also Turkish citizens, with its racist agenda[60]. As a result, German agitation triggered anti-Semitism from the minority Christian community as well as Armenian nationalists[61]. While Turkey was grappling with the influence of this German inspired anti-Semitism, it was simultaneously facing the complexities of a new state searching for a national identity, and beleaguered with religious, social, and economic challenges.

Under these circumstances, the German mindset began to spread quickly throughout Turkey and neighboring territories. In the summer of 1934, a series of attacks and boycotts on Jews took place in Thrace, the perception being that Jews controlled too much of the economy[62]. Moreover, Jews had been present in Thrace since the 4th century, and thrived throughout the years of the Ottoman Empire[63]. Instigated by German propaganda, members of the community believed Jews were not only resisting Turkification, but also controlling the economy, which made them a prime target for retribution[64]. The unrest was prompted when General Inspector Ibrahim Tali Ongoren issued a report after touring the region:

> The Jew of Thrace is so morally corrupt and devoid of character that it strikes one immediately. . . . In the Jewish value system, honor and dignity have no place . . . . [I]t is of the utmost necessity that this element [the Jews], whose hands are grabbing for all the treasures of Thrace, not be allowed to continue to suck out the Turks' blood. The Jews represent a secret danger. . . . And for Turkish Thrace to be able to recover, to finally solve the [Jewish] problem in the most radical way[65].

---

[60] Turkey and the Holocaust, *supra* note 5, at 36–37.

[61] The Jews of the Ottoman Empire, *supra* note 15, at 254.

[62] Bali, *supra* note 32, at 9. Thrace is an area comprised of territory shared by Greece, Bulgaria, and Turkey.

[63] The Jews of the Ottoman Empire, *supra* note 15, at 95.

[64] Bali, *supra* note 32, at 9.

[65] Guttstadt, *supra* note 3, at 67–68.

As a result, Jewish businesses and homes were destroyed, and there were violent physical attacks. Most of the Jews fled their homes to Istanbul, leaving all their possessions behind[66]. The government reacted by banning a key anti-Semitic publication, and firing the local Mayor and Police Chief[67]. Lastly, Prime Minister Ismet Inönü shut down numerous groups and associations engaged in pro-Nazi propaganda, and addressed the Grand National Assembly:

> In Turkey every individual is under the protection of the laws of the Republic. Anti-Semitism is neither a Turkish product nor part of the Turkish mind. At certain periods it penetrates our country from foreign countries but we reject it. This disturbance is most likely a contagion of this sort[68].

Immediately after his speech, Inönü issued a press release advising Jews to seek justice and pursue their attackers[69].

Although anti-Semitism reared its ugly head on occasion, the poisonous racism promoted by the Germans, which had taken root in Europe, was rejected in Turkey[70]. In fact, the Germans noted that "it would be a mistake to think that there would be anti-Jewish laws or regulations [in Turkey] in the near future"[71].

Nationalism and German Influence Cause Shift in Turkish Immigration Laws

Eventually, the sustained evolution of nationalism, combined with the impact of German racist ideology, gave way to anti-minority poli-

---

[66] *Id.* at 62.
[67] TURKEY AND THE HOLOCAUST, *supra* note 5, at 19.
[68] *Id.* at 15.
[69] *Id.* at 16.
[70] GUTTSTADT, *supra* note 3, at 313.
[71] BAHAR, *supra* note 7, at 1111 (citing German State Archives, Politische Archiv Inland II, A/ B R99446, (13 Dec. 1938)) (quoted by Rıfat Bali, Sarayın ve Cumhuriyetin Dişçibaşısı Sami Günzberg [The Chief Dentist of the Court and Republic, Sami Günzberg] 131 (Istanbul: Kitabevi, 2007)).

tics and immigration reform as Jews were fleeing Germany and other European nations. In response, Turkey revised and tightened its existing passport and residence restrictions on refugees and foreigners[72]. Jewish residents, such as the scholars who lost their German citizenship as a result of Nuremberg Laws, were told to leave the country; and Turkish Jews who lived abroad were denied entry back into the country, even if their passports were in proper order[73]. In addition, laws were proposed that would cut-off Jewish immigration and even deport naturalised Turkish Jews if they could not learn to read or write Turkish within a year[74]. In the end, these measures were defeated and Prime Minister Celal Bayar responded to a growing anti-Semitic drumbeat, "There is no Jewish problem in our country. There is no minority problem at all. We do not intend to artificially create a Jewish problem because of external influences. We will not allow external influences to influence us"[75].

The Nazi strategy was clear: revoke the citizenship of German refugees and their families living in Turkey, thereby leaving them technically stateless. This, in turn, would affect their residency status, as Turkish law prevented people from entering or remaining in Turkey if they lost their citizenship in their country of origin[76]. However, when Turkish authorities realised that these laws would have the effect of deporting Jews back to countries in which they would be persecuted, the government issued new residency permits allowing them to stay for up to five years[77]. Even German Ambassador Franz von Papen, based in Istanbul, understood this scheme would not fly with the Turks, writing in his memoirs:

[72] BAHAR, *supra* note 7, at 1637–57; GUTTSTADT, *supra* note 3, at 99–106.

[73] GUTTSTADT, *supra* note 3, at 104–06; TURKEY AND THE HOLOCAUST, *supra* note 5, at 25.

[74] Kemal Atatürk commented: "A person who does not speak Turkish is not to be trusted, even if he claims to have a bond with the Turkish culture". *See* GUTTSTADT, *supra* note 3, at 16 n.47 (quoted in Sadoglu, Turkiye de Ulusculuk, 214); *see also* Rifat N. Bali, *Politics of Turkification During the Single Party Period, available at* http://www.rifatbali.com/images/stories/dokumanlar/basel.pdf.

[75] THE JEWS OF THE OTTOMAN EMPIRE, *supra* note 15, at 254.

[76] GUTTSTADT, *supra* note 3, at 101.

[77] TURKEY AND THE HOLOCAUST, *supra* note 5, at 25. Again, it is noted that these refugees were privileged because of their immense contribution to academia in Turkey. *See* GUTTSTADT, *supra* note 3, at 89–90.

Hitler ordered me to withdraw passports from all German Émigrés in Turkey and deprive them of German citizenship. I resisted this order ... the majority of émigrés had left Germany with the full permission of the Government ... I could not see my way to carry out his instructions ... the Turkish government would consider such a step inexplicable. Not a single émigré was molested in any way[78].

Although these oppressive reforms were ultimately voted down in the Grand National Assembly[79], they were emblematic of the disarray of Turkish politics regarding Jewish immigration and refugee issues. Turkish Prime Minister Refik Saydam attempted to assure the Jewish community by reiterating that "Jews of Turkish nationality who reside in Turkey enjoyed the same constitutional rights as all other Turkish citizens"[80]. He denied anti-Semitism existed in Turkey, but also paradoxically noted, "Turkey does not permit foreign Jews to move here and refuses to grant entry to Jewish emigrants"[81]. The contradictory policies of the Turkish government during the Holocaust demonstrate why observers lament that more lives should have been saved[82].

V. WORLD WAR II BEGINS: TURKEY DECLARES ITS NEUTRALITY

Turkey's Foreign Policy Centred on Peace not War

By the end of May 1939, Nazi Germany had invaded and occupied France, Denmark, Norway, Belgium, Luxembourg, the Netherlands, Czechoslovakia, and Poland. In response, Britain and France declared war on Germany, and later that year entered a tripartite agreement with

---

[78] *Id.* at 13–14.
[79] TURKEY AND THE HOLOCAUST, *supra* note 5, at 24. The Grand National Assembly is Turkey's Parliament, founded during the War of Liberation.
[80] GUTTSTADT, *supra* note 3, at 106.
[81] *Id.* It has been advanced that economic conditions prevented Turkey from taking on more refugees. REISMAN, *supra* note 5, at 29, 37–38.
[82] GUTTSTADT, *supra* note 3, at 309–13.

Turkey for mutual defense and cooperation[83]. At the inception of the war, it appeared as if Germany was unstoppable, and Turkey dexterously moderated its relations between the Allied and Axis powers to preserve its independence and security.

Above all, Turkey was determined to stay neutral after the devastating economic and political effects of both WWI and the War of Liberation; and after Italy's entry into the war on the side of the Germans, it issued a declaration of non-belligerence[84]. Moreover, the dismantling of the Ottoman Empire, and the Capitulations imposed by the Treaty of Sèvres, created severe debt and inflation for the newly formed republic[85]. Complicating matters, over 1.4 million Greeks left Turkey, leaving a depleted professional and skilled workforce and further damaging the outlook of a financial recovery[86]. The nation's leaders recognised their security, military, and fiscal vulnerabilities, and Turkey's foreign policy became centred on the theory, "Peace at Home, Peace Abroad"[87]. Although it proclaimed its neutrality, numerous historians believed that the Turkish government was essentially pro-German, which was a view certainly held by the British[88]. Throughout the war, both Germany and the Allies continually exerted pressure on Turkey to enter the war on

---

[83] *See* Treaty of Mutual Assistance between Turkey, France and the United Kingdom in DERINGIL, *supra* note 10, at 189–92.

[84] ABOUL-ENEIN & ABOUL-ENEIN, *supra* note 10, at 118, 120–21; *see also*, Murat Metin Hakki, *Surviving the Pressure of the Superpowers: An Analysis of Turkish Neutrality During the Second World War*, CHRONICON 44–62 (2005), *available at* http://www.ucc.ie/chronicon/3/hakkfra.html.

[85] DERINGIL, *supra* note 10, at 14–15. Capitulations were a series of hard-to-swallow economic, legal, social, and political concessions that were imposed on Turkey in the Treaty of Sèvres. *Id.* at 68–70. The Treaty of Lausanne, entered into at the end of the War of Liberation, superseded the Treaty of Sèvres and ended capitulations, but economic hardships continued. *Id.* at 14. For full text of Treaty of Sèvres, *see* Treaty of Peace with Turkey (1920), *available at* http://treaties.fco.gov.uk/docs/pdf/1920/TS0011.pdf.

[86] DERINGIL, *supra* note 10, at 15.

[87] *Id.* at 3 (cited quote in Winston Churchill, *The Grand Alliance*, at 484); "Menemencioglu's primary aim as foreign minister was to keep Turkey out of the war". *Id.* at 52 (quoting Weisband, Turkish Foreign Policy, at 50).

[88] *Id.* at 52, 53, 55. *See also*, GUTTSTADT, *supra* note 3, at 35; Hakki, *supra* note 84.

their respective sides[89]. In short, independent Turkey found itself engaged in a delicate balancing act, as Nazi aggression quickly escalated,
drawing surrounding countries into the conflict[90].

By the time the United States entered the war in 1941, German
soldiers were positioned on the borders of western Turkey, and the
potential for a Nazi invasion dictated the nation's anxieties and politics[91]. In order to balance its interests between the Allied and Axis
powers, Turkey likewise signed friendship and non-aggression agreements with both Germany and the Soviet Union[92]. Equally important,
Turkey's foreign policy was driven by economic considerations, as it
was the Nazi regime's sole supplier of chromium, an essential component to manufacture military hardware[93]. So critical was the supply of
chromium that Albert Speer, Germany's Minister of Armaments and
War Production, wrote Hitler, "should supplies of chromium from
Turkey be cut off, the manufacture of tanks, U-boats and other war
machines would cease, the current reserve would be sufficient only for
5-6 months"[94]. Moreover, Turkey relied on Germany as its main trading
partner not only for chromium, but also for wool and cotton, all of
which were critical to its besieged economy[95].

---

[89] DERINGIL, *supra* note 10, at 95, 115, 140, 154, 161.

[90] *Id.* at 100–03, 140, 142, 144. Turkey placed a premium value on its independence and neutrality, and philosophically believed constancy in the region was in
its best self-interest. Foreign Minister Menemencioglu remarked: "We have no use
for either a total English or a total German victory, because for us the existence of a
central stabilized Europe remains a basic prerequisite". *Id.* at 134. Turkey was also
clever enough to procure military equipment from both Germany and the Allies. *Id.*
at 135.

[91] DERINGIL, *supra* note 10, at 121, 124, 130, 149. Turkey was also concerned about
hostilities with Italy. *Id.* at 32, 71–72, 89. *See also* Hakki, *supra* note 84.

[92] For full text Turkish-German Friendship Treaty, *see* Turkish–German Friendship Treaty, 18 June 1941, *available at* http://www.ibiblio.org/pha/policy/1941/410618a. html.

[93] ABOUL-ENEIN & ABOUL-ENEIN, *supra* note 10, at 121. In an effort to balance its
trade dependence and facilitate friendly relations with both the Allied and Axis
factions, Turkey also provided Britain with with chromium and, at one juncture,
offered the British its entire output. *See* DERINGIL, *supra* note 10, at 27–28.

[94] ABOUL-ENEIN & ABOUL-ENEIN, *supra* note 10, at 121.

[95] DERINGIL, *supra* note 10, at 23–24.

It is probable that the pro-German sentiment can be explained not only by financial dependence, but also by a common enemy, the Soviet Union[96]. There were approximately forty million people of Turkish ethnicity living in the Soviet Union, and Turkey had a keen interest in their status, and consequently had a stake in the outcome of military action between the Russians and Nazis[97]. Additionally, the concessions forced upon Turkey in the Treaty of Sèvres, created empathy for the German predicament of having their hands tied by the Treaty of Versailles[98].

Despite neutrality pacts with Germany, Russia, and the Allies, Turkey was apprehensive about being forced into the war, and felt compelled to maintain a large army, which placed financial strains on its fragile economy[99]. In order to generate revenue, a "wealth tax" was passed known as Varlik Vergisi, which had the effect of taxing wealthy non-Muslims, disproportionately Jews[100]. Furthermore, this oppressive tax was viciously levied, and forced many successful Jews to sell their companies at deep discounts to Muslims, or file bankruptcy, risk confiscation, and even be sent to labor camps[101]. Eventually the tax was repealed, but it was another shock to a reeling Jewish community already feeling the full impact of the Holocaust and Turkey's ever-changing policies.

---

[96] Although Turkey signed a non-aggression treaty with the Soviet Union, there was a significant amount of distrust of the Russians. This was more evident at the inception of the War in 1939 when the Nazis and the Soviets signed a non-aggression pact clouding Turkey's foreign policy. *See* DERINGIL, *supra* note 10, at 7, 73, 78.

[97] Hakki, *supra* note 84; GUTTSTADT, *supra* note 3, at 32–33; DERINGIL, *supra* note 10, at 130.

[98] GUTTSTADT, *supra* note 3, at 29.

[99] DERINGIL, *supra* note 10, at 13, 115, 145, 154, 161; REISMAN, *supra* note 5, at 32; THE JEWS OF THE OTTOMAN EMPIRE, *supra* note 15, at 255.

[100] BALI, *supra* note 32, at 12–13.

[101] TURKEY AND THE HOLOCAUST, *supra* note 5, at 38–45; GUTTSTADT, *supra* note 3, at 72–81.

VI. GERMANY DEMANDS TURKEY REPATRIATE ITS JEWS

Nazi Expulsion and Final Solution Policies Send Jews Fleeing Europe

During the early years of the war, Germany was focused on expulsion of the Jews, and issued an "ultimatum" to neutral countries and its allies, to repatriate its Jewish citizens from occupied territories[102]. Jews, who were not repatriated, would be adjudicated stateless, and transported to death camps [103]. But the strategy of expulsion soon mutated into a doctrine of extermination; and when Hermann Goering[104] ordered the Final Solution[105], he established a deadline of 31 January 1943 for countries to finish their repatriation. Of importance, the Turkish Foreign Minister Menemencioglu, was personally warned by the German Embassy to repatriate its Jews[106].

As a result, evacuations continued to escalate throughout occupied Europe; but since Turkey was a neutral country, Jews whose citizenship papers were in order were theoretically exempt from deportation and could be repatriated[107]. Until the deadline imposed by the Final Solution, Germany had honoured this exemption in order to maintain excellent diplomatic channels, as Turkey was geographically strategic

[102] GUTTSTADT, *supra* note 3, at 146–48.

[103] *Id.* at 153.

[104] Goering was one of the architects of Hitler's Final Solution. *See Hermann Goering*, JEWISH VIRTUAL LIBRARY, http://www.jewishvirtuallibrary.org/jsource/ Holocaust/goering.html (last visited 1 June 2015).

[105] The Final Solution was Hitler's plan to exterminate the Jews of Europe. *See* THE HOLOCAUST EXPLAINED, http://www.theholocaustexplained.org/ks3/the-final-solution/#.VIXfAouNT9s (last visited 1 June 2015). For complete transcript of the actual "Conference Record, The Final Solution of the Jewish Problem, Berlin, January 20,1942," *see Translation of Document*, TRUMANLIBRARY.ORG, http:// www.trumanlibrary.org/whistlestop/study_collections/nuremberg/documents/ index.php?documentdate=1945-00-00&documentid=C194-3-9&studycollectionid=&page number=1 (last visited 1 June 2015).

[106] BAHAR, *supra* note 7, at 2766, 2775.

[107] GUTTSTADT, *supra* note 3, at 153–55, 236. In this historical context, deportation refers to Jews being transported to concentration camps.

to its war efforts and the Nazis were still dependent on chromium to produce weapons[108]. In fact, Hitler was convinced that Turkey would inevitably join the war effort on the side of the Axis powers[109].

Diplomatic Efforts to Save Turkish Jews in France

For Turkish Jews living in occupied Europe, the issue of whether they properly maintained their citizenship and were eligible for repatriation would determine life or death as the Final Solution geared into full force[110]. The Turkish Constitution permitted individuals who lived abroad to remain citizens, provided they followed the required steps including registering with the nearest consulate every five years[111]. However, citizenship laws required Turks living outside the country who did not participate in the War of Liberation to return within five years, or they would lose their citizenship[112].

Because of continuous fluctuation in laws, Turkish Jews living in Europe had many distinctive citizenship issues, and their status was crucial to escaping the claws of death camps. At the onset of the war, there were between 20,000-50,000 Turkish Jews living in Europe, but only 5,000-10,000 had their citizenship papers up to date[113]. Turkey referred to them as "regular" Jews[114]. On the other hand, "irregular" Jews[115] often had no passports, or they had expired. Some irregular Jews, however, had valid passports, but failed to register with the local consulate as required by law, making repatriation complicated[116]. Al-

---

[108] DERINGIL, *supra* note 10, at 139, 128–29.

[109] *Id.* at 136.

[110] GUTTSTADT, *supra* note 3, at 144.

[111] BAHAR, *supra* note 7, at 2303.

[112] *Id.*; TURKEY AND THE HOLOCAUST, *supra* note 5, at 47–58; *see* CONSTITUTION OF THE REPUBLIC OF TURKEY JULY 23, 1995, art. 88, *available at* http://global.tbmm. gov.tr/docs/constitution_en.pdf.

[113] GUTTSTADT, *supra* note 3, at 157–58.

[114] BAHAR, *supra* note 7, at 2303; GUTTSTADT, *supra* note 3, at 135, 153.

[115] BAHAR, *supra* note 7, at 2303; TURKEY AND THE HOLOCAUST, *supra* note 5, at 64.

[116] GUTTSTADT, *supra* note 3, at 48–53.

though there were only 700 Turkish Jews living in Germany[117], France, by way of contrast, had the largest European population of Turkish Jews, estimated between 10,000-50,000, many of whom left Turkey after the establishment of the republic because of economic conditions and the discriminatory policies of Turkification[118]. Nonetheless, Turkey allowed for dual citizenship; but after decades of living abroad, many Jews let their citizenship lapse as roots were established in their new homelands[119]. Unfortunately, this caused countless numbers to perish, as they were unable to be repatriated, were then classified stateless, and, finally, transported to death camps[120].

After the armistice between Germany and France, the French National Assembly dissolved and adopted legislation in close cooperation with the Nazi Regime[121]. As a consequence, France was divided into a northern zone occupied by Germany and a southern, free zone governed by the Vichy puppet government[122]. In short order, the Vichy government adopted Germany's Nuremberg laws, including revocation of citizenship for all French Jews naturalised after 1927, who were then classified as stateless[123]. The Turkish Embassy was forced to move to Vichy, and its diplomats made it known to both the Germans and the French that as a neutral country, they objected to anti-Jewish laws

---

[117] *Id.* at 159.

[118] Guttstadt places the number at 20,000 but indicates others have estimated between 20,000–50,000. *Id.* at 180. Reisman estimates the number of Turkish Jews in France approximated 20,000. REISMAN, *supra* note 5, at 132. Shaw places the figure at 10,000 but notes that this figure excludes Jews who let their citizenship expire. TURKEY AND THE HOLOCAUST, *supra* note 5, at 46–47.

[119] AN AMBASSADOR AND A MENSCH, *supra* note 8, at 119.

[120] BAHAR, *supra* note 7, at 4354–405; GUTTSTADT, *supra* note 3, at 151.

[121] BAHAR, *supra* note 7, at 2126. High-ranking French government officials Pierre Laval and Joseph Petain, who had known anti-Semitic leanings, enthusiastically cooperated with the Germans. *See* AN AMBASSADOR AND A MENSCH, *supra* note 8, at 86–87.

[122] AN AMBASSADOR AND A MENSCH, *supra* note 8, at 84.

[123] GUTTSTADT, *supra* note 3, at 185. *See also The Destruction of the Jews of France*, HOLOCAUSTRESEARCHPROJECT.ORG, http://www.holocaustresearchproject.org/nazi occupation/frenchjews.html (last visited 1 June 2015). Further, see 20 Dec. 1942 article in New York Times regarding Jews in Vichy, AN AMBASSADOR AND A MENSCH, *supra* note 8, at 108.

being applied to Turkish citizens[124].

At the onset of the war, it was more advantageous to be a Turkish Jew than a French Jew, since Turkey was neutral and its citizens came under the protection of the embassy. Consequently, Turkish Jews were exempt from the full range of German anti-Jewish measures[125]. French Jews, however, were treated the same as German Jews and stripped of their basic human and civil rights. Moreover, the French government in Vichy was even more heavy-handed than their German counterpart in administrating anti-Jewish regulations[126]. Although treatment of Jews varied from region to region, they inevitably were terminated from civil employment positions; prohibited from engaging in certain trades, businesses, or professions; forced to register all assets, wear marks on clothing identifying them as Jews when in public, and receive permission for leaving their homes; prohibited from owning radios or telephones, riding bicycles, or attending movies; and subjected to a special Jewish curfew. Jewish businesses and homes were confiscated and sold and safety deposit boxes looted[127].

Moreover, Turkish Jews living in France represented a large professional class, and their affluence provided the necessary pretext for anti-Semitic attitudes to prevail amongst the French population. This, in turn, created the necessary atmosphere to enable the Germans to gain support for their racist policies[128]. Turkish diplomats struggled

[124] Jews with Turkish citizenship living in France are distinguished from French Jews. The former were exempt from many anti-Jewish laws until the end of the war. GUTTSTADT, *supra* note 3, at 192, 236.

[125] *Id.* at 192. However, these exemptions were often ignored by Germany. *Id.* at 202; AN AMBASSADOR AND A MENSCH, *supra* note 8, at 133.

[126] Paul Webster, *The Vichy Policy on Jewish Deportation*, BBC.CO.UK, http://www.bbc.co.uk/history/worldwars/genocide/jewish__01.shtml (last updated 2 Jan. 2011); *The Destruction of the Jews of France*, HOLOCAUSTRESEARCHPROJECT. ORG, http://www.holocaustresearchproject.org/nazioccupation/frenchjews.html (last visited 1 June 2015).

[127] TURKEY AND THE HOLOCAUST, *supra* note 5, at 48–51. The Vichy government passed *Statute de Juifs*, stating in part, "it was unacceptable that followers of a minority cult could exercise an influence in countries of Christian civilization". *Id.* at 56.

[128] Webster, *supra* note 126.

to obtain information regarding its citizens in order to ascertain their status and protect Turkish Jews and their property that had been subject to anti-Jewish laws[129]. For example, there were situations where apartments of Jews, who were detained or deported, were confiscated by authorities that sought to liquidate those assets. When notified, some Turkish diplomats were able to intervene to secure the properties and protect the interests of its citizens[130]. In fact, diplomats took the position that these assets were part of Turkey's "national wealth" and should remain in the hands of Turks[131]. Representatives were also in communication with German and French authorities attempting to track down Jews who were detained and sent to labor or concentration camps[132]. Turkish officials even went so far as to advise its Jews to ignore the Vichy government's identification policies and other anti-Jewish restrictions[133].

Before the Nazis' extermination policies were employed, it was less challenging for Turkey to provide the necessary documentation to German authorities to repatriate its Jews[134]. But as the war proceeded, embassies were closed and Jews were imprisoned, which made it difficult for them to contact their consulates or families. Of importance, communication between family members was often necessary for assistance to retrieve citizenship papers, as Jews were often rounded up without notice or time to assemble their belongings[135]. Once the Final Solution

[129] TURKEY AND THE HOLOCAUST, *supra* note 5, at 89–90, 78–99; BAHAR, *supra* note 7, at 3889.

[130] BAHAR, *supra* note 7, at 3766–3821. For an example of the nature of the correspondence between Turkish diplomats and German and French representatives regarding rights of Turkish Jews, *see* The Vitali Benbassa file in TURKEY AND THE HOLOCAUST, *supra* note 5, at 99–111; GUTTSTADT, *supra* note 3, at 189.

[131] BAHAR, *supra* note 7, at 3749.

[132] TURKEY AND THE HOLOCAUST, *supra* note 5, at 89, 128, 131; GUTTSTADT, *supra* note 3, at 191–92.

[133] TURKEY AND THE HOLOCAUST, *supra* note 5, at 86. Guttstadt takes a contrary position, questioning the efforts of Turkish diplomats in assisting to repatriate Turkish Jews. GUTTSTADT, *supra* note 3, at 149, 197–99.

[134] TURKEY AND THE HOLOCAUST, *supra* note 5, at 123.

[135] *See, e.g.,* The Menahem Hatem File, correspondence between Turkish-Consulate General, German authorities and Hatem family regarding issues of citizenship and

strategies were implemented and extinction was the goal, Germans paid much more attention to citizenship papers to ensure everything was in order before releasing any Jews[136].

In 1942, the Vichy government began a process to classify almost 10,000 Turkish Jews living in southern France as stateless and subject to deportation. It had been determined that the citizenship of these Jews had been revoked because of a failure to register, as required by Turkish immigration law[137]. However, Turkish diplomats intervened, and the Vichy government capitulated after Foreign Minister Menemencioglu threatened to remove its ambassador in Paris[138]. At the Second Yad Vashem International Historical Conference on Rescue Attempts during the Holocaust, Dr Chaim Pazner shared:

> Chaim Barlas notified me from Istanbul that . . . approximately ten-thousand Jews who were Turkish citizens, but had been living in France for years had neglected to register and renew their Turkish citizenship . . . were in danger of being deported to the death camps . . . the Turkish Foreign ministry in Ankara submitted a detailed memorandum . . . and requested urgent action by the Turkish Legation in Paris . . . . We later received word from Istanbul and Paris that . . . these ten thousand Jews had been saved from extermination[139].

Notwithstanding that Ankara lacked both the commitment and a strategy to repatriate its Jewish citizens, individual Turkish diplomats throughout occupied Europe, especially in France, have been credited

---

personal property confiscated by the Nazis in Turkey and the Holocaust, *supra* note 5, at 155–68.

[136] Guttstadt, *supra* note 3, at 234, 240. Bahar, *supra* note 7, at 2793; Turkey and the Holocaust, *supra* note 5, at 123.

[137] Turkey and the Holocaust, *supra* note 5, at 124. *See also* Memorandum from War Refugee Board attaché Ira Hirschman regarding diplomats' efforts concerning these 10,000 Jews in An Ambassador and a Mensch, *supra* note 8, at 228, 272.

[138] Turkey and the Holocaust, *supra* note 5, at 125.

[139] *Id.* at 126–27.

with saving the lives of Jews[140]. As evacuations accelerated, the Germans extended the repatriation deadline at numerous stages. Turkish diplomats often negotiated with the Nazis for additional time it needed to administrate the repatriation of Jews, which drew the ire of Adolph Eichmann[141]. The German Embassy eventually informed Turkey that the absolute deadline for the evacuation of Jews in France was 25 May 1944, and any remaining thereafter would be subject to deportation[142]. In response, the Turkish Ministry of Foreign Affairs gave each individual counsel general flexibility to generate passports, visas and even the authority to restore citizenship in emergency situations[143]. Some consulates went to the extraordinary effort of placing advertisements in newspapers, informing its citizens of their options regarding repatriation, and as a result, many Turkish Jews were able to escape the death camps[144]. However, various scholars believe that Turkey, as part of a public relations campaign, has exaggerated the efforts and accomplishments of Turkish diplomats[145].

Nevertheless, there is ample evidence to suggest that Ankara[146] objected to a substantial influx of Jews[147]. Many who were attempting to be repatriated had their applications denied or fatally delayed,

---

[140] *Turks Saved Jews from Nazi Holocaust, supra* note 8; SHOAH: TURKEY, THE US AND THE UK, *supra* note 5, at 234–39. For a list of Turkish diplomats who have been identified for saving Jews, *see id.* at 241–42. Turkish diplomats worked to save Jews in Belgium, the Netherlands, Italy, Greece and the Aegean Islands. However, rescue activities and efforts by diplomats throughout occupied Europe varied significantly. *See* GUTTSTADT, *supra* note 3, at 148, 248–308.

[141] TURKEY AND THE HOLOCAUST, *supra* note 5, at 151–52. Eichmann was Hitler's right-hand man in charge of exterminating the Jews. For more on Eichmann, *see Adolf Eichmann,* USHMM.ORG, http://www.ushmm.org/wlc/en/article.php?ModuleId=10007412 (last visited 21 Jan. 2015).

[142] TURKEY AND THE HOLOCAUST, *supra* note 5, at 204; GUTTSTADT, *supra* note 3, at 157, 236.

[143] TURKEY AND THE HOLOCAUST, *supra* note 5, at 60–62, 127–28.

[144] *Id.* at 135, 145, 147–49; BAHAR, *supra* note 7, at 4297.

[145] BAHAR, *supra* note 7, at 2233–98; GUTTSTADT, *supra* note 3, at 149–51.

[146] Ankara is the capital of Turkey, home to the Grand National Assembly, and seat of the central government.

[147] BAHAR, *supra* note 7, at 4386–405; GUTTSTADT, *supra* note 3, at 157–58.

despite the efforts of individual consulates[148]. The government was requiring "undisputable Turkish citizenship" to permit repatriation[149], granting preferential treatment only to Jews who were returning for military service or had some unique contribution to offer the country[150]. Furthermore, Germany continued to demand information from the Turkish government identifying Jews eligible for repatriation, but repeatedly failed to obtain adequate responses from Turkey resulting in deportations to death camps[151]. Laws passed over the years revoking citizenship, now created barriers that in many cases were insurmountable[152]. Moreover, although ninety percent of all Turkish Jews who met the criteria for repatriation resided in France, the government clearly was dead set against large numbers of refugees and instructed the Turkish Ambassador Behic Erkin "not to send back Jews by the train load"[153]. Not surprisingly, the rejection of repatriation was interpreted by the Nazis as a green light to deport, and between 2,000–3,000 Jews lost their citizenship and most probably their lives because of Turkey's obstructive governmental processes[154].

VII. TURKISH DIPLOMATS WHO HAVE BEEN RECOGNISED FOR SAVING JEWS

Ambassador Behic Erkin

Despite Ankara's policies that impeded the repatriation of Turkish Jews, the fortitude and humanitarian efforts of several individual diplomats have been internationally recognised. The Turkish Ambassador to France, Behic Erkin, was a close friend of Atatürk[155]. When laws were

[148] GUTTSTADT, *supra* note 3, at 211–13, 232, 310–13.

[149] BAHAR, *supra* note 7, at 2615, 2773. Most of the evidence indicates that primarily "regular" Turkish Jews were repatriated.

[150] GUTTSTADT, *supra* note 3, at 157, 230, 232.

[151] *Id.* at 153–57; BAHAR, *supra* note 7, at 2755–812.

[152] BAHAR, *supra* note 7, at 2348–99, 5743–77; GUTTSTADT, *supra* note 3, at 151–52.

[153] BAHAR, *supra* note 7, at 2687; GUTTSTADT, *supra* note 3, at 211, 225.

[154] GUTTSTADT, *supra* note 3, at 242–44. It is estimated that only 550 Jews were repatriated from France. *Id.* at 242.

[155] SHOAH: TURKEY, THE US AND THE UK, *supra* note 5, at 240; AN AMBASSADOR AND

enacted that made having a Turkish last name mandatory, Atatürk gave Behic his last name with the annotation, "[a] person of independent mind who can make his own correct decisions under all conditions"[156].

As French Jews became casualties of the anti-Jewish restrictions, Erkin and the Turkish Embassy often received information that these laws were also being enforced on Turkish citizens. Frequently, he would contact the Vichy government to make Turkey's position clear,

> The Republic of Turkey does not discriminate among its citizens on the basis of race, ethnicity, religion . . . the Republic of Turkey is concerned about the laws by which the French government is forcing our citizens to abide . . . we hereby inform [the French authorities] that we reserve all of our rights with regard to our Jewish citizens[157].

Erkin's exemplary determination included meeting with Nazis to ascertain the identities and whereabouts of Turkish Jews who were being deported to death camps[158]. Towards that end, he often placed advertisements in newspapers in Marseilles, Nice, and Lyon, letting Turkish Jews know that the embassy could assist in repatriation[159]. Erkin's efforts often paid off, and he and his staff were responsible for saving the lives of thousands of Jews by arranging the necessary documentation for escape by rail[160]. As a result, the Raoul Wallenberg Foundation documented these efforts: "Behic Erkin was the Turkish Ambassador to Paris when France was under Nazi occupation. In order to prevent the Nazis from rounding up the Jews, he gave them documents saying their property, houses, and businesses, belonged to Turks. He saved many lives in this way"[161].

A MENSCH, *supra* note 8, at 13–14, 73–74.

[156] AN AMBASSADOR AND A MENSCH, *supra* note 8, at 5.

[157] *Id.* at 110.

[158] *Id.* at 121; GUTTSTADT, *supra* note 3, at 141.

[159] AN AMBASSADOR AND A MENSCH, *supra* note 8, at 129.

[160] *Id.* at 122.

[161] *Turks Saved Jews from Nazi Holocaust*, *supra* note 8.

Turkish Vice Consul Necdet Kent

Another Turkish diplomat who helped rescue Jews was Necdet Kent, who served as Turkish Vice Consul in Marseilles during the occupation of France. When the Germans rounded up eighty Turkish Jews and boarded them on cattle cars heading for the concentration camps, Kent protested and entered one of the trains refusing to get off[162]. The Germans released the Jews and apologised to Kent for the misunderstanding[163]. After the war, Kent recalled this incident,

> there was a mistake that more than eighty Turkish citizens had been loaded on to these animal wagons because of their Jewishness, and as a representative of a government that rejected such treatment of religious beliefs, I could not consider leaving them alone[164].

Additionally, Necdet Kent was credited with arranging documentation for Jews in southern France, whose passports were invalid, and objecting to the Nazis' stripping males in public to determine whether they were Jews[165]. Later on, Kent was awarded the Supreme Service Medal from Turkey, and Israel recognised him with a special medal that read, "Saving one's life is like saving all the world"[166]. When Necdet Kent died in 2002, the Israeli consulate and Istanbul's Deputy Chief Rabbi attended his funeral[167].

---

[162] TURKEY AND THE HOLOCAUST, *supra* note 5, at 132–33. *See also id.* at 341–44, app. 4, Testimony of Retired Ambassador Necdet Kent Regarding the Rescue of Jewish Turks at Marseilles During World War II.

[163] *Id.*; *Necdet Kent*, JEWISHVIRTUALLIBRARY.ORG, http://www.jewishvirtuallibrary. org/jsource/biography/NecdetKent.html (last visited 1 June 2015).

[164] AN AMBASSADOR AND A MENSCH, *supra* note 8, at 154–61. Guttstadt casts a shadow of doubt on Kent's version of events. GUTTSTADT, *supra* note 3, at 219–21.

[165] *Necdet Kent, supra* note 163.

[166] AN AMBASSADOR AND A MENSCH, *supra* note 8, at 155. *Necdet Kent, supra* note 163. *See Obituaries: Necdet Kent, 91; Turkish Diplomat Saved Jew in WWII*, L.A. TIMES (21 Sept. 2002), http://articles.latimes.com/2002/sep/21/local/me-kent21. Kent's story of having saved Jews has been met with some skepticism. *See* GUTTSTADT, *supra* note 3, at 219–21.

[167] *Necdet Kent, supra* note 163. *See Obituaries: Necdet Kent, 91; Turkish Diplomat*

Turkish Consul General Selattin Ulkumen, The Turkish Schindler

In Greece, Selahattin Ulkumen, known as the Turkish Schindler[168], served as Turkish Consul General on the Island of Rhodes, which was occupied initially by the Italians, and then by the Germans. The Jews of Rhodes had enjoyed wealth and opportunity throughout the years of the Ottoman Empire up until the onset of war[169]. When the Germans arrived, they started to deport all of the Jews on the island for extermination, and refused to make any distinction between Jews of different nationalities. Ulkumen interceded, informing the commander that Ankara's position was that, "under Turkish law, all citizens were equal. We didn't differentiate between citizens who were Jewish, Christian, or Muslim"[170]. He further explained to the German officials, "I would advise my Government if he didn't release the Jewish Turks ... it would cause an international incident. Then he agreed"[171].

In an attempt to inflate the list of Turkish Jews whose citizenship was in order, Ulkumen added an additional 25–30 Jews who were no longer citizens. In all, 50 Jews were saved, only 13 of which were Turkish citizens[172]. Ultimately, the Nazis realised too late that they had been deceived; and as a consequence of Ulkumen's heroic efforts, the Gestapo bombed his home, killing his wife[173].

Saved Jew in WWII, L.A. Times (21 Sept. 2002), http://articles.latimes.com/2002/sep/21/local/me-kent21.

[168] Interestingly, Necdet Kent has also been referred to as the Turkish Schindler. Guttstadt, *supra* note 3, at 220.

[169] *Obituaries: Selahattin Ulkumen*, The Telegraph (18 Jul. 2003, 12:01 AM), http://www.telegraph.co.uk/news/obituaries/1436384/Selahattin-Ulkumen.html.

[170] Turkey and the Holocaust, *supra* note 5, at 253.

[171] *Id.*

[172] *The Righteous Among the Nations: Selahattin Ulkumen*, yadvashem.org, http://www.yadvashem.org/yv/en/righteous/stories/ulkumen.asp (last visited 1 June 2015); *Turks Saved Jews from Nazi Holocaust*, *supra* note 8. Germans deported 1,673 Jews from Rhodes, only 150 survived.

[173] An Ambassador and a Mensch, *supra* note 8, at 194.

In a speech, Ulkumen's son Mehmet explained his father's actions and motivation:

> For him, it was not just the right thing, but the only possible thing he could do. He always used to say, "We Muslims are like Jews. Share the same father and same God. We also share the same belief which as we know is deeply rooted in Jewish teaching, that he who saves a life saves a whole world"[174].

Ulkumen was awarded the honor "Righteous Gentile" by Yad Vashem in 1989[175].

Erkin, Ulkumen, and Kent were not alone. The Raoul Wallenberg Foundation has identified eighteen Turkish diplomats credited with helping Jews not only in France but also in Germany, Greece, Prague, Budapest, Romania, Czechoslovakia and Bulgaria[176]. In recognition of the efforts of Turkey, the Anti-Defamation League presented the *Courage to Care* award to honor Turkish diplomats who took extraordinary efforts to save Jews during the Shoah[177]. Abraham H. Foxman, ADL National Director who is also a Holocaust survivor, presented the award:

> Turkey's role in saving Jews has been ignored for too long. With the millions upon millions of words that have been written about the Holocaust, and about those who upheld the honor of humanity at a time when that word had become utterly grotesque, Turkey's role in the forefront of those few

---

[174] Mehmet Ülkümen, Speech at Geneva Non-Governmental Gathering for First Annual U.N. Day of Commemoration in Memory of the Victims of the Holocaust: Muslim Hero Saved Jews in Holocaust (27 Jan. 2006), transcript *available at* https://www.facinghistory. org/rescuers/mehmet-%C3%BClk%C3%BCmen%E2%80%9Cmuslim-hero-saved-jews-holocaust%E2%80%9D-transcript-speech.

[175] *The Righteous Among the Nations, supra* note 172.

[176] *Turks Saved Jews from Nazi Holocaust, supra* note 8.

[177] *The Holocaust: Definition and Preliminary Discussion*, YADVASHEM.ORG, http://www.yadvashem.org/yv/en/holocaust/resource_center/the_holocaust.asp (last visited 1 June 2015). Shoah is word used in the Bible to mean "destruction".

nations who provided refuge and rescue to the tragic Jews of Europe has been largely omitted or overlooked. While millions were murdered before the eyes of an indifferent world, Turkey was one of the tiny handful of nations who acted in the name of conscience and community[178].

In accepting the award, then Turkish Prime Minister Recep Tayyip Erdogan reiterated, "Anti-Semitism has no place in Turkey. It is alien to our culture"[179].

VIII. TURKEY INFLUENCED BY ALLIED POLICIES CONCERNING JEWISH REFUGEES

A study of Turkey's reluctant policies towards repatriation of Jews and refugee traffic cannot be judged in a vacuum, or outside the context of the restrictive approach embraced by the United States and Great Britain. Bound by treaty and the common interest of thwarting German domination, their strategies were interrelated, and pressure exerted by America and Britain had a direct effect on Turkey's options pertaining to Jewish refugees[180]. Since the maintenance of Turkey's neutrality was of utmost importance, the Turkish government required a measured and disciplined approach to this sensitive issue, to avoid provoking unnecessary conflict between world powers.

Even before the official declaration of war, the issue of refugees was becoming an international crisis; and in 1938, delegates from thirty-two nations convened in France for the Evian Conference[181].

---

[178] *Prime Minister Erdogan, supra* note 8.

[179] *Id.* Ironically, the American Jewish Congress recently asked Erdoğan to return the Profile in Courage award bestowed upon him in 2004 after he compared Israel's policies to that of Hitler. Yitzhak Benhorin, *American Jewish Congress Asks Erdogan to Return Award*, YNETNEWS.COM (23 Jul. 2014, 12:14 AM), http://www.ynetnews.com/articles/0,7340,L-4550062,00.html.

[180] The policy of Turkey was not to accept Jewish refugees unless the British had issued immigration certificates for entry into Palestine. OFER, *supra* note 5, at 164, 305.

[181] At the Evian conference, negotiations were entered into with the Germans for a humanitarian solution to the Jewish refugee problem, but the Nazi regime offer was

Moreover, to the astonishment of Hitler, the meetings failed to generate significant measures to resolve the Jewish refugee problem, because most participant nations balked at resettling Jews in their countries, which, in turn, reinforced the Nazi propaganda that no one wanted them[182]. Subsequent to news of Hitler's Final Solution, and the systematic murder of Jews became public, Britain and the U.S. initiated another summit in Bermuda in April 1943 to once again address the refugee crisis[183]. Historical accounts of these meetings were unequivocal that "[t]he real purpose of the Bermuda Conference ... was to silence critics of the official do-nothing policies, pay lip-service to humanitarian principle, and perpetuate the status quo by stalling for time"[184]. Although these gatherings were held contemporaneously with the world's notice of Hitler's blueprint to exterminate European Jewry, strikingly, it failed to produce a comprehensive rescue plan[185]. Interest-

more of a "ransom". *See* HENRY L. FEINGOLD, BEARING WITNESS 74–77 (1995).

[182] The failure of the conference to aid Jewish refugees was noted by Hitler. *See Evian Conference*, ZIONISM-ISRAEL.COM, http://www.zionism-israel.com/dic/Evian_conference.htm (last visited 1 June 2015); AN AMBASSADOR AND A MENSCH, *supra* note 8, 165–66. *See also* RICHARD BREITMAN & ALLAN J. LICHTMAN, FDR AND THE JEWS 109–10, 122–23 (2013).

[183] The U.S. and Britain were just going through the motions at Bermuda. "Their purpose was to eliminate any risk of being saddled with a large-scale exodus of Jews from enemy-controlled Europe. The two governments refused to make substantial new asylum commitments to Jews who had a genuine chance of escaping". LOUISE LONDON, WHITEHALL AND THE JEWS, 1933-1948, 223 (2003). Furthermore, the Agenda of the Bermuda Conference had called for England to revisit its immigration policies regarding Palestine. *See* Item VII at *U.S. Policy During WWII: Jewish Organizations Plan for Rescue of European Jewry*, JEWISHVIRTUALLIBRARY, http://www.jewishvirtuallibrary.org/jsource/Holocaust/jewplan.html (last visited 1 June 2015).

[184] AGOSTINO VON HASSELL, ET. AL, ALLIANCE OF ENEMIES 158 (2006). *See also* DAVID S. WYMAN, THE ABANDONMENT OF THE JEWS 143 (1984); FEINGOLD, *supra* note 181, at 83.

[185] "The two governments had decreed that the focus of their conference would be on 'refugees' rather than 'Jews'. The most important reasons for playing down the Jewish aspect . . . was to discourage pressure to undertake a special effort to save Jews". LONDON, *supra* note 183, at 212. Also, the plans of the Nazis to exterminate Jews were first published in New York Times on 25 November 1942, and an editorial on 2 December stated that 2,000,000 were already dead and 5,000,000 more at risk. LAUREL LEFF, BURIED BY THE TIMES 156, 157 (2005). On 17 December 1942, the United Nations issued a statement regarding the genocide of Jews in Europe. LONDON, *supra* note 183, at 203; RAFAEL MEDOFF, BLOWING THE WHISTLE ON GENOCIDE 11

ingly, Turkey did not have representatives at either conference and after Evian, it tightened up its immigration laws to prevent Jewish refugees from entering the country[186].

American Anti-Semitism and the Roosevelt Administration

At Evian, the United States suggested that "no country would be expected or asked to receive a greater number of immigrants than is permitted by its existing legislation"[187]. The administration's position was self-serving; America had reformed its immigration laws to limit settlers from any one country not to exceed three percent of existing immigrants from that nation, already living in the U.S. For example, in 1938, the maximum refugee quota was 27,370 from Germany, and only 6,542 from Poland, whereas 3,300,000 Polish Jews eventually perished in the Holocaust[188]. One of the reasons advanced for this legislation was to limit the influx of Jews and Italians[189]. In fact, anti-Semitism in America was mainstream, and conspiracy theories represented views that Jews were communists and wielded too much political and economic power[190]. Furthermore, opinion polls indicated that one-third of Americans held anti-Semitic views, which, in turn, affected public policy[191].

For the first five years of the Holocaust, Roosevelt convened 430 press conferences, and mentioned the Jewish refugees only one time[192]. Moreover, the administration and Congress refused to alter immigra-

---

(2009).

[186] BAHAR, *supra* note 7, at 5473; GUTTSTADT, *supra* note 3, at 101.

[187] MEDOFF, *supra* note 185, at 6.

[188] *Id.* at 4. *See also The "Final Solution": Estimated Number of Jews Killed*, JEW-ISHVIRTUALLIBRARY, http://www.jewishvirtuallibrary.org/jsource/Holocaust/ killed-table.html (last visited 1 June 2015).

[189] MEDOFF, *supra* note 185, at 3; *See also* FEINGOLD, *supra* note 181, at 61–62.

[190] Even American hero Charles Lindberg weighed in on Jewish influence. BREIT-MAN & LICHTMAN, *supra* note 182, at 187–88. *See also* FEINGOLD, *supra* note 181, at 196–99; WYMAN, *supra* note 184, at 9–15; MEDOFF, *supra* note 185, at 2–3.

[191] MEDOFF, *supra* note 185, at 3; FEINGOLD, *supra* note 181, at 61–62.

[192] MEDOFF, *supra* note 185, at 5–6.

tion quotas for fear of too many Jews entering America, or to pressure Britain to change its policies to allow more refugees into Palestine[193]. President Roosevelt's feeble efforts to liberate Jews were highlighted by his refusal to bomb German railways and transit lines, known at the time to be carrying Jews to death camps[194]. In particular, America's tactics to block immigration to the United States was underscored by a well-known incident regarding the ship, *St. Louis.* This vessel, carrying 900 Jewish refugees from Nazi Germany, was denied entry into the United States with the full knowledge of President Roosevelt and State Department officials. The ship eventually had to return to Europe, where many of the passengers eventually were sent to death camps[195]. Additionally, the United States even took steps to deport Jews back to occupied countries, because of alleged immigration violations[196]. In a cruel twist of fate, American immigration laws prohibited granting of visas for anyone with a criminal record, which was interpreted to include persons who were in labor or concentration camps[197]. In sum, these intentional and obstructive actions to prevent the rescue of Jews

---

[193] *Id.* at 10; WYMAN, *supra* note 184, at 190.

[194] FEINGOLD, *supra* note 181, at 151. The party line by officials was that a bombing campaign would require resources that would divert from the greater war efforts. For a detailed discussion of the decision to forgo bombing of transit lines to death camps and Auschwitz, *see* WYMAN, *supra* note 184, at 288–307. Furthermore, the World Jewish Congress requested the Administration to bomb Auschwitz. *The World Jewish Congress in New York Asks the War Department to Bomb the Crematoria At Auschwitz*, PBS.ORG, http://www.pbs.org/wgbh/amex/holocaust/filmmore/reference/ primary/bombworld.html (last visited Jan. 22, 2015).

[195] SHOAH: TURKEY, THE US AND THE UK, *supra* note 5, at 38–46. The ship was originally headed to Cuba, but was denied entry and headed to the United States instead. FEINGOLD, *supra* note 181, at 63, 79.

[196] United States ex rel. Weinberg v. Schlotfeldt, 26 F. Supp. 283 (D. Ill. 1938). The court stated, "[u]nder conditions as they now exist it would be cruel and inhuman punishment to deport this petitioner to Czechoslovakia, belonging as he does to the race which is thus being persecuted and exiled". *Id.* at 284.

[197] SHOAH: TURKEY, THE US AND THE UK, *supra* note 5, at 12. Another reason advanced for America's refusing refugees was the economic factor. The property of Jews had been confiscated in Europe, consequently many refugees had limited resources. Immigration laws at the time prohibited entry for individuals likely to become a public charge (LPC), and neither the Administration nor Congress was motivated to make exceptions. *Id.*

were commonplace, and part of a broader strategy on the part of the Roosevelt administration[198].

It later became public that the State Department was infiltrated with anti-Semitism at very high levels; and in an internal communication, Assistant Secretary Adolf Berle dictated the tactic to block Jewish immigration into the United States:

> We can delay and effectively stop for a temporary period of indefinite length the number of immigrants into the United States. We could do this by simply advising our Consuls to put every obstacle in the way and to require additional evidence and to resort to various administrative advices which would postpone and postpone and postpone the granting of the visas[199].

Near the end of the war, Josiah Dubois, a young attorney in the Treasury Department, cataloged the intentional concealment by State and Treasury officials concerning their knowledge of Hitler's "Final Solution". Dubois prepared a memorandum for President Roosevelt entitled "The Acquiescence of this Government in the Murder of the Jews", and threatened to go to the press[200]. In this detailed document to the President, Dubois wrote,

> The tragic history of this Government's handling of this matter reveals that certain State Department officials are guilty of the following: . . . They have not only failed to use Government machinery at their disposal to rescue Jews from Hitler but have even gone so far as to use this Government machinery to prevent the rescue of these Jews[201].

---

[198] WYMAN, *supra* note 184, at xx-xxi; FEINGOLD, *supra* note 181, at 200.
[199] AN AMBASSADOR AND A MENSCH, *supra* note 8, 172–73; MEDOFF, *supra* note 185, at 22–23.
[200] *See* Dubois' full report, handed to Treasury Secretary Henry Morgenthau, Jr., for President Roosevelt, in MEDOFF, *supra* note 185, at 40–52.
[201] *Id.* at 41.

Roosevelt, facing humiliation in an election year, was forced to capitulate, and formed the War Refugee Board,[202] which would operate out of Istanbul to facilitate the immigration of Jewish refugees.

Britain, Arab Appeasement, and Turkey

Britain's conduct in blocking Jewish immigration to Palestine takes on special meaning because of its historical relationship with the Jewish people. In 1917, Britain proclaimed in the Balfour Declaration that "His Majesty's Government view[s] with favour the establishment in Palestine of a national home for the Jewish people, and will use their best endeavors to facilitate the achievement of this object"[203]. Thus, in 1922, the League of Nations resolution for the Mandate for Palestine recognised the "historical connection of the Jewish people with Palestine", and charged Britain with the responsibility of facilitating a "national home for the Jewish people"[204]. In fulfillment of these obligations, Britain administered immigration into Palestine in cooperation with the Jewish Agency, which was created in 1929[205]. Although the Mandate was silent as to limits of Jewish immigrants, Britain issued its White Paper of 1922, establishing quotas based on a complex formula of economic criteria[206]. Afterwards, they published another White Paper in 1930, which introduced an additional factor that would limit Jewish immigration: Arab employment benchmarks. This new scheme to limit immigration was premised on the negative impact of Jewish

---

[202] The War Refugee Board was comprised of officials from the Departments of State, War, and Treasury. Their responsibility was to facilitate the rescue of Jewish refugees. OFER, *supra* note 5, at 269. *See also* SHOAH: TURKEY, THE US AND THE UK, *supra* note 5, at 179–81; WYMAN, *supra* note 184, at 204–06.

[203] *See* The Balfour Declaration, *available at* http://avalon.law.yale.edu/20th_century/balfour.asp (last visited 1 June 2015).

[204] The Palestine Mandate, *available at* http://avalon.law.yale.edu/20th_century/palmanda.asp (last visited 1 June 2015).

[205] The Jewish Agency was created pursuant to the Mandate for Palestine as the Jewish representative for the establishment of the Jewish homeland. *See id.*, art. 4.

[206] OFER, *supra* note 5, at 5. *See* full text of British White Paper of June 1922, *available at* http://avalon.law.yale.edu/20th_century/brwh1922.asp (last visited 22 Jan. 2015).

refugees on Arab employment opportunities[207].

As a direct transit route to Palestine through the Balkan states, Turkey was often caught in the quagmire of Britain's politics regarding the resettlement of Jewish refugees. After the Holocaust began, immigration to Palestine increased dramatically, and the resulting Arab protests caused Britain once again to reassess its policies, and conclude it had already satisfied the basic requirements of the Balfour Declaration[208]. This policy shift culminated in the White Paper of 1939, which established a hard quota of Jewish immigration: 75,000 over the next five years, at the same time millions of Jews were being sent to death camps[209]. Thereafter, the British revoked immigration approvals that were granted before the war began, and refugees attempting to escape the gas chambers in Europe for Palestine became the new "enemy aliens" of Britain[210]. Meanwhile, America's Ambassador to Turkey, Laurence Steinhardt noted, "There is a problem of visas, none too much enthusiasm on the part of the British for a large number of Jewish refugees in Palestine as they have their eyes on the Arab world"[211]. In the end, these new immigration restrictions would have a devastating result for Jewish refugees and a direct effect on the foreign policy of Turkey.

Over the course of the war, the British took extraordinary steps to thwart the escape of Jews headed for concentration camps in order to pacify the Arab population in Palestine[212]. Britain's prolific naval block-

---

[207] OFER, *supra* note 5, at 6.

[208] *Id.* at 128. Furthermore, approximately 170,000 Jewish immigrants arrived in Palestine between 1935–1939. GUTTSTADT, *supra* note 3, at 108.

[209] The 75,000 quota enforced by Britain was broken down to 50,000 for immigrants with legal immigration certificates, and 25,000 for war refugees. GUTTSTADT, *supra* note 3, at 108. *See* full text of British White Paper of 1939, *available at* http:// avalon.law.yale.edu/20th_century/brwh1939.asp (last visited 1 June 2015).

[210] OFER, *supra* note 5, at 129.

[211] SHOAH: TURKEY, THE US AND THE UK, *supra* note 5, at 261 (referencing Laurence Steinhardt papers, Library of Congress, Container 82).

[212] *Id.* at 53–57. For a comprehensive discussion on the British White Paper of 1929 and Britain's exhaustive efforts to block immigration to Palestine, *see id.* at 128–46. *See* memorandum excerpts from Colonial Secretary re Britain's position on illegal immigration. *Id.* at 56–57. There were at least forty-six vessels with Jewish

ades to prevent "illegal" immigration often took place in Turkish waters, notably, incidents such as the sinking of the *Salvador* and the *Struma*, received worldwide attention[213]. To cover all bases, and prevent Jews from immigrating to Palestine, Britain continually exerted pressure on Turkey to limit assistance to Jewish refugees, but often these threats were ignored. Regardless of intimidation, some refugees without proper documentation were allowed to enter and remain in Turkey until the end of the war[214].

Disgracefully, in May 1944, Britain rejected Adolf Eichmann's offer to the Jewish Agency in Istanbul, to trade one million Jews from Hungary, Romania, Poland, and Czechoslovakia for money and supplies, because it "would involve our being pressed to receive unmanageable numbers into Palestine, and thereby introduce the dangerous complication that the immigration quota would be exceeded at a particularly critical time"[215]. Besides, Britain also had its own demons regarding anti-Semitism, and it was clear there would be no immigration to the UK "unless in some quite rare and exceptional cases it can be shown that the admission of the refugee will be directly advantageous to our war effort"[216]. In the meantime, Britain's politics played directly into the hands of Hitler and substantially contributed to the mass extermination of Jews[217].

---

refugees intercepted by the Royal Navy. *Id.* at 271–72.

[213] *Id.* at 51–63; Ofer, *supra* note 5, at 147–56. Turkey received much of the blame for the sinking of the Struma, a rescue ship from Romania carrying 769 refugees, because of their refusal to let the ship disembark in Istanbul and continue to Palestine. Turkey was steadfast in blaming Britain for this incident as a result of their immigration policies. Ofer, *supra* note 5, at 166. Further, Britain even went to the extent of blocking ships carrying refugees that the Nazis permitted to leave from Germany and Czechoslovakia. *Id.* at 31.

[214] Turkey and the Holocaust, *supra* note 5, at 286, 289; Ofer, *supra* note 5, at 286–89.

[215] Turkey and the Holocaust, *supra* note 5, at 286.

[216] London, *supra* note 183, at 200.

[217] Turkey and the Holocaust, *supra* note 5, at 280. British policies, embodied in the British White Paper of 1939, prevented Jewish refugees from immigrating to Palestine. As a result, many were unable to escape Nazi Germany and the occupied territories. Ofer, *supra* note 5, at 128–38.

IX. ISTANBUL: AN ESCAPE ROUTE FOR JEWISH REFUGEES TO PALESTINE

Turkey's Neutrality and Geographic Location Helps Jews Escape the Holocaust

Turkey's neutrality enabled Istanbul to operate as a central locale for relief organisations such as the Jewish Agency and War Refugee Board, as well as international embassies, the Red Cross and Vatican representatives[218]. Most importantly, because of its Mediterranean location and proximity to Palestine, Turkey was the most essential transit route for Jewish refugees[219]. During the course of the war, it is estimated that over 100,000 refugees passed through Turkey by land and sea, with both the government and private citizens providing ships and other means of provision, despite tenacious interference by the British[220]. After banning refugee transit in 1938, Turkey eventually became more flexible as the war progressed, but maintained strict controls[221].

Although the Jewish Agency had offices in Geneva, neutral Switzerland had its own struggles with anti-Semitism and provided significant logistical support for the German war effort, including blocking escape routes for Jews[222]. As a result, it deemed Turkey a much friendlier environment to carry out its rescue activities[223], and senior

---

[218] TURKEY AND THE HOLOCAUST, *supra* note 5, at 257. Further, it has been reported that the War Refugee Board was responsible for saving 200,000 Jews. AN AMBASSADOR AND A MENSCH, *supra* note 8, at 182.

[219] OFER, *supra* note 5, at 163; SHOAH: TURKEY, THE US AND THE UK, *supra* note 5, at 181.

[220] TURKEY AND THE HOLOCAUST, *supra* note 5, at 266. Also, Britain opposed the War Refugee Board as inconsistent with its policies regarding Palestine. OFER, *supra* note 5, at 269.

[221] BAHAR, *supra* note 7, at 5774, 5980, 6331–400.

[222] Jonathan Petropoulos, *Co-Opting Nazi Germany: Neutrality in Europe During WWII*, ADL.ORG, http://archive.adl.org/braun/dim_14_1_neutrality_europe.html#. VGdnceeZOqR (last visited 1 June 2015); Roger Cohen, *The (Not So) Neutrals of World War II*, N.Y. TIMES (26 Jan. 1997), http://www.nytimes.com/1997/01/26/weekin review/the-not-so-neutrals-of-world-war-ii.html.

[223] Turkey replaced Switzerland as the primary headquarters for Jewish Agency efforts. TURKEY AND THE HOLOCAUST, *supra* note 5, at 257.

representative Chaim Barlas successfully lobbied Turkey to loosen up its immigration and visa restrictions[224]. Afterward, Turkey instructed its consulates in Bucharest, Belgrade, Geneva, Kaunsas, Stockholm, and Salonica to issue the necessary immigration and visa documentation for refugee transit to Palestine[225]. Of crucial importance, Turkey enacted Transit Law no. 2/15132 in 1941 that allowed more flexibility in facilitating transit for European Jews to Palestine[226]. In his memoirs, Barlas noted the importance of Turkish support,

> One of the most important reasons for the success of the Jewish immigration to Palestine was the consent of the Turkish government which even though subject to German influence and under danger of invasion by sea and land, enables Jewish immigrants to pass through Turkey in accordance with requests made by the Jewish Agency. The "Transit Law" which was passed by the Turkish cabinet on 12 February 1941, became the primary basis of this immigration movement[227].

Moreover, Turkey assisted the Red Cross's efforts to ship humanitarian aid throughout Europe, and the Ministry of Finance allowed the banking system to be used to purchase food, transportation fares, and other material aid for the refugees[228]. In turn, this enabled Jewish relief organisations to act as communication hubs that gathered information about deportations and other Nazi atrocities, while also serving as processing centers for passports, visa, and other citizenship related documents. Furthermore, members of the "Rescue Committee" used Istanbul as an indispensable location and traveled throughout occupied Europe gathering intelligence and planning escapes routes with the

---

[224] BAHAR, *supra* note 7, at 5851; GUTTSTADT, *supra* note 3, at 110–11.

[225] For the complete text of Barlas Memorandum to Turkish government, *see* TURKEY AND THE HOLOCAUST, *supra* note 5, at 259–61. Also, Turkey permitted its banks in Istanbul to be used as depositories for funds to assist relief efforts, including money used for bribery. *Id.* at 275.

[226] *Id.* at 261–63.

[227] TURKEY AND THE HOLOCAUST, *supra* note 5, at 264.

[228] *Id.* at 274–75.

assistance of Turkish diplomatic channels[229].

In addition, the Vatican had a diplomatic mission in Istanbul, which was staffed by Monsignor Angelo Roncalli, who was affectionately referred to as the Turkish Pope[230]. Roncalli spoke out boldly against the Nazi persecution of Jews, and has been credited with intervening on behalf of persecuted Jews with numerous foreign governments, including Bulgaria, Italy, Romania, Slovakia, Greece, Croatia, France, Germany, and Hungary[231]. The Turkish government worked with Roncalli to arrange for humanitarian aid and he encouraged the Vatican to engage with neutral countries to accept Jewish refugees[232]. Moreover, Roncalli and Ira Hirschman of the War Refugee Board concocted "Operation Baptism" to save Hungarian Jews[233] and were even able to convince the German Ambassador in Istanbul, Franz von Papen, to use his position to help rescue Jews[234]. Ultimately, the Wallenberg Foundation recognised Monsignor Roncalli's achievements: "He did not only exercise direct action to save thousands of men, women and children condemned to extermination but also . . . was restless in the act of revealing to the Holy See and allied countries . . . the horrendous

---

[229] *Id.* at 276–77. The Rescue Committee was also known as the Committee of Four to save Polish Jews. Peter Landé & Joyce Field, *"Jews for Sale": The Rudolph Kasztner Transports,* JEWISHGEN.ORG, http://www.jewishgen.org/databases/ Holocaust/0172_Kasznter_Jews.html (last visited 1 June 2015).

[230] *Roncalli, The "Turkish Pope",* GARIWO.NET, http://en.gariwo.net/righteous/ rescuers/roncalli-the-turkish-pope-9694.html (last visited 1 June 2015).

[231] *Humanitarian actions of Monsignor Angelo Roncalli,* RAOUL WALLENBERG FOUND., http://www.raoulwallenberg.net/general/humanitarian-actions-monsignor/ (last visited 1 June 2015).

[232] TURKEY AND THE HOLOCAUST, *supra* note 5, at 277–78; SHOAH: TURKEY, THE US AND THE UK, *supra* note 5, at 211.

[233] Roncalli organised fake baptisms for Jews in Hungary to avoid deportation to concentration camps. TURKEY AND THE HOLOCAUST, *supra* note 5, at 297–98; SHOAH: TURKEY, THE US AND THE UK, *supra* note 5, at 219–33.

[234] Michael Curtis, *Honoring Pope John XXIII, a Righteous Man,* AMERICAN THINKER (31 May 2014), http://www.americanthinker.com/articles/2014/05/ honoring_pope_john_xxiii_a_righteous_man.html. At the Nuremburg trials, Von Papen most likely did not receive the death sentence as a result of assisting Roncalli in rescuing Jews.

genocide that was taking place"[235]. Angelo Roncalli became Pope John XXIII on 28 October 1958.

Some of the refugees who arrived in Turkey were the first survivors of the concentration camps. With the support of the government, these evacuees were able to communicate to the world details regarding the massacres taking place in Europe[236]. Over time, fifteen relief organisations dedicated to the Jewish refugee problem were based in Istanbul, many illegally, while the government looked the other way[237]. Likewise, the Mossad operated extensively in Istanbul and was intricately involved in negotiating with Turkish officials and local shippers to transport "illegal" refugees by boat[238]. Later on, after they terminated diplomatic relations with Germany in 1944, Turkish authorities ordered consuls in occupied regions to issue 400 visas every ten days for travel to Turkey[239]. The Jewish Agency also convinced Turkey to delay entering the war as to not interfere with Germany's "expatriation ultimatum", which permitted more Turkish Jews to leave occupied territories[240].

However, the effectiveness of Turkey as a transit route was drastically limited by pressure exerted by Britain, the U.S., and the war efforts of Germany[241]. There were frequent impediments involving the

---

[235] Horacio Moreno, *Remembering Monsignor Angelo Giuseppe Roncalli*, RAOUL WALLENBERG FOUND. (4 Dec. 2001), http://www.raoulwallenberg.net/ roncalli/ tributes-29/programs/remembering-monsignor-angelo/.

[236] This information was compiled and known as the "Istanbul Lists". TURKEY AND THE HOLOCAUST, *supra* note 5, at 266.

[237] *Id.* at 256; SHOAH: TURKEY, THE US AND THE UK, *supra* note 5, at 203.

[238] OFER, *supra* note 5, at 238–66. Mossad was a Jewish organisation significantly involved in transporting illegal immigrants from Europe to Palestine. Today, Mossad is Israel's intelligence agency similar to the CIA in the United States. Refugees were deemed illegal if they did not have immigration certificates to enter Palestine that were approved by Britain. *Id.* at 5–7, 11–17.

[239] TURKEY AND THE HOLOCAUST, *supra* note 5, at 298. Ambassador Steinhardt believed Turkey would accept up to 500 refugees per week. OFER, *supra* note 5, at 28, 131–33.

[240] TURKEY AND THE HOLOCAUST, *supra* note 5, at 296. Finally, Turkey, under pressure from the Allies, declared war on Germany and the Axis powers in February 1945. *Id.*

[241] *Id.* at 255–56, 287. In fact, U.S. Ambassador Steinhardt felt rescue efforts were

government's constraints prohibiting vessels to pass through its waters. Turkey's tendency was to raise concerns about safe passage due to wartime hostilities, or yield to unbending British pressure regarding illegal immigration[242]. Additionally, because of the limitations imposed by the White Paper, many refugees who passed through Turkey to Palestine did not have proper documentation and were deemed "illegal" by the British. Complicating matters, the United States was in full support of Britain's immigration policies regarding the Jews[243].

In order to appease the British, Turkey often relented by denying Jews entry, and created obstacles for private ships participating in transporting Jews from occupied territories[244]. Also, Turkey was known to be extremely diligent in inspecting the paperwork of refugees, and to delay or deny entrance if documentation was not in order[245]. The primary concern of Ankara was a scenario whereby Jews would arrive in Turkey and remain there because they were subsequently refused admission to Palestine by the British[246]. While this may be true, Turkey was generally amenable to avail itself as a transit route for refugees on their way to Palestine; but the government, not unlike Britain or the United States, was not receptive to "opening its doors" to Jewish refugees[247].

---

hampered by the inability to procure transit visas through the Baltic States to Turkey. OFER, *supra* note 5, at 270–71.

[242] OFER, *supra* note 5, at 128–38, 278. *See also* WYMAN, *supra* note 184, at 215–20. Turkey was also concerned about its ships being attacked by the Germans. The Nazis sank the *Mefkura*, a privately owned Turkish rescue ship, and all 295 refugees were lost, including one-hundred children. *Id.* at 195–98.

[243] WYMAN, *supra* note 184, at 159.

[244] BAHAR, *supra* note 7, at 5660–77, 6015–66.

[245] OFER, *supra* note 5, at 163–64, 279. Ira Hirschman believed officials were deliberately dragging their feet in approving refugee transit visas because of anti-Semitic leanings. *Id.* at 272.

[246] GUTTSTADT, *supra* note 3, at 132–33.

[247] SHOAH: TURKEY, THE US AND THE UK, *supra* note 5, at 61.

CONCLUSION

The relationship between Turkey and its Jewish population has a long and rich history. Jews in the Ottoman Empire flourished and integrated into society, but the collapse of the empire at the end of WWI gave way to nationalism and the Turkification of society. This seismic shift produced a destabilising environment, triggering almost fifty percent of Turkish Jews to emigrate, mostly to European countries. Moreover, Turkey's preference to populate and expand its economy with Muslims, as opposed to minorities, also affected its policies regarding immigration and repatriation. Domestically, Turkey's economy was in crisis mode, and gearing up for war created additional economic concerns.

Remaining neutral was the centerpiece of Turkey's foreign policy during the Holocaust and WWII, and its politics reflected its determination to act in its own self-interest. After Hitler's conquest and occupation of Europe, Jews of Turkish descent were looking to either return to Turkey or immigrate to Palestine. Wartime politics, combined with German-inspired anti-Semitism and Turkey's nationalistic tendencies, resulted in the tightening of citizenship laws, which had catastrophic consequences for Turkish Jews living in occupied Europe who were attempting to repatriate. For exiles without a nexus to Turkey, the conferences at Evian and Bermuda demonstrated that Turkey was not alone in refusing Jewish refugees a humanitarian place of sanctuary.

On the other hand, Turkey's efficacy as a transit route for refugees to Palestine was dictated, for the most part, by Britain's immigration policies and Germany guaranteeing safe passage, whether by sea or rail. As long as refugees were just passing through on their way to Palestine, Turkey's objections were diminished. But, as often was the case, the quandary occurred when Jews escaping occupied Europe would make their way into Turkey without proper certificates to Palestine. For the most part, Turkey objected to refugees entering the country unless their stay was short, and their paperwork to Palestine was in order. Ultimately, when the United States and Britain altered their immigration strategies towards the end of the war, Istanbul served as an important location for humanitarian relief organisations and a critical transit route for refugees escaping occupied Europe.

There is significant evidence that individual Turkish diplomats, especially in France, were actively engaged in attempting to secure the rights of and repatriate Turkish Jews. There is a conflict of opinion whether or not the activities of these diplomats were the result of individual humanitarian concerns, or a consequence of affirmative directives from Ankara. Most of the research leads to the conclusion that Turkey was not interested in a large influx of Jews and that these officials, for the most part, acted out of their own compassion with minimal directives from government officials.

The question remains, could Turkey have done more to repatriate its Jews, provide a more effective transit route to Palestine or open its doors to refugees. Over 80 years later, the answer is clearly, yes. But, at the time, Turkey's skillful diplomacy was focused predominantly on independence, stability, and survival, while the complexities of domestic and international policy were exacerbated by war. However, unlike some of its European contemporaries, the fabric and backbone of Turkey's moral compass allowed it to steadfastly resist active collaboration with Hitler's Final Solution. That, in and of itself, provides an essential mitigating factor when rigorously critiquing Turkey's political maneuvering during the Holocaust.

Turkey's Support for Hamas: A Bridge Too Far?

David Benjamin[*]

INTRODUCTION

Turkey has long aspired to serve as a bridge between civilisations: between East and West, between Europe and Asia, between Islam and Christianity. Turkey's geographic location, its democracy, its previously secular and now purportedly moderate-Islamic outlook, its close ties with the West—including its membership in the North Atlantic Treaty Organisation—are factors that make this seem viable. Turkey's bid to join the European Union (EU) reflects this desire while U.S. President Obama, during his visit to Turkey in 2009 spoke of a "model partnership"[1], a sentiment that has since been echoed consistently by former

*David Benjamin is a Senior Fellow of the the the Centre for the Study of Law & Public Policy at Oxford. He is a member of the Israel Bar specializing in International Law, the Law of Armed Conflict and Counter-Terrorism and a former senior officer in the Israel Defence Forces Military Advocate General's Corps. He lectures widely both in Israel and abroad. Mr Benjamin holds a Bachelor of Arts (B.A.) in Political Studies and a Bachelor of Laws (LL.B.) from the University of Cape Town as well as a Master of Laws (LL.M.) from Tel Aviv University. He is also a graduate of the Israel Defence Forces Command and Staff College.

[1] Press Release, Office of the Press Sec'y, the White House, Joint Press Availability with President Obama and President Gul of Turk. (6 Apr. 2009), https:// www. whitehouse.gov/the-press-office/joint-press-availability-with-president-obama-and-president-gul-turkey.

Turkish Prime Minister and ideologue Ahmet Davutoğlu[2].

For Turkey to fulfil this bridging role effectively, it needs good relationships on both sides of the Bosphorus. This may require a delicate balancing act, but the potential to benefit from both worlds would seem to justify the effort.

The Justice and Development Party (AKP), since coming to power in 2002, has added a major agenda item to the Turkish vision—the desire to bolster Turkey's leadership role in the Islamic world. Needless to say, this aspiration does not always square easily with Turkey's bridging role.

To a large extent, Turkey has arguably succeeded in "having its cake and eating it too". It has pursued its cause on the Islamic front while retaining most of its friends. However, its leadership of President Recep Tayyip Erdoğan and Prime Minister Ahmet Davutoğlu has consistently and increasingly put its relationship with the West and others under strain. Such is the case regarding Turkey's support for Hamas—the violent, Islamist, rejectionist Palestinian faction that controls the Gaza Strip—an adversary of both Israel and the Fatah-led Palestinian Authority (PA) and an outlawed terrorist organisation in the U.S., the EU, and other countries.

This article examines the history and nature of Turkey's ties with Hamas, the former's motivations for pursuing the relationship and the implications for Turkey's relations with other actors as well as for the Israeli-Palestinian "Peace Process". What emerges clearly from the analysis is that Turkey's current conduct vis-à-vis Hamas is incompatible with the constructive international bridging role to which Turkey aspires. In conclusion, the article looks at considerations which might persuade Turkey to change course in this regard.

[2] *See* Press Release, Republic of Turk. Ministry of Foreign Affairs, Foreign Minister Davutoğlu, "The model partnership between Turkey and the U.S. will continue forever," http://www.mfa.gov.tr/foreign-minister-davutoglu-the-model-partnership-between-turkey-and-the-u_s_-will-continue-forever.en.mfa (last visited 16 May 2016).

I. HOW THE TURKEY-HAMAS RELATIONSHIP DEVELOPED

Before the AKP came to power in Turkey in 2002, there was no Turkish relationship to speak of with Hamas. In 2006, Turkey hosted its first Hamas conference and such events took place with increasing frequency in successive years[3]. The Gaza conflict of 2008-2009 brought about a downturn in the hitherto flourishing relations between Turkey and Israel with Erdoğan accusing the Israelis of atrocities in the Hamas-controlled Gaza Strip[4]. This was compounded by the "Mavi Marmara Affair" in May 2010. The Mavi Marmara was a cruise ship sent by IHH[5], a prominent NGO with close ties to Turkey's ruling AKP party, to spearhead a protest flotilla aimed at breaking the Israeli naval blockade of the Hamas-ruled Gaza Strip. Israeli naval commandos boarding the vessel were attacked by some of the protesters. The bloody clash that ensued claimed the lives of nine Turkish nationals[6]. Diplomatic relations between Turkey and Israel have been poor ever since, despite several brief attempts at reconciliation[7]. In parallel, the ties between Turkey and Hamas have become steadily stronger.

Hamas has been bolstered by a series of high-profile meetings that have taken place between Turkish and Hamas leaders since 2012.

[3] Soner Cagaptay, *The AKP's Hamas Policy: Transformation of Turk Foreign Policy and the Turk View of the West,* THE FAO JOURNAL (2010) http://www.washingtoninstitute.org/uploads/Documents/opeds/4b7c32f9b0278.pdf.

[4] *See* Katrin Bennhold, *Leaders of Turkey and Israel Clash at Davos Panel,* N.Y. TIMES (29 Jan. 2009), http://www.nytimes.com/2009/01/30/world/europe/30clash.html.

[5] The IHH is an abbreviation for *İnsan Hak ve Hürriyetleri ve İnsani Yardım Vakfı,* meaning Foundation for Human Rights and Freedoms and Humanitarian Relief in English.

[6] Yaakov Katz, *Nine Dead in Vicious Conflict Aboard 'Mavi Marmara',* JERUSALEM POST (01 June 2010), http://www.jpost.com/Israel/Nine-dead-in-Vicious-conflict-aboard-Mavi-Marmara; *see* Robert Weston Ash, *The Mavi Marmara Trial: Politicising the Turkish Justice System,* 1 J. CTR. FOR STUDY OF L. & PUB. POL'Y at Oxford 49 (2015), for a more detailed account and legal analysis of the incident and its aftermath, including the show trial conducted by Turkish Authorities.

[7] *See* Jay Alan Sekulow, *Turkey-Israel Relations,* 1 J. CTR. FOR STUDY OF L. & PUB. POL'Y at Oxford 1 (2015), for background on Turkish-Israeli relations.

For example, in January 2012, the leader of Hamas in Gaza, Ismail Haniyeh, visited Turkey where he met Turkish Premier Erdoğan at his Istanbul residence. He was also cheered by the Turkish Parliament[8]. In April 2012, both Erdoğan and Davutoğlu met with Hamas off-shore leader Khaled Mashaal in Qatar. This came on the heels of a visit by Mashaal to Ankara in March 2012[9]. Then in July 2012, Mashaal met again with Erdoğan in Ankara[10]. He was there once more in September 2012 and attended the Congress of the ruling AKP party with Erdoğan[11]. After the hostilities of November 2012[12], Davutoğlu joined a delegation of Arab ministers for a highly publicised visit to Gaza[13].

In June 2013, both Mashaal and Haniyeh travelled to Ankara where they met with Erdoğan and Davutoğlu[14]. Mashaal met with Erdoğan once again in Ankara in October of that year[15]. During the Gaza–Israel conflict in July-August 2014, Davutoğlu met with

[8] *Gaza's Hamas PM Warmly Welcomed in Turkish Parliament*, DAILY STAR (03 Jan. 2012), http://www.dailystar.com.lb/News/Middle-East/2012/Jan-03/158702-gazas-hamas-pm-warmly-welcomed-in-turkish-parliament.ashx.

[9] *Turkish FM Talks Palestine with Hamas Chief*, DAILY NEWS (23 Apr. 2012), http://www.hurriyetdailynews.com/turkish-fm-talks-palestine-with-hamas-chief.aspx?pageID=238&nID=19042&NewsCatID=338; *Hamas Leader Meets with Erdoğan in Surprise Visit*, CIHAN (16 Mar. 2012), https://www.cihan.com.tr/en/hamas-leader-meets-erdogan-in-surprise-visit-hd-video-647915.htm.

[10] *Erdoğan Holds Surprise Talks with Hamas Leader*, TODAY'S ZAMAN (25 July 2012), http://www.todayszaman.com/diplomacy_erdogan-holds-surprise-talks-with-hamas-leader_287633.html. NOTE: The Erdoğan government has recently closed down the *Today's Zaman* news outlet. Accordingly, until the Erdoğan government reverses its decision, access to *Today's Zaman* articles is unavailable.

[11] Elior Levy, *Mashaal: Resistance is Only Path Towards State*, YNET NEWS (30 Sept. 2012), http://www.ynetnews.com/articles/0,7340,L-4287181,00.html.

[12] Dubbed *"Operation Pillar of Defence"* by Israel.

[13] Press Release, Republic of Turk. Ministry of Foreign Affairs, Foreign Minister Davutoğlu "Your Pain is Our Pain and Your Future is Our Future, http:// www.mfa.gov.tr/foreign-minister-davutoglu-your-pain-is-our-pain-and-your-future-is-our-future.en.mfa (last visited 16 May 2016).

[14] *Hamas Leaders Meet with Erdoğan in Ankara*, TODAY'S ZAMAN (18 June 2013), http://www.todayszaman.com/latest-news_hamas-leaders-meet-with-erdogan-in-ankara_318567.html.

[15] *Turkey's Erdoğan Meets Hamas Leader Mashaal*, TODAY'S ZAMAN (8 Oct. 2013), http://www.todayszaman.com/latest-news_turkeys-erdogan-meets-hamas-leader-meshaal_328470.html.

Mashaal in Qatar[16]. Mashaal visited Turkey in December 2014 and had a highly publicised meeting which can aptly be described as a "lovefest". In what can only be interpreted as a sign of growing intimacy, Mashaal was taken by Prime Minister Davutoğlu to a gathering of the AKP party in his home town of Konya. In addition to a display of hand-holding and mass adulation by the party faithful, Mashaal received a private audience lasting no less than four-and-a-half hours with the Turkish Prime Minister[17]. The most recent publicised high-level meeting took place between Erdoğan and Mashaal in Istanbul in December 2015[18].

The meetings mentioned above are those which the parties saw fit to publicise. Needless to say, lower-profile and lower-level contacts have been taking place continuously[19].

Erdoğan has famously stated that he does not view Hamas as a terrorist organisation. In a 2011 interview on a U.S. television channel, Erdoğan said:

> Let me give you a very clear message. I don't see Hamas as a terror organisation. Hamas is a political party. And it is an organisation. It is a resistance movement trying to protect its country under occupation. So we should not mix terrorist organisations with such an organisation[20].

In a speech given in January 2015, in Germany, Davutoğlu reiterated his government's position that "Hamas is not a terrorist organisation

---

[16] *Israel Is Disingenuous about Peace: Turkish FM*, ANADOLU AGENCY (26 July 2014), http://www.aa.com.tr/en/politics/365086--Israel-is-disingenuous-about-peace-Turkish-FM.

[17] Burak Bekdil, *Davutoğlu and Mashaal: A Marriage Made in Heaven*, GATESTONE INST. (01 Jan. 2015), http://www.gatestoneinstitute.org/4997/davutoglu-mashaal.

[18] *Erdoğan Meets Hamas Leader Meshaal in Istanbul*, HURRIYET DAILY NEWS (20 Dec. 2015), http://www.hurriyetdailynews.com/Default.aspx?PageID=238&NID=92747&NewsCatID=352.

[19] This was confirmed to the writer by an opposition member of the Turkish parliament.

[20] Tovah Lazaroff, *Erdoğan: Hamas is Not a Terrorist Organization*, JERUSALEM POST (13 May 2011), http://www.jpost.com/Middle-East/Erdogan-Hamas-is-not-a-terrorist-organization.

and has not carried out any terrorist acts"[21].

In December 2011, a Palestinian website posted the news that Erdoğan had directed Turkey's finance ministry to donate $300 million to the Hamas government in Gaza[22]. Turkey also pledged $200 million for reconstruction in Gaza after the conflict in 2014[23] although a World Bank report from May 2015 showed that Turkey had so far failed to meet this pledge[24]. Turkish Foreign Ministry spokesman, Tanju Bilgic subsequently insisted that the aid was still on track and confirmed that Turkish aid to Gaza over the previous 10 years had reached $369 million[25]. According to Israeli sources, Turkey has been giving financial support to Hamas to the tune of $250 million per year. This money has been reportedly channelled mostly through private sources with the full coordination of Erdoğan and his aides, mostly to Hamas in the West Bank[26]. Also, the powerful Turkish NGO, IHH is known to be part of Hamas' fundraising network[27].

Reports from early 2016 show Hamas in a financial crisis which has forced it to cut back on salaries, including even in its military wing, the Al-Kassam Brigades. The crisis has been attributed to Egypt's destruction of smuggling tunnels running between Gaza and its terri-

---

[21] Bekdil, *supra* note 17.

[22] Saed Bannoura, *Turkey to Grant Hamas $300 Million*, IMEMC (03 Dec. 2011), http://www.imemc.org/article/62607.

[23] *Turkey Pledges $200 Million for Gaza's Reconstruction*, Today's Zaman (13 Oct. 2014), http://www.todayszaman.com/anasayfa_turkey-pledges-200-million-for-gazas-reconstruction_361515.html.

[24] Deniz Arslan, *World Bank Report: Turkey Fails to Honour Pledge to Gaza*, Today's Zaman (24 May 2015), http://www.todayszaman.com/anasayfa_world-bank-report-turkey-fails-to-honor-pledge-to-gaza_381631.html.

[25] *Turkey Says Keeping Promise on Aid to Gaza*, Anadolu Agency (27 May 2015), http://www.aa.com.tr/en/news/517739--turkey-says-keeping-promise-on-aid-to-gaza.

[26] *Turkey Replaces Iran as Primary Funding Source for Hamas*, World Tribune (22 Dec. 2013), http://www.worldtribune.com/2013/12/22/turkey-replaces-iran-as-primary-funding-source-for-hamas.

[27] *The Union of Good – Analysis and Mapping of Terror Funds Network*, Israeli Sec. Agency, http://www.shabak.gov.il/English/EnTerrorData/Reviews/Pages/coalition.en.aspx (last visited 16 May 2016).

tory as well as a lack of foreign financial support[28]. The situation with respect to donations from Turkey is unknown.

In early 2015, Turkey was reportedly prepared to host the offices of Khaled Mashaal, who, according to various sources, was asked by Qatar to relocate from his headquarters in Doha due to pressure from the U.S. and others. Publicly, Hamas has denied the existence of any moves to expel Mashaal from Qatar[29].

II. TURKEY BECOMES AN OPERATIONAL BASE FOR HAMAS

Over and above the political and financial support for Hamas from the Turkish government, Turkey has in recent years become a base for Hamas terror-related activity. Reportedly set up in 2011, after Hamas was expelled from Damascus, the so-called "West Bank and Jerusalem Headquarters" of the organisation is located in Istanbul.

The kingpin of Hamas' Turkish operation has been Saleh al-Arouri, the founder of Hamas' armed wing in the West Bank, deported from the West Bank in 2010 after lengthy prison terms. Arouri is believed to have directed and financed Hamas operatives in the West Bank to carry out kidnappings, car bombings and roadside attacks. In August 2014, Arouri publicly claimed responsibility on behalf of Hamas for the abduction and murder of three Israeli teenagers in June of that year[30]. He has also been alleged to be plotting kidnappings of Israelis abroad. In early 2015, the Israeli secret service (*Shin Bet*) confirmed the arrest

---

[28] Kifa Ziboun, *Hamas' Financial Crisis Affects its Military Wing for the First Time*, ASHARQ AL-AWSAT (15 Mar. 2016), http://english.aawsat.com/2016/03/article55348538/hamas-financial-crisis-affects-its-military-wing-for-the-first-time.

[29] *Report: Hamas' Mashaal Expelled from Qatar, Heading for Turkey*, TODAY'S ZAMAN (06 Jan. 2015), http://www.todayszaman.com/anasayfa_report-hamas-mashaal-expelled-from-qatar-heading-for-turkey_369063.html.

[30] Saleh al-Arouri, *Hamas Leadership Acknowledges Responsibility for Kidnapping Three Israeli Teens*, THE MIDDLE EAST MEDIA RESEARCH INST. (20 Aug. 2014), http://www.memritv.org/clip/en/4437.htm.

of a terror network in the West Bank which had been planning mass casualty attacks on a Jerusalem Soccer stadium and the City's light rail system. This network had been built and funded by the then Turkey-based Arouri. Arouri is also suspected of involvement in a Hamas ring which conspired to overthrow the Fatah–led government of Mahmoud Abbas in the West Bank in the summer of 2014. The ring, comprising over 90 operatives, was exposed by the Shin Bet. In July 2015, Palestinian Authority security forces claimed to have arrested some 250 Hamas operatives who had been planning to kidnap Israelis, fire at vehicles on main routes in the West Bank and launch attacks on IDF checkpoints. The object was to provoke an Israeli reaction which would lead to a deterioration of ties between Israel and the PA. The Hamas cells also planned to assassinate senior PA security officials. Again, Arouri was fingered as being behind the plot[31].

Hamas in Turkey is also known to be actively recruiting operatives from among Gaza and West Bank residents and Israeli Arabs who are studying in Turkey, Jordan, Syria and other Arab countries. Such recruiting efforts are reportedly under way as far afield as Malaysia[32]. The students are said to undergo initial screening in Jordan and Turkey and are then sent to the headquarters in Istanbul, where they receive security clearances and training in light weapons, bomb-making and covert operations, which takes place just outside the city—all with the knowledge of Turkish intelligence officials. The recruits, allegedly hundreds every year, are then sent for additional training in Syria and from there, to the West Bank to engage in terror operations.

The Istanbul Headquarters receives ongoing reports from the West Bank from intelligence-gathering agents working in the field, and is be-

---

[31] Avi Issacharoff, *Hamas Plot to Attack Israel, PA in West Bank Foiled by Mass Arrests*, Times of Israel (19 July 2015), http://www.timesofisrael.com/hamas-plot-to-attack-israel-pa-in-west-bank-foiled-by-mass-arrests/.
[32] *Hamas Activity in Malaysia*, The Meir Amit Intelligence and Terrorism Info. Ctr. (06 May 2015), http://www.terrorism-info.org.il/Data/articles/Art_20805/E_085_15_936313463.pdf.

lieved to have been behind several of the violent incidents taking place in Jerusalem since the last quarter of 2014. Moreover, many of the illicit arms in the hands of West Bank Hamas members were purchased and shipped by Hamas' Turkish operation[33].

Arouri has been known to have several dozen operatives assisting him. These include Imad alAlami, Hamas' erstwhile representative in Iran, and around 20 deportees from the 2011 Shalit Deal, among them Zaher Jabarin and Jihad Yarmur, who were involved in the murder of IDF soldier Nachshon Wachsman in 1994[34].

There is a further dimension to Hamas in Turkey which aggravates an already grave situation: There are indications that Arouri has been operating as a law unto himself and has not always coordinated with the Hamas top leadership. Thus for example, Arouri is understood to have initiated the 2014 kidnapping of three Israeli teens without the knowledge of Mashaal or Hamas in Gaza. True to form, the organisation closed ranks after the fact and voiced its support for Arouri's action, but it appears that the branch of Hamas hosted by Turkey is in fact more extreme and even less pragmatic than the Hamas mainstream[35].

Turkey is apparently also home to Hamas financial operatives Bakri Hanifa and Maher Ubeid. The former was said to be heavily involved in an ongoing operation to move "tens of millions of dollars" from Qatar to Turkey which are then sent on to Hamas' political and military wings. The latter was believed to be engaged in the transfer of funds from Turkish official sources to Hamas in Gaza via Turkish money changers[36].

---

[33] Alex Fishman, *Forced from Damascus, Hamas Establishing Itself in Turkey*, YNET NEWS (25 Feb. 2015), http://www.ynetnews.com/articles/0,7340,L-4630331,00.html.
[34] *Id.*
[35] Shlomi Eldar, *Turkey's Hamas 'Bureau'*, AL-MONITOR (01 Dec. 2014), http://www.al-monitor.com/pulse/originals/2014/12/saleh-al-arouri-khaled-meshaal-hamas-leadership-turkey-gaza.html#.
[36] Jonathan Schanzer & David Andrew Weinberg, *The Turkey-Hamas Nexus*,

Reports from August 2015 indicate that Arouri was asked to leave the country by the Turkish government. At the time of writing, Arouri is understood to have relocated to Qatar. A Hamas source has said that Arouri left voluntarily so as not to embarrass Turkey which was under significant pressure from the U.S. and Israel. The source maintained that Turkey had not placed restrictions on Hamas activities or its officials living in that country and that Arouri had not been banned from entering Turkey[37]. Press reports confirm that despite the departure of Arouri, Erdoğan has clarified that he has no intention of closing Hamas offices in Turkey or of ceasing Turkey's financial and moral support for Hamas[38]. In addition, there are reports claiming that since relocating, Arouri has been shuttling freely between Qatar and Turkey[39].

The continued presence of Hamas operations in Turkey has been a key sticking-point in reconciliation efforts between Israel and Turkey. Interestingly, some commentators say the shutting-down of Hamas in Turkey would also serve the interests of the mainstream Hamas leadership due to the rogue nature of the Turkish operation[40].

III. TURKEY'S MOTIVATIONS FOR ITS TIES WITH HAMAS

Analysts of Turkish foreign policy routinely point to Ahmet Davu-

THE NAT'L INTEREST (16 Jan. 2015), http://nationalinterest.org/feature/the-turkey-hamas-nexus-12044.

[37] Herb Keinon & Khaled Abu Toameh, *Hamas Activity in Turkey an Obstacle to Ankara – Jerusalem Reconciliation*, JERUSALEM POST (21 Dec. 2015), http:// www.jpost.com/Israel-News/Politics-And-Diplomacy/Hamas-activity-in-Turkey-an-obstacle-to-Ankara-Jerusalem-reconciliation-438011.

[38] Smadar Perry & Itamar Eichner, *Hamas Leader Expelled from Turkey*, YNET NEWS (22 Dec. 2015), http://www.ynetnews.com/articles/0,7340,L-4742831,00.html.

[39] Aaron Klein, *Exiled Hamas Terror Kingpin Back in NATO-Member Turkey*, BREITBART (06 Jan. 2016), http://www.breitbart.com/middle-east/2016/01/06/exiled-hamas-terror-kingpin-back-in-nato-member-turkey/.

[40] Alex MacDonald, *What does the Turkey–Israel Détente Mean for Hamas?* MIDDLE EAST EYE (23 Dec. 2015), http://www.middleeasteye.net/news/what-does-turkey-israel-detente-mean-hamas-1595659569.

toğlu's book "Strategic Depth" for an explanation of what Turkey under the AKP is trying to achieve. Essentially, the book sets out a vision of "neo-Ottomanism" which is the idea that Turkey should re-establish itself as the leader and epicentre of the Islamic world in much the same way as the Ottoman Empire fulfilled this role for about five centuries. To this end, Turkey has set about a process of Islamisation of its foreign policy which runs counter to Turkish policies of previous decades which were more in line with a Western approach[41].

Initially, upon coming to power in 2002, the AKP had a declared policy of "zero problems with neighbors". However, with the advent of the inaptly named "Arab Spring", Turkey saw an opportunity to advance its agenda and support the creation of like-minded regimes. Accordingly, Turkey saw the Muslim Brotherhood as a kindred spirit and was one of the chief supporters of the Morsi government in Egypt, while it lasted. Despite the overthrow of the Brotherhood in Egypt, Turkey remains a die-hard supporter of the movement and is, to date, the only country in the region which has not recognised the regime of Abdel Fatah el-Sisi in Egypt[42].

It is possible to explain Turkey's affinity for Hamas as a natural extension of the former's support of the Muslim Brotherhood. Hamas is recognised as having a deep connection with the Brotherhood. It has even been asserted that "Hamas *is* the Muslim Brotherhood"[43].

In addition to the ideological kinship, it has also been suggested that Turkey has several political motivations for its attitude to Hamas. One of these is the desire to position Turkey as an independent

[41] Amanda Paul, *The Folly of Turkey's Ideological Foreign Policy*, TODAY'S ZAMAN (06 Jan. 2015), http://www.todayszaman.com/columnist/amanda-paul/the-folly-of-turkeys-ideological-foreign-policy_369047.html.

[42] *Id.*

[43] *See, e.g.*, Andrew C. McCarthy, *Hamas Is the Muslim Brotherhood*, NAT'L REVIEW (29 Jan. 2011), http://www.nationalreview.com/corner/258381/hamas-muslim-brotherhood-andrew-c-mccarthy.

thought-leader, with its own defiantly-held opinions, unsusceptible to pressure from Washington or other sources, even at the cost of international isolation. In this respect, Erdoğan has been said to be an admirer of Russia's Vladimir Putin and can perhaps be seen as trying to emulate the latter's seeming nonchalance towards international opinion[44]. Erdoğan's chief policy adviser, Ibrahim Kalin, has branded Turkey's situation as "precious loneliness," arguing that it stems from "Turkey's principled and ethical stance" on international issues[45]. Certainly, in the Muslim world, which Turkey aspires to lead, an outspokenly militant stance on the Palestinian issue is generally considered a political asset, if not a necessity.

Another possibility is that Turkey identifies Iran as its main competitor for the Muslim world's top-spot and attaches importance to preventing the latter from establishing too big a footprint on the Palestinian issue—the one cause that unites Muslims everywhere. The significance of this rivalry has increased since the two countries have become embroiled on opposite sides of Syria's protracted civil war. Turkey may be taking advantage of the fallout between Hamas and Tehran over the former's opposition to Syria's Assad, while mindful that Hamas could well end up in Iranian arms again after possibly losing Doha. The London-based newspaper *Al-Hayat* reported that shortly after the July-August 2014 hostilities between Israel and Gaza, Hamas leader Khaled Mashaal met in Turkey with the commander of the Quds Force of the Iranian Revolutionary Guard, Qassem Soleimani. According to the report, after the meeting, a Hamas delegation travelled to Iran to discuss the resumption of financial and military aid from Tehran[46].

---

[44] Semi Idiz, *Some See Snubs, Erdoğan Sees Envy.*, Al-Monitor (17 Feb. 2015), http://www.al-monitor.com/pulse/originals/2015/02/turkey-international-isolation-erdogan.html#ixzz3SHB3j4Wt. Whether the crisis in Turkey-Russia relations following the November 2015 downing of a Russian jet by Turkey has affected Erdoğan's opinion of Mr Putin, is open to speculation.

[45] *Id.*

[46] Elior Levy, *Hamas and Iran Said to be Renewing Ties*, Ynet News (17 Feb. 2015), http://www.ynetnews.com/articles/0,7340,L-4627643,00.html.

Press reports from April 2015 claimed that Iran's financial and military aid to Hamas had indeed been resumed;[47] yet, a senior Hamas official complained in January 2016 that Hamas had not received financial aid from Iran since 2009[48]. Given that Iran has been emboldened and strengthened economically by the deal it signed with the P5+1 in July 2015, it can be anticipated that Iran will seek to further consolidate its influence in the Palestinian arena. Since Iran has reportedly severed its ties with the Palestinian Islamic Jihad organisation, the second largest militant faction in Gaza after Hamas, it seems natural that Iran will try to get Hamas, the heavier hitter, on board again. In a meeting reportedly held in March 2016 between Hamas leaders and senior Iranian officials, the Iranians explained the drop in aid as a result of economic difficulties and insisted that their support for the Palestinian cause was as strong as ever[49]. One can surmise that Turkey is watching these developments closely.

Iran is not Turkey's only competitor for influence in the Palestinian sphere. Qatar, with its vast disposable income, continues to host the Hamas Headquarters (albeit somewhat reluctantly) and remains notably active in initiatives relating to Gaza[50].

[47] Con Coughlin, *Iran Rekindles Relations with Hamas*, WALL ST. J. (21 Apr. 2015), http://www.wsj.com/articles/iran-rekindles-relations-with-hamas-1429658562; Con Coughlin, *Iran 'is Intensifying Efforts to Support Hamas in Gaza'*, THE TELEGRAPH (04 Apr. 2015), http://www.telegraph.co.uk/news/worldnews/middleeast/iran/11515603/Iran-is-intensifying-efforts-to-support-Hamas-in-Gaza.html; *see also Israel: Iran Steps up Arms Shipments to Hezbollah, Hamas*, TIMES OF ISRAEL (13 Apr. 2015), http://www.timesofisrael.com/israel-iran-steps-up-arms-shipments-to-hezbollah-hamas/.

[48] Maayan Groisman, *Report: Senior Hamas Official Blames Iranian "Liars" for Deserting Hamas*, JERUSALEM POST (31 Jan. 2016), http://www.jpost.com/Middle-East/Report-Senior-Hamas-official-blames-Iranian-liars-for-deserting-Hamas-443 356.

[49] Maayan Groisman, *Commander of Elite Iranian Quds Force Meets Secretly with Hamas Delegation*, JERUSALEM POST (17 Mar. 2016), http://www.jpost.com/Middle-East/Commander-of-elite-Iranian-Quds-Force-meets-secretly-with-Hamas-delegation-448286.

[50] Avi Issacharoff, *Turkey Joins Qatari Bid to Broker Israel-Hamas Deal*, TIMES OF ISRAEL (28 Apr. 2015), http://www.timesofisrael.com/qatar-turkey-try-to-broker-israel-hamas-ceasefire/.

Another regional power looking to fortify its position and influence, particularly in light of the Iran–P5+1 deal, is Saudi Arabia. This country, noticeably anxious about a stronger Iran, has also reached out to Hamas. A high-level Hamas delegation headed by Khaled Mashaal, visited Riyadh in July 2015 to meet with King Salman, Crown Prince Muhammad bin Nayef, and other Saudi officials. Significantly, Arouri was included in the Hamas delegation along with Mashaal's deputy, Moussa Abu Marzouk. This was the first such meeting in over three years[51]. The Hamas publication *al-Resalah* explained that the Saudi King had requested that Hamas and Fatah empower him to replace Egypt as mediator in the reconciliation efforts between the two groups. Mashaal, the report said, came to Riyadh carrying a written "letter of empowerment" for Salman. However, Iran's *Fars* news outlet, voicing Iranian displeasure at the visit, reported that the Saudi king had asked Mashaal to send hundreds of trained Hamas gunmen to Yemen to fight alongside the Saudi army against the Houthi separatists, who are backed by Iran[52]. Hamas spokesman Sami Abu Zuhri denied the *Fars* report as "pure lies"[53].

A Turkish commentator has suggested that Hamas would prefer an Arab country as its base, because, among other things, it isn't keen on the idea of Turks leading Arabs[54]. In this respect, Turkey and Iran are in the same boat, while Saudi Arabia has the edge. Turkey therefore may be tempted to be as accommodating as possible towards Hamas, even to the extent of allowing it to operate a terror base in Turkey, in order to get ahead of the pack on the Palestinian front.

Domestic political considerations may also be behind Turkey's

---

[51] Elhanan Miller, *In Hamas' Embrace of Sunni Saudi Arabia a Slap to Iran*, Times of Israel (21 July 2015), http://www.timesofisrael.com/in-hamass-embrace-of-sunni-saudi-arabia-a-slap-to-iran/.

[52] *Id.*

[53] *Id.*

[54] *Suspicions of Turkey Hamas Alliance Stoke Fears in Israel*, Fox News (04 Mar. 2015), http://www.foxnews.com/world/2015/03/04/turkey-red-carpet-for-hamas-stokes-fears-in-israel/.

support for Hamas. Sympathy for the Palestinians is shared across the entire political spectrum in Turkey and championing the "Palestinian cause" has traditionally played well at the polls while religiously conservative voters, who constitute the AKP's power base, feel empathy with Islamic Arab actors[55]. Even Turkey's main opposition party, the Kemalist CHP (Republican People's Party), has shown a willingness to engage with Hamas. In January 2012, party chairman Kemal Kılıçdaroğlu held a meeting with Ismail Haniyeh at the party headquarters in Ankara[56]. With that, a CHP member of the Turkish parliament told this writer he doubted whether the average Turkish voter would be happy about Turkey hosting an operational base of a foreign terrorist organisation. This is borne out by polls showing that some 80% of Turks disapprove of Hamas and a majority oppose violence against civilians[57]. Indeed, an opposition party member of the National assembly did ask, after Arouri appeared to take responsibility for the kidnapping and murder of three Israeli teenagers in July 2014, whether it was true that the person responsible was resident in Turkey[58]. However, by and large, the issue has not been the subject of public discussion in Turkey.

After the first round of voting in the Turkish general election in June 2015, it appeared that the ruling AKP party might be forced to make political concessions having failed to achieve a majority of seats in the National Assembly. The AKP gained only 258 seats out of 550,

---

[55] Gallia Lindenstrauss & Süfyan Kadir Kıvam, *Turkish-Hamas Relations: Between Strategic Calculations and Ideological Affinity*, 17 STRATEGIC ASSESSMENT 1, 10–11 (2014); *see also* Bekdil, *supra* note 17.

[56] *Turkish CHP Leader Meets Hamas Leader in Ankara*, WORLD BULLETIN (03 Jan. 2012), http://www.worldbulletin.net/haber/83809/turkish-chp-leader-meets-hamas-leader-haniyeh-in-ankara.

[57] Jacob Poushter, *The Turkish People Don't Look Favorably Upon the U.S., or Any Other Country, Really*, PEW RESEARCH CENTER (31 Oct. 2014), http://www.pewresearch.org/fact-tank/2014/10/31/the-turkish-people-dont-look-favorably-upon-the-u-s-or-any-other-country-really/.

[58] *Loğoğlu Asks if Hamas Leader Accused of Kidnappings Lives in Turkey*, TODAY'S ZAMAN (09 July 2014), http://www.todayszaman.com/diplomacy_logoglu-asks-if-hamas-leader-accused-of-kidnappings-lives-in-turkey_352583.html.

which led to coalition talks with the other political parties[59]. All the potential coalition partners (the CHP with 132 seats, the left-wing pro-Kurdish HDP with 80 seats and the right-wing Nationalist MHP also with 80 seats) had criticised Erdoğan's hostile attitude towards Israel, arguing that Turkey should be standing together with Israel against Iran[60]. Thus, for a while it seemed possible that the AKP could shift its stance on Israel and Hamas. Indeed, it appears that Saleh Al-Arouri received his marching orders during this period. In November 2015, however, a second round of voting was held which gave the AKP a clear majority.

Since his election victory, Erdoğan and his AKP have moved to restrict opposition voices, including those which have criticised his policies towards Israel and Hamas. A major development was the forcible closure in March 2016, of the daily newspaper *Zaman* which was aligned with Turkish opposition cleric in exile, Fethulla Gülen. Gülen was a vocal critic of the Turkish-led Gaza Flotilla which had resulted in the *Mavi Marmara* incident[61].

Given the AKP's post-election position, one can assume that any previous domestic electoral considerations militating against Turkey's support of Hamas no longer carry much weight.

Some observers explain Turkey's deepening of relations with Hamas and the corresponding downturn in relations with Israel as connected to advancements in the peace process between Turkey

[59] Raziye Akkoc, *Turkey PM Ends First Round of Coalition Talks with Only One Choice of Partner*, The Telegraph (15 July 2015), http://www.telegraph. co.uk/news/worldnews/europe/turkey/11742251/Turkey-PM-ends-first-round-of-coalition-talks-with-only-one-choice-of-partner.html.

[60] *Erdogan's Loss Could Result in Better Turkey-Israel Ties*, i24 News (08 June 2015), http://www.i24news.tv/en/news/international/middle-east/74117-150608-erdo gan-s-loss-could-result-in-better-turkey-israel-ties; Tova Dvorin, *Turkish Elections: What's Next for Israel?*, Israel Nat'l News (07 June 2015), http://www. israelnationalnews.com/News/News.aspx/196380#.VbzoN_mqqko.

[61] Joe Lauria, *Reclusive Turkish Imam Criticizes Gaza Flotilla*, Wall St. J. (04 June 2010), http://www.wsj.com/articles/SB10001424052748704025304575284721 280274694.

and the Kurdish Workers' Party (PKK). The AKP with its Islamic religious orientation would always have felt a natural affinity with Hamas. However, as long as Turkey was employing harsh measures in response to the violence of the PKK, it found itself relatively isolated and was happy to have that isolation relieved by a warming of ties with Israel which was enabled by the Oslo Process. Since the 2013 official ceasefire purporting to end its conflict with the PKK, so the argument goes, AKP-ruled Turkey is simply following its natural inclination of sympathy towards Hamas and hostility towards Israel[62]. If this analysis is correct, then circumstances may once again be ripe for a warming of Turkey-Israel relations.

The end of July 2015 saw a sudden deterioration in the Turkey-PKK relationship. On July 25th, Turkey launched bombing raids on PKK positions in Northern Iraq as well as a domestic crackdown against the group involving hundreds of arrests. This was in response to an attack on Turkish troops in South East Turkey. Subsequently the PKK has said on its website: "The truce has no meaning anymore after these intense air strikes by the occupant Turkish army"[63].

Turkey is also facing an additional terror threat in the form of the Islamic State of Iraq and al-Sham (ISIS) which is suspected of carrying out a suicide bombing in the border town of Suruc on July 20th which killed 32. Turkey responded to the attack by bombing ISIS targets in Syria as well as rounding up local suspects. Interestingly, Turkey had previously been roundly criticised both at home and abroad for not acting against ISIS and has even stood accused by some of covertly supporting ISIS in its confrontations with Kurdish forces.

The latter half of 2015 and the first quarter of 2016 saw a massive

---

[62] Barçin Yinanç, *Turkey's Talk with the PKK Justifies its Ties to Hamas*, HURRIYET DAILY NEWS (02 Apr. 2013), http://www.hurriyetdailynews.com/turkeys-talk-with-the-pkk-justifies-its-ties-to-hamas.aspx?pageID=449&nID=44061&NewsCatID=412.

[63] *Turkey Extends Airstrikes to Kurdish Targets*, SKY NEWS (26 July 2015), http://news.sky.com/story/1525357/turkey-extends-airstrikes-to-kurdish-targets.

upsurge in terror attacks on Turkish soil. Among these, the bombing outside the Ankara Central Railway Station in September 2015 which caused 103 fatalities in addition to some 400 injured was the deadliest terror attack in modern Turkish history. The Kurdish TAK group claimed responsibility for two further mass-casualty terrorist attacks in Ankara in February and March 2016 while ISIS perpetrated attacks in Istanbul in January and March 2016.

It should be noted that Turkey has already sought Western support in its fight against ISIS and Kurdish nationalist terrorism. It is also possible that the recent spike in terror threats to Turkey has, at least in part, motivated it to seek an improvement in relations with Israel, which may in turn affect its relationship with Hamas.

There are also official explanations for Turkey's ongoing support of Hamas. As Prime Minister Davutoğlu said shortly after the terror attacks in Paris in early 2015:

> Turkey is friends with Palestine and we have a strong mutual relationship with its leaders" ... "Hamas has not launched any terror attack and they even condemned the recent attacks in Paris. If their land was not conquered there would be no need for the existence of Hamas and that is the reason why we do not see them as a terrorist movement[64].

Turkey has also made much of Hamas' electoral successes in the Palestinian parliamentary elections of 2006. In an interview to the Washington Post in January 2009, Erdoğan stated:

> Hamas entered the elections as a political party. If the whole world had given them the chance of becoming a political player, maybe they would not be in a situation like this after the elections that they won. The world has not respected the

---

[64] *Turkey Defends Ties with Hamas*, Rudaw (13 Jan. 2015), http://rudaw.net/english/ middleeast/turkey/13012015.

political will of the Palestinian people[65].

Ibrahim Kalin, Advisor to the Turkish Premier, has explained the Turkish Policy vis-à-vis the Israeli–Palestinian issue as follows: "Turkey will continue to actively work for a two-state solution based on 1967 borders. For that to be achieved it will first push for Palestinian reunification and then for talks to resume for a solution"[66].

This statement is in line with the official Turkish policy as stated on its Ministry of Foreign Affairs' website:

> Turkey supports a negotiated settlement to the Israeli–Palestinian conflict on the basis of the UN Security Council Resolutions 242, 338, 1397 and 1515, the principle of land for peace, the Arab Peace Initiative and the Road Map that would ensure two states living side by side within secure and recognised borders.

> Turkey is concerned with the ongoing division in Palestine since June 2007. Turkey encourages for national reconciliation and also calls on the international community for taking a constructive attitude that would focus on a national agreement rather than separation and isolation[67].

Indeed, Turkey appears to have been active in pushing for reconciliation between the Palestinian factions and has justified its contacts with Hamas, in part, as being directed towards this end. Foreign Minister Mevlüt Cavuşoğlu has claimed for Turkey a pivotal role in establishing the Palestinian national unity government:

---

[65] Lally Weymouth, *Palestine Today is an Open-Air Prison*, WASH. POST (31 Jan. 2009), http://www.washingtonpost.com/wp-dyn/content/article/2009/01/30/AR2009013002809.html?sid=ST2009020200054.

[66] Yinanç, *supra* note 62.

[67] *Turkey's Political Relations with the State of Palestine*, REPUBLIC OF TURK. MINISTRY OF FOREIGN AFFAIRS, http://www.mfa.gov.tr/turkey_s-political-relations-with-the-palestinian-national-authority.en.mfa (last visited 16 May 2016).

Since this government will be an important signal for the independent state of Palestine, Israel doesn't accept it. . . . Is there anyone else who objects to unity in Palestine? If so, they may criticise our work with Hamas and Al Fatah, yet everyone who wants unity in Palestine shouldn't object to our relations with Hamas in this matter[68].

Turkey is also claiming to have had a "moderating" effect on Hamas, with Foreign Minister Cavuşoğlu asserting that Hamas is now "mainstream":

Everyone sees how Hamas' attitude in the past was and how different it is now. Turkey is the strongest contributor for this change. We have even convinced Hamas to recognise Israel as an independent state when there is resolution. . . . Turkey wants peace in the Middle East and connects everyone who wants to contribute. We try to convince each side. Our connection with Hamas in fact is important for peace and dialogue. Even though everyone accepts this, we don't understand why they don't want Hamas leader[s] to come [to] Turkey[69].

Although Turkish leaders have not been hesitant to defend their support for Hamas on ideological grounds, there are also practical considerations involved if Turkey is to have any impact on the *cause célèbre* of the Gaza Strip. Activism with regard to the plight of the people of Gaza is a *sine qua non* for a country striving to lead the Muslim world. Since Hamas are the *de facto* rulers of Gaza, it follows that any action to ameliorate conditions in Gaza must, of necessity, go through Hamas. A notable Turkish project which commenced long before the warming of ties with Hamas has been the Ankara Forum, a forum for cooperation between Turkey, Israel and the Palestinian Authority whose

---

[68] *Turkey Says Had Convinced Hamas to Recognise Israel*, World Bulletin (12 Jan. 2015), http://www.worldbulletin.net/haber/152783/turkey-says-had-convinced-hama s-to-recognise-israel.
[69] *Id.*

flagship project was to reconstruct and rehabilitate the Erez Industrial Area in the Northern Gaza Strip after the Israeli disengagement from Gaza in 2005. Any leeway on this project would necessitate the cooperation of Hamas. So far, due to a lack of progress in Gaza, the focus of the forum moved to Jenin in the West Bank. Also, the Turkish International Cooperation and Development Agency (TIKA) has been active in various projects in the Palestinian-controlled territories.

As mentioned above, Turkey also pledged large sums for reconstruction in Gaza after the 2014 conflict, although some reports claim that Turkey has been slow to meet its commitments. In April 2015, Mehmet Gormez, Turkey's President of Religious Affairs, visited Gaza and pledged to finance the rebuilding of 19 mosques destroyed during the conflict. During the visit, the Hamas leader in Gaza, Ismail Haniyeh, praised Turkey for its "reliable and sacred bond"[70].

IV. IMPLICATIONS FOR TURKISH–ISRAELI RELATIONS

Israel–Turkey relations are characterised by a glaring paradox. On the one hand, trade relations between the two countries have been booming at record levels. By way of illustration, for the first third of 2014, the Israeli Ministry of Economy stated that exports to Turkey were running ahead of 2013's record level, with the figure climbing nearly 25% to $949.2 million in the first four months of the year. Imports from Turkey grew to $956 million, a 21% increase from the same time in 2013[71]. Incredibly, Turkey's national flag carrier Turkish Airlines has more flights into and out of Tel Aviv than any other foreign airline[72]. By contrast, on the diplomatic front, relations between

[70] Tzvi Ben-Gedalyahu, *Turkey to Help Hamas Rebuild 19 Destroyed 'Missile Mosques'*, THE JEWISH PRESS (18 May 2015), http://www.jewishpress.com/news/breaking-news/turkey-to-help-hamas-rebuild-19-destroyed-mosques-missile-sites/ 2015/05/18/.

[71] Ora Coren, *Israeli Trade with Turkey on Track to Reach Record*, HAARETZ (04 July 2014), http://www.haaretz.com/business/.premium-1.603035.

[72] Danny Sadeh, *Turkish Airlines Remains Most Active Foreign Airline in Israel*, YNET NEWS (12 Jan. 2015), http://www.ynetnews.com/articles/0,7340,L-4613890,

Turkey and Israel have arguably never been worse. While there has been much bad blood over the *Mavi Marmara* Affair and Israel's military operations in Gaza as well as Erdoğan's unbridled anti-Israel and anti-Semitic ranting[73], never before has Israel directly accused Turkey of material support for Hamas terror attacks. Israel's former Defence Minister, Moshe Ya'alon, complained to the U.S. Secretary of Defense that Turkey is "playing a cynical game" and that "Hamas now has two command centres, one in Gaza and one in Turkey"[74].

Further, Israel's Strategic Affairs Minister, Yuval Steinitz, has stated that Israel expects the U.S. and NATO to pressure Turkey to dismantle Hamas infrastructure in Turkey. For its part, Turkey has rejected the Israeli allegations. Turkish officials have said: "Turkey has dialogue with Hamas but will absolutely not allow a terror organisation

---

00.html.

[73] Recep Tayyip Erdoğan, President of Turkey, Speech Made Prior to his Election as President of Turkey (03 Aug. 2014), http://www.memritv.org/clip_transcript/en/4484.htm. Erdoğan stated,

> [j]ust like Hitler tried to create a pure Aryan race in Germany, the State of Israel is pursuing the same goals right now. . . . This is really amazing. They kill the women so that they will not be able to give birth to Palestinian babies. They kill the babies so that they will not be able to grow up to be men. They kill the men so that they will not be able to defend their homeland. They are even afraid of babies in cribs. They are even afraid of children playing in parks or on beaches. They are even afraid of the wounded or the wheelchair-ridden in hospitals. Rest assured that the more they kill, the more they will be afraid. The more they shed blood, the more they will drown in the blood that they shed. No cruelty lasts forever. The day is sure to come when they will be held accountable for their atrocities. We impatiently await this day of reckoning. We believe, from the bottom of our hearts, that laws will be implemented and that justice will prevail. We know that these baby killers – this Israel – will sooner or later be held accountable for all their deeds in accordance with the law.

Id.

[74] Ricky Ben-David, *Ya'alon: Hamas Has Two Command Centres – in Gaza and Turkey*, Times of Israel (22 Oct. 2014), http://www.timesofisrael.com/yaalon-hamas-has-command-centers-in-gaza-turkey/.

to operate on Turkish soil"[75]. Of course, such a response rings hollow when taken in the context of Turkey's stated position that Hamas is not a terror organisation[76].

The current state of Turkey–Israel relations stands in stark contrast to the situation prior to 2009. Until then, since the early 1990s and including the initial years of the AKP's ascendency, the relationship had been exceptionally warm—encompassing even extensive military cooperation. At present, neither country has an ambassador in the other, military cooperation is non-existent, and, incredibly, a Turkish opinion poll released in May 2015 found that 42.6% of respondents view Israel as the number one threat to Turkey[77]. Notwithstanding, both sides have consistently expressed an interest in rapprochement, each blaming the other for the impasse.

In a sign that a change in Turkey's attitude to Israel might be pending, a mere two weeks after the June 2015 elections, a low-key meeting took place in Rome between Feridun Sinirlioğlu, Director General of the Turkish Foreign Ministry, and his Israeli counterpart, Dore Gold[78]. Soon afterwards, Turkish Foreign Minister Mevlüt Cavuşoğlu confirmed that reconciliation talks were underway. However, according to Cavuşoğlu, "The ball is in the court of the other side on our two demands"[79].

The first demand in question is compensation to the families of the casualties of the *Mavi Marmara* incident. All indications are that

---

[75] Itamar Eichner, *Turkey Denies Harboring Hamas Terror Command*, YNET NEWS (28 Nov. 2014), http://www.ynetnews.com/articles/0,7340,L-4597286,00.html.

[76] Bekdil, *supra* note 17; Lazarof, *supra* note 20.

[77] *Survey: Israel and US Biggest Threats for Turkey*, TODAY'S ZAMAN (27 May 2015), http://www.todayszaman.com/diplomacy_survey-israel-and-us-biggest-threats-for-turkey_381906.html.

[78] *Foreign Ministry Chief Meets Turkish Counterpart in Sign of Thaw*, TIMES OF ISRAEL (22 June 2015), http://www.timesofisrael.com/foreign-ministry-chief-meets-turkish-counterpart-in-sign-of-thaw/.

[79] *Turkey Confirms Reconciliation Talks with Israel*, TIMES OF ISRAEL (24 June 2015), http://www.timesofisrael.com/turkey-confirms-reconciliation-talks-with-israel/.

the parties are close to agreement on this issue. The other demand is much more problematic and appears to flow directly from the Turkey–Hamas relationship, namely the lifting of the Israeli blockade on the Gaza Strip.

In December 2015, Turkey and Israel renewed talks on restoring diplomatic ties. A second round of talks was reportedly commenced in Geneva in February 2016. Subsequently, and particularly in the wake of the 2015-2016 terror attacks in Turkey, statements by the leaders of both countries have reflected a mutual willingness to improve relations[80]. For example, after the March 2016 Ankara bombing, Prime Minister Benjamin Netanyahu condemned the attack and expressed Israel's "solidarity with the Turkish people in the war against terrorism and calls on the international community to unite in the fight against terror"[81].

In a gesture mirroring Netanyahu's, subsequent to the March 2016 terror attack in Istanbul in which three Israelis were killed, Erdoğan sent a message to Israeli President Reuven Rivlin in which he conveyed his "deepest condolences to the people of Israel and to the families of Israeli citizens who lost their lives in this treacherous attack"[82]. A further gesture which did not go unnoticed in Israel was the prompt sacking of an AKP official who on Twitter wished death on the Israelis hurt in the attack[83]. In addition, a statement by the Director-General of Israel's Foreign Ministry praised the Turkish government for its cooperation in the aftermath of the attack and asserted that "Turkey and Israel

---

[80] *Netanyahu Condemns Attack on Ankara, Calls for International Unity in War on Terror*, JERUSALEM POST (13 Mar. 2015), http://www.jpost.com/Israel-News/Politics-And-Diplomacy/Netanyahu-condemns-Ankara-attack-calls-for-international-unity-in-war-on-terror-447802.

[81] *Id.*

[82] *Erdogan Sends Condolences to Rivlin over Istanbul Blast Victims*, TIMES OF ISRAEL (20 Mar. 2016), http://www.timesofisrael.com/erodgan-sends-condolences-to-rivlin-over-istanbul-blast-victims/.

[83] *Turkish Official Fired after Wishing Death on Israelis Hurt in Bombing*, TIMES OF ISRAEL (19 Mar. 2016), http://www.timesofisrael.com/turkish-official-fired-after-wishing-death-on-israelis-hurt-in-bombing/.

stand united in the front against terror and in dealing with the shared regional challenges"[84].

In spite of these overtures, scepticism still abounds. The following comments made in March 2016 by the Israel Defence Forces Deputy Chief of Staff, Major-General Yair Golan, are probably reflective of the thinking in the Israeli establishment: "As long as Turkey is ruled by a party with a strong Islamist orientation—basically the Muslim Brotherhood—and by a ruler as contrarian as Erdoğan; as long as this is the situation, we can expect problems and we can expect challenges"[85].

Indeed, major obstacles still remain in the path of a full rapprochement: Israel is unlikely to relinquish its demand that Turkey shut down all Hamas terror activity on its soil; and as long as Hamas controls Gaza and shows no sign of renouncing its terror campaign against Israel, it is highly unlikely that Israel will agree to a lifting of the blockade. This is because such a move would enable a massive influx of arms into Gaza by sea. Israel is likely to insist that all imports to Gaza pass through an Israeli inspection process. Whether a formula can be found that satisfies all parties remains to be seen. One idea that has been proposed in talks involving Turkey and Qatar has been a floating port on which international inspections would take place, but no progress has been reported on this initiative. It is also anticipated that Egypt would baulk at any move which would give Turkey a foothold in Gaza and thereby bolster the presence of the Muslim Brotherhood and its supporters in the region.

Israel is reportedly also demanding that any reconciliation agreement with Turkey include Hamas' return of the bodies of two Israeli soldiers who fell in 2014 *Operation Protective Edge.*

Clearly, therefore, the prospects for Turkish-Israeli reconciliation

---

[84] *Id.*
[85] Judah Ari Gross, *Top Israeli General: 'Expect problems' So Long as Erdogan in Power*, TIMES OF ISRAEL (18 Mar. 2016), http://www.timesofisrael.com/top-israeli-general-expect-problems-so-long-as-erdogan-in-power/.

are closely bound to the Turkey-Hamas relationship. Hence, it should come as no surprise that Turkey is coordinating its stance towards Israel with the leaders of Hamas. Davutoğlu even went so far as to profess publicly that Turkey's "sole goal" in the rapprochement process with Israel was to "bring solutions to the problems of our Palestinian brothers"[86].

V.   IMPLICATIONS FOR TURKISH–PALESTINIAN RELATIONS

Although Hamas was nominally a partner in forming the "Palestinian Unity Government" in June 2014, the relationship between Hamas and Mahmoud Abbas' Fatah faction is so fractious that, at time of writing, it appears that the "Unity Government" led by Prime Minister Rami Hamdalla is that in name only, if it exists at all[87]. Protestations of Palestinian unity are unconvincing at the best of times, but particularly so since successive Hamas plots to destabilise and overthrow the Fatah-led Palestinian Authority in the West Bank were exposed in August 2014 and July 2015, respectively[88]. It is also instructive to read what Mahmoud Abbas had to say about Hamas in an interview given on November 30, 2014, to the Egyptian daily *Akhbar Al-Yawm*, wherein he slammed Hamas' conduct which sparked and prolonged the Gaza war of July-August 2014. At one point he stated: "I want to say here that no one lies more than them [Hamas] and the MB [Muslim

---

[86] Dalit Halevy, *Hamas Says Turkey Consulted with it on Israel Talks*, Israel Nat'l News (23 Dec. 2015), http://www.israelnationalnews.com/News/News.aspx/205494#.Vzt0PvkrKUk; see also Ari Yashar, *Turkish PM: Israel Deal only Meant "to Help Gaza"*, Israel Nat'l News, (22 Dec. 2015), http://www.israelnationalnews.com/News/News.aspx/205330#.Vzt0n_krKUk.

[87] Khaled Abu Toameh, *Hamas Threatens to Exit National Unity Government with PA*, Jerusalem Post (13 Jan. 2015), http://www.jpost.com/Arab-Israeli-Conflict/Hamas-threatens-to-exit-national-unity-government-with-PA-387543; see also *Palestinian Unity Government Resigns*, Al Jazeera (17 June 2015), http:// www.aljazeera.com/news/2015/06/palestinian-unity-government-resigns-150617125314649.html.

[88] *See supra* Section II.

Brotherhood]"[89]. In December 2014, the Turkish newspaper *Zaman* reported that Abbas had warned Turkey about its ties with Hamas in a July 2014 visit to Istanbul[90].

Palestinian Authority officials are reportedly also peeved at being left out of the loop in indirect talks between Hamas and Israel during 2015, mediated by Turkey, Qatar and the EU[91].

Regarding the discussions on Gaza in the context of the Turkish–Israeli negotiations, Fatah Central Committee member Azzam al-Ahmad has clarified the PA's position: "The mediations from outside the framework of the PA are unacceptable, since they consecrate division. Turkey or any other country is not entitled to negotiate with Israel on any part of our country. The legitimate Palestinian leadership did not ask Turkey to intervene and negotiate on our behalf"[92]. Hamas, in turn, has branded the PA position as "unpatriotic"[93].

Given the tensions between the PA leadership and Hamas, it follows that Turkey–PA relations are not well served by Turkey's supporting and harbouring Hamas. This is indubitably compounded by the fact that the plot to overthrow the PA in the West Bank was directed by Hamas headquarters in Turkey.

VI. IMPLICATIONS FOR THE ISRAELI–PALESTINIAN PEACE PROCESS

Hamas is arguably the single biggest impediment to progress in the

---

[89] *Abbas in Interview*, THE MIDDLE EAST MEDIA RESEARCH INSTITUTE (05 Dec. 2014), http://www.memri.org/report/en/0/0/0/0/0/0/0/8323.htm.

[90] Deniz Arslan, *Abbas Asked Erdoğan to Mend Ties with Egypt*, TODAY'S ZAMAN (14 Dec. 2014), http://www.todayszaman.com/anasayfa_abbas-asked-erdogan-to-mend-ties-with-egypt_366915.html.

[91] *Palestinian Unity Government Resigns*, *supra* note 87.

[92] Ahmad Melhem, *Will Israel, Turkey decide the fate of Gaza?*, AL MONITOR (15 Mar. 2016), http://www.al-monitor.com/pulse/originals/2016/03/israel-turkey-negoti ations-floating-harbor-gaza.html#.

[93] *Id.*

stalled Israeli-Palestinian peace process. While its counterpart Fatah has stated its belief in a negotiated two-state solution to the conflict, Hamas remains fixated on its goal of destroying the State of Israel by violent means[94]. Hamas is a powerful actor on the Palestinian scene; and just as the Gaza Strip fell to a violent Hamas overthrow of the PA, there is a very real danger that the same fate could befall the West Bank. The reality is that even if Israel and the PA could succeed in working out a peace agreement, any arrangement for ceding territory to the PA could be exploited by Hamas to turn the West Bank into an additional platform from which to attack Israel. Thus, there are only two possible ways forward: either Hamas is dismantled or weakened to a degree that it is no longer relevant, or Hamas "changes its spots".

While many would view the latter option as a practical impossibility owing to Hamas' extremist, religious-based ideology, Turkey has defended its engagement with Hamas by professing to be pushing this option. However, despite Turkey's claims to have "moderated" Hamas, the organisation has shown no outward sign whatsoever of flexibility. On the contrary, all indications are that Hamas is digging-in (quite literally), having already commenced the rebuilding of its terror tunnel network and other military capabilities[95], as well as intensifying its terror operations in Jerusalem and the West Bank. Press reports from April 2015 describe efforts by Turkey and Qatar to broker a long-term ceasefire deal between Israel and Hamas; yet, all indications are that Hamas only wants an easing of restrictions to buy time to enable the organisation to reconstruct and regroup militarily[96]. Furthermore, even if one were to accept the Turkish argument that its relationship with Hamas can somehow contribute to the peace process, this would at most justify Turkey's maintaining a dialogue with Hamas. There can be no justification whatsoever for Turkey providing material support and harbouring

---

[94] Hamas Covenant 1988, 18 Aug. 1988, http://avalon.law.yale.edu/20th_century/hamas.asp.
[95] Elior Levy, *Hamas Reconstructing Terror Tunnels Using Israeli* Material, YNET NEWS (19 Dec. 2014), http://www.ynetnews.com/articles/0,7340,L-4605504,00.html.
[96] Issacharoff, *supra* note 50.

a base for Hamas terrorist activity, as has been exposed. As described above, this terror activity has not only been directed at Israel but also towards undermining the Palestinian factions who espouse non-violent compromise. This is seriously undercutting chances for intra-Palestinian unity, which Turkey itself has espoused as a *sine qua non* for peace.

In the final analysis, therefore, Turkey's current conduct vis-à-vis Hamas can only be seen as detrimental to the peace process.

VII. IMPLICATIONS FOR TURKEY'S RELATIONSHIP WITH THE WEST

U.S. President Obama, on a visit to Turkey soon after taking office in 2009, had the following to say about the U.S.–Turkey relationship:

> This is a country that has been often said lies at the cross-roads between East and West. It's a country that possesses an extraordinarily rich heritage but also represents a blend of those ancient traditions with a modern nation state that respects democracy, respects rule of law, and is striving toward a modern economy.

> I think that where there's the most promise of building stronger U.S.–Turkish relations is in the recognition that Turkey and the United States can build a model partnership in which a predominantly Christian nation, a predominantly Muslim nation—a Western nation and a nation that straddles two continents—that we can create a modern international community that is respectful, that is secure, that is prosperous, that there are not tensions—inevitable tensions between cultures—which I think is extraordinarily important[97].

Obama's sentiments were echoed by Ahmet Davutoğlu, then the Turkish Foreign Minister[98].

---

[97] Office of the Press Sec'y, *supra* note 1.
[98] Republic of Turk. Ministry of Foreign Affairs, *supra* note 2.

Over and above its "model partnership" with the U.S., Turkey also has close ties with the European Union—having applied for membership in that organisation. Turkey is also a long-standing member of NATO (since 1952).

The upgrade of Turkey's relationship with Hamas, in particular the support and hospitality provided to Hamas terror operations, flies in the face of policies held by the U.S. and EU[99], where Hamas is designated as a terrorist organisation. It does not bode well for the "model partnership" vision or for Turkey's European aspirations.

Upon learning of Khaled Mashaal's December 2014 visit to Turkey, U.S. State Department Spokesperson, Jen Psaki, articulated the U.S. position as follows:

> Our position on Hamas has not changed. Hamas is a designated foreign terrorist organisation that continues to engage in terrorist activity and demonstrated its intentions during the summer's conflict in—with Israel. . . .
>
> We continue to raise our concerns about the relationship between Hamas and Turkey with senior Turkish officials, including after learning of Mashaal's recent visit there. And we have urged the government of Turkey to press Hamas to reduce tensions and prevent violence[100].

In a daily press briefing given during the 2014 Gaza-Israel hostilities, Deputy Spokesperson Marie Harf, who was asked why Secretary of State Kerry was frequently holding talks with Davutoğlu despite his

---

[99] Hamas was recently removed from the EU's terror organisations' list by the EU Court due to what EU officials have described as a "technicality". However, the EU still holds the position that Hamas is a terrorist organisation and has appealed the decision. *EU Keeps Hamas on Terror List Despite Court Ruling*, YNET NEWS (27 Mar. 2015), http://www.ynetnews.com/articles/0,7340,L-4641700,00.html.

[100] *US 'Concerned' over Hamas-Turkey Relations*, HURRIYET DAILY NEWS (9 Jan. 2015), http://www.hurriyetdailynews.com/us-concerned-over-hamas-turkey-relations.aspx?PageID=238&NID=76702&NewsCatID=510.

and Erdoğan's offensive comments about Israel, had this to say:

> Because the Turks have a role to play. We've said these com-
> ments make it harder for them to play a role, but they do
> have a role to play and they have a relationship with Hamas. I
> mean, they can have conversations that we can't. So obviously
> the Turkish Foreign Minister is a key player in the region and
> has some leverage he can bring to bear on the situation. Those
> two things aren't mutually exclusive[101].

Israel has appealed to NATO to take action against Turkey.
Official communiqués sent from Jerusalem to NATO Headquarters
in Brussels have said it was inconceivable that a member of the alliance
would maintain ties with a terrorist organisation[102].

Mashaal's December 2014 visit also provoked a response from
the senior German parliamentarian, Volker Beck, who criticised the
German government for failing to rebuke Turkey over the visit. The
German Foreign Ministry clarified that "Hamas is in the eyes of the
Federal Government and the European Union a terrorist organisation"
and stated that the Federal Government had expressed "surprise" about
the presence of Mashaal in Turkey[103].

Following the July 2015 suicide bombing in Suruc and the subsequent attacks on Turkish soldiers, Turkey requested an emergency

---

[101] Sevil Erkus, *Turkish FM to Meet Hamas Leader in Bid to Secure Week-Long Humanitarian Cease-Fire*, HURRIYET DAILY NEWS (25 July 2014), http://www. hur-riyetdailynews.com/turkish-fm-to-meet-hamas-leader-in-bid-to-secure-week-long-humanitarian-cease-fire.aspx?pageID=549&nID=69602&NewsCatID=510.

[102] Shlomo Cesana, *Israel Livid Over New Hamas Headquarters in Turkey*, ISRAEL HAYOM NEWSLETTER (26 Nov. 2014), http://www.israelhayom.com/site/newsletter_article.php?id=21733.

[103] Benjamin Weinthal, *Top German MP: Merkel Should Condemn Turkey for Host-ing Hamas Official*, JERUSALEM POST (31 Dec. 2014), http://www.jpost.com/Interna-tional/Top-German-MP-Merkel-should-condemn-Turkey-for-hosting-Hamas-offi-cial-386205.

meeting of NATO to obtain support for its actions against ISIS and the PKK. In that meeting, NATO Secretary General Jens Stoltenberg expressed NATO's solidarity with Turkey. These developments have also triggered discussions between the U.S. and Turkey about military cooperation against ISIS. Notably, Turkey has agreed to allow the U.S. military to make use of the İncirlik air base for its strikes against ISIS[104]. Also, the U.S. has expressed solidarity with Turkey in light of subsequent terror attacks[105].

As of yet, neither the U.S. nor any of the EU states have commented publicly on the disclosures about the Hamas operational headquarters in Turkey. Also, the matter has received no significant mainstream press coverage outside of Israel. It is worthy of note, however, that in September 2015, the U.S. Treasury Department placed Saleh Al-Arouri on its Counter-Terrorism Designations List[106].

It is not publicly known whether these issues have been raised with Turkey through discreet channels, although according to press reports from June 2015, Turkish intelligence reportedly requested Arouri to cut back on his anti-Israel activity, apparently due to concerns about U.S. disapproval[107]. Indeed, Arouri's eventual departure from Turkey has been attributed to U.S. and Israeli pressure being brought to bear on Turkey[108].

---

[104] 'NATO Allies Stand in Solidarity with Turkey', WORLD BULLETIN (28 July 2015), http://www.worldbulletin.net/politics/162510/nato-allies-stand-in-solidarity-with-turkey.

[105] US Deplores 'Vicious Terrorist Attack' in Istanbul, TIMES OF ISRAEL (19 Mar. 2016), http://www.timesofisrael.com/us-deplores-vicious-terrorist-attack-in-istanbul/.

[106] U.S. DEP'T OF THE TREASURY, OFFICE OF FOREIGN ASSETS CONTROL, Counter Terrorism Designations, https://www.treasury.gov/resource-center/sanctions/OFAC-Enforcement/Pages/20150910.aspx (last visited 16 May 2016).

[107] Amos Harel, Turkey Sends Message to Local Hamas Operatives to Cut Back on Anti-Israel Terror, HAARETZ (10 June 2015), http://www.haaretz.com/news/diplomacy-defense/.premium-1.660431.

[108] Klein, supra note 39.

CONCLUSION

Turkey's courtship with Hamas has for some time troubled Israel, the PA, the U.S., the EU, and others in the international community. Moreover, the situation has worsened dramatically since Turkey allowed Hamas to establish and operate a base on its soil. Yet, instead of being roundly condemned or sanctioned for its conduct, Turkey has, for the most part, received mixed messages from the international community.

The U.S. in particular has sought to exploit the Turkey-Hamas relationship on occasions when it wanted an interlocutor with Hamas. Thus, from time to time, the U.S. has urged Turkey to exert pressure on Hamas while at the same time condemning the existence of the relationship. One may criticise the U.S. position which essentially legitimises Turkey's defence of the relationship. Any possible advantage to having Turkey as an interlocutor is surely outweighed by the active terrorist threat posed by Hamas operations in Istanbul. Accordingly, one would expect more robust objections to Turkey's conduct.

A positive development has been the pressure reportedly brought to bear by the U.S. and Israel on Turkey to curb the activities of Saleh al-Arouri. Indeed, Arouri's departure from Turkey was an important step, yet the remainder of Hamas' Turkish infrastructure remains intact with Arouri allegedly still calling the shots and even visiting from time to time from his new base in Qatar.

What incentives, if any, exist for Turkey to pull back its support for Hamas? One might expect that developments in late July 2015 which saw Turkey approaching NATO and the U.S. for backing in its campaign against ISIS might provide some leverage with which to pressure Turkey to rein in Hamas activity on its soil.

However, another development in the region has, meanwhile, strengthened Turkey's hand and its ability to resist NATO and EU pressure, namely the European migration crisis. Turkey is seen as the key to solving the crisis, and this has had the effect of muting international criticism of Turkish behaviour on other issues[109].

At the time of writing, it appears that the strongest incentive for Turkey to curb Hamas activity on its soil is the former's desire to normalise relations with Israel. Analysts have pointed to a variety of factors that have rekindled Turkey's interest in rapprochement with Israel since late 2015. One has been the crisis with Russia after the Turkish downing of a Russian jet in November 2015. Russia is a key supplier of natural gas, and Turkey is urgently seeking alternative sources for this crucial commodity to reduce its dependency on Russia[110]. Nearby Israel with its recently discovered natural gas reserves is an obvious option.

Others point to Turkey's political isolation, not only as a result of the crisis with Russia, but also due to disagreements with the U.S. over the latter's support for the Kurds. Turkey is also estranged from much of the Arab world as a result of its fall-out with Egypt over the former's continued backing of the Muslim Brotherhood and needless to say, it is at odds with Iran over the civil war in Syria. In such a situation, Turkey needs whatever friends it can get[111].

Another factor, according to Turkish defence sources, is a Turkish desire to acquire Israeli military hardware, in particular advanced UAV's and fighter jet systems. Turkey may also be interested in benefiting from Israel's counter-terrorism experience in a period when Turkey

[109] Mark Mardell, *Turkey Has European Union over a Barrel*, BBC News (17 Mar. 2016), http://www.bbc.com/news/world-europe-35819675.

[110] Mehmet Cetingulec, *Will Russia's Economic Restrictions on Turkey Backfire?*, Al Monitor (13 Dec. 2015), http://www.al-monitor.com/pulse/originals/2015/12/turkey -russia-steep-costs-of-downing-of-russian-jet.html#.

[111] Eyal Zisser, *Terror, Refugees, Diplomatic Fallout*, Israel Hayom Newsletter (16 Mar. 2016), http://www.israelhayom.com/site/newsletter_opinion.php?id=15519; Yossi Melman, *Analysis: A Weakened Turkey Seeks Israel's Help to Break Growing Isolation*, Jerusalem Post (01 Mar. 2016), http://www.jpost.com/Israel-News/Politi cs-And-Diplomacy/Analysis-A-weakened-Turkey-seeks-Israels-help-to-break-growin g-isolation-446549.

is once again facing serious terror threats from Kurdish militant factions as well as from ISIS[112].

There are also those—Arab sceptics in particular—who attribute Turkey's latest overtures to Israel to Turkey's neo-Ottoman agenda whereby Turkey aspires to expand its influence into areas ruled by the former Ottoman Empire. They see Turkey as standing to gain a highly influential foothold in the Palestinian arena if the negotiations with Israel result in a lifting of the Gaza blockade, thereby positioning Turkey as a key presence in the Gaza Strip[113]. This theory gels with official Turkish protestations that helping the Palestinians is the "sole" objective of the reconciliation attempt.

In return for some or all of the above benefits, Turkey may well be prepared to deny Hamas an operational base in Turkey. This would not necessarily entail a souring of relations between Turkey and Hamas. In fact, as already mentioned, it may suit the mainstream leadership of Hamas in Gaza and Doha who view Hamas in Turkey as a rogue operation[114].

The question now to be asked is whether Israel is interested enough in a reconciliation with Turkey. The answer is probably in the affirmative, but not at any cost. The Israelis have experienced Erdoğan's fickleness and will be sceptical about Turkey's motives and reliability. Moreover, the closing of Hamas' terror base in Turkey is more likely to be demanded as a precondition for negotiations rather than as a *quid pro quo.*

---

[112] Ari Yashar, *Turkey Wants Normalization to Buy Israeli Weapons*, ISRAEL NAT'L NEWS (24 Dec. 2015), http://www.israelnationalnews.com/News/News. aspx/205437# .VvaqSfl97IU.

[113] Lee Gancman, *Hamas Denies Rumours of Turkish Designs on Gaza*, TIMES OF ISRAEL (29 Dec. 2015), http://www.timesofisrael.com/hamas-denies-rumors-of-turkish-designs-on-gaza/.

[114] MacDonald, *supra* note 40.

The analysis in this article suggests that Turkey's current policy towards Hamas is of no benefit to anyone other than to Saleh Al-Arouri's rogue faction of Hamas. Hence, regardless of whether international pressure is brought to bear, it is unclear why Turkey would wish to persist with its current course. Certainly, if Turkey wants to fulfil the international bridging role that has been a cornerstone of its foreign policy, it must acknowledge that allowing Hamas to operate a terror base on its soil is "a bridge too far".

TURKEY AND THE UNITED STATES: FRIENDS OR FOES?

NATHANAEL BENNETT*

INTRODUCTION

The United States has long viewed its alliance with Turkey as one of significant strategic importance. The reasons for this view are many, and include economic, symbolic, and security components. The importance of this relationship is clearly articulated in President Dwight Eisenhower's words as he prepared to leave Turkey after a visit in 1959: "We stand together on the major issues that divide the world, and I see no reason whatsoever that we shouldn't be two of the sturdiest partners standing together always for freedom, security, and the pursuit of peace"[1].

---

*Mr Bennett is a Research Associate of the Centre for the Study of Law & Public Policy at Oxford. He is the Director of Government Affairs for the American Center for Law & Justice (ACLJ), as well as the Main Representative to the United Nations in New York, NY, for the European Centre for Law & Justice (ECLJ). He also assists the ECLJ in its work before the UN Human Rights Council in Geneva, Switzerland. In his current capacity, Mr Bennett represents the ACLJ in matters involving the U.S. Congress and the Executive Branch. Mr Bennett received his Bachelor of Science (Business Management) (B.S.) degree from National Louis University, where he graduated *summa cum laude*.

[1] Michael Rubin, *The Trouble with Turkey*, AEI (3 Oct. 2011), http://www.aei.org/publication/the-trouble-with-turkey.

Economically, Turkey is important to the U.S. due to the enormous size of its still emerging market. While Turkey currently has a population of more than seventy-two million[2] and a projected population of ninety-five million by 2050[3], it presently consumes less than the Netherlands, which has a population of just seventeen million[4]. Even before any of its population and consumption growth potential is realised, Turkey boasts the 17th largest (and among the fastest growing) economy in the world[5].

Symbolically, Turkey's alliance is crucial to the U.S. for two principal reasons: geography and culture. Geographically, Turkey is literally the bridge between Europe and Asia, with Greece and Bulgaria on its western border and Georgia and Armenia on its eastern border. To the south, Turkey shares a border with the Middle East nations of Syria, Iraq, and Iran. This strategic positioning makes Turkey a pivotal player in the geopolitical affairs of Europe, Asia, and the Middle East. Culturally, the U.S. has a vested interest in the success of democracy in a significant Muslim-majority nation like Turkey. This was one of the main themes of President Barrack Obama's 6 April 2009 address to the Turkish Parliament, in which he called Turkey a "strong, vibrant, secular democracy"[6].

As important as the economic and symbolic components of the U.S./Turkey alliance are, it is reasonable to believe that the security component is the most critical to both nations. The current military alliance between the U.S. and Turkey dates back to 1947 and the emergence of the threat posed by the Soviet Union during the early stages of the Cold War[7]. Today, Turkey sits in the heart of a region that breeds

---

[2] *Countries of the World*, WORLDATLAS, http://www.worldatlas.com/aatlas/populatio ns/ctypopls.htm (last visited 11 Feb. 2015).
[3] ANDREW FINKEL, TURKEY: WHAT EVERYONE NEEDS TO KNOW 6 (2012).
[4] *Id.* at 6.
[5] *Id.* at 43.
[6] Remarks to the Grand National Assembly of Turkey in Ankara, Turkey, 2009 DAILY COMP. PRES. DOC. 1 (6 Apr. 2009).
[7] Pelin Baysal & Cansu Akbiyikli, *What U.S. Counsel Should Know About*

sectarian strife and Islamic terrorism—much of which is ultimately aimed at the U.S. and its allies. Clearly, the security importance of the alliance has never been greater, and yet recent years have seen an erosion of that alliance. In the years since Recep Tayyip Erdoğan's Justice and Development Party (AKP) took power in 2002[8], there have been a number of security-related disputes between the two nations. The first major sign of division may have been on 1 March 2003, when Turkey denied a U.S. request to launch a northern front into Iraq from Turkish bases[9]. Fast forward to 2016, and Turkey is by most accounts completely unwilling to halt the flow of Islamic State[10] fighters into and out of Turkey along its border with Iraq and Syria[11].

Clearly, Turkey holds tremendous strategic importance for the U.S. There is little doubt that President Obama had this in mind when in January 2012, he listed then-Prime Minister Erdoğan as one of five world leaders with whom he has been able to forge a "bond of trust"[12]. But given recent events, there is reason to question whether Turkey is moving away from the West and toward U.S. foes. Nowhere is this question more relevant than in the ongoing War on Terror.

I. TURKEY: BRIDGING THE EAST AND THE WEST

On 6 April 2009, during a diplomatic visit to Turkey, President Obama said:

Strengthening Bilateral Commercial Relations Between U.S. and Turkey (Part 1), INSIDE COUNSEL (8 Jan. 2015), http://www.insidecounsel.com/2015/01/08/what-us-counsel-should-know-about-strengthening-bi.

[8] FINKEL, *supra* note 3, at 72.

[9] *Id.* at 2.

[10] The Islamic State is also known as both the Islamic State of Iraq and Syria (ISIS) and the Islamic State of Iraq and the Levant (ISIL).

[11] Michael Rubin, *On ISIS and Our 'Allies,' the Turks*, AEI (22 Sept. 2014, 9:21 AM), http://www.aei.org/publication/on-isis-and-our-alllies-the-turks.

[12] Fareed Zakaria, *Inside Obama's World: The President Talks to TIME About the Changing Nature of American Power*, TIME (19 Jan. 2012), http://swampland.time.com/2012/01/19/inside-obamas-world-the-president-talks-to-time-about-the-changing-nature-of-american-power.

I'm trying to make a statement about the importance of
Turkey not just to the United States but to the world. This is a
country that has been often said lies at the crossroads between
East and West. It's a country that possesses an extraordinarily rich heritage, but also represents a blend of those ancient
traditions with a modern nation state that respects democracy,
respects rule of law, and is striving toward a modern economy.
... I think that where there's the most promise of building
stronger U.S.–Turkish relations is in the recognition that
Turkey and the United States can build a model partnership in
which a predominantly Christian nation and a predominantly
Muslim nation, a Western nation and a nation that straddles
two continents—that we can create a modern international
community that is respectful, that is secure, that is prosperous; that there are not tensions—inevitable tensions between
cultures, which I think is extraordinarily important[13].

President Obama's words describe the significant symbolic value
of the U.S. alliance with Turkey. They also, however, allude to the main
challenge facing the alliance: that of overcoming dramatic differences in
culture, ideology, and heritage.

The Islamic identity of Turkey is nearly ubiquitous, because
approximately 99.7% of Turks are Muslim[14]. This phenomenon has
occurred slowly but steadily since the turn of the 20th century, at which
time only about 44% of Istanbul's population was Muslim[15]. Turkey's
first Constitution, adopted in 1924, declared Islam as the official religion, but this designation was removed in 1928[16]. The current Constitution does not establish a religion, and grants all citizens equality

---

[13] The President's News Conference with President Abdullah Gul of Turkey in
Ankara, Turkey, 2009 Daily Comp. Pres. Doc. 2, 5 (6 Apr. 2009).
[14] Finkel, *supra* note 3, at 10.
[15] *Id.*
[16] *Id.* at 9.

under the law, regardless of creed or gender[17]. Further, Article 24 of the Constitution grants freedom of religious belief and conscience so long as the exercise of that freedom does not threaten the integrity of the secular state[18]. In practice, however, only Muslims who speak Turkish are considered "Turks" and have any realistic chance of obtaining a state-appointed position[19].

Despite these deep cultural and religious ties to the Middle East, Turkey is a member of the North Atlantic Treaty Organization (NATO)[20] and is generally viewed as leaning politically toward the West. This perception would seem to be out of step with a recent MetroPOLL survey that found 43% of Turks view the U.S. as Turkey's greatest threat[21]. The same survey found that only 3% of Turks view Iran as any threat at all[22]. Moreover, a tracking poll conducted by the Pew Research Center has consistently found Turks to have a significantly unfavourable view of the U.S. The most recent version of this poll indicates that U.S. favourability may be on the rise in Turkey, but still just 29% of Turks respond favourably to the U.S.[23] The Turkish public's wariness of the U.S. was reinforced in 2005 by a wildly popular novel titled *Metal Storm*[24], in which Turkey was invaded by the U.S.[25] To further complicate its diplomatic ties with the West, Turkey has significant allegiances to the Arab world, as evidenced by the 2004 selection of Turkish professor Ekmeleddin Ihsanoglu as the new Secretary General of the Organisation of Islamic Cooperation (OIC)—a

[17] *Id.* at 10.
[18] CONST. OF THE REPUBLIC OF TURKEY 7 Nov. 1982, art. 24.
[19] FINKEL, *supra* note 3, at 10.
[20] *NATO Member Countries*, NATO (27 Mar. 2014), http://www.nato.int/cps/en/natohq/nato_countries.htm.
[21] FINKEL, *supra* note 3, at 80.
[22] *Id.*
[23] Richard Wike, Bruce Stokes, & Jacob Poushter, *America's Global Image*, PEW RESEARCH CTR. (23 June 2015), http://www.pewglobal.org/2015/06/23/1-americas-global-image.
[24] ORKUN UCAR & BURAK TURNA, METAL FURTINA (2004).
[25] Karl Vick, *In Many Turks' Eyes, U.S. Remains the Enemy*, WASH. POST, 10 Apr. 2005, at A21.

post he held until 2013[26].

Turkey's relationship with Europe contains many similarly conflicting characteristics. Turkey began the process of ascending to the European Union (EU) alongside Croatia in 2005. Croatia completed the process and became a full member in 2011. Meanwhile, Turkey is nowhere close to finishing the process[27]. Given the incredibly slow progress being made, there is room to speculate about how badly Erdoğan really wants to finish the ascension process.

As a way of surviving in this "crossroads of the world" region, Turkey has adopted a "Policy of Zero Problems with our Neighbors"[28]. While the wording of the policy portrays Swiss-like neutrality, implementation has been challenging, marked by conflict, and in many ways has led to more isolation than cooperation[29].

II. The Erdoğan Effect

President Erdoğan is commonly viewed as the most influential political figure in Turkish history since Kemal Atatürk founded Turkey[30]. This is likely due to both his charismatic personality and the economic resurgence that Turkey has experienced during his time in power. Yet, Erdoğan's past conduct is anything but noncontroversial.

---

[26] *General Secretariat*, Organisation of Islamic Cooperation, http://www.oic-oci. org/oicv2/page/?p_id=38&p_ref=14&lan=en (last visited 11 Feb. 2015).
[27] Kemal Kirisci, *Turkey's Strategic Choices*, Brookings (19 Dec. 2014), http:// www.brookings.edu/research/opinions/2014/12/19-turkeys-strategic-choices-kirisci.
[28] *Policy of Zero Problems with our Neighbors*, Republic of Turk. Ministry of Foreign Affairs, http://www.mfa.gov.tr/policy-of-zero-problems-with-our-neighbor s.en.mfa (last visited 16 May 2016).
[29] Burak Bekdil, *Turkey: "Zero Problems with Neighbors"*, Gatestone Inst. (6 Apr. 2015, 4:00 AM), http://www.gatestoneinstitute.org/5471/turkey-zero-problems-neigh bors.
[30] *Turkish President Erdoğan on ISIS and Regional Security: A Conversation with Recep Tayyip Erdoğan*, Council on Foreign Relations (22 Sept. 2014), http://cfr. org/turkey/turkish-president-erdogan-isis-regional-security/p33488 [hereinafter *Turkish President Erdoğan on ISIS*].

For starters, Erdoğan's AKP "is the latest in a succession of parties descended from an overtly Islamic movement founded in the 1960s"[31]. In 1983, after Turkey's constitutional court banned two previous parties that were modeled after the Muslim Brotherhood, Islamist ideologue Necmettin Erbakan formed the Welfare Party (also known as Refah or RP)[32]. Erdoğan was elected Mayor of Istanbul in 1994 as a member of the Welfare Party[33]. In 1998, the court also dissolved the Welfare Party, and Erdoğan joined the Virtue Party (FP)[34]. Later the same year, Erdoğan was imprisoned on charges of religious incitement[35]. After his release four months later[36], Erdoğan founded the AKP[37]. Perhaps none of these Islamist associations should be surprising given that Erdoğan has been "photographed sitting at the feet of the proto-Taliban Afghan warlord Gulbeddin Hekmatyar"[38], has referred to himself as the "Imam of Istanbul" and a "servant of shari'a"[39], and has even espoused the idea that Muslims discovered America[40]. It is also highly probable that these views were formed—or at least solidified—during his imam-hatip education[41].

Despite these hard-line Islamist roots, Erdoğan's tenure as the most powerful figure in Turkey began with a fairly resounding secular tone. When the AKP swept to power in 2002 (garnering two-thirds of

---

[31] FINKEL, *supra* note 3, at 73.

[32] Rubin, *supra* note 1.

[33] Hakan Aslaneli, *Erdoğan Goes to Prison*, HURRIYET DAILY NEWS (27 Mar. 1999), http://www.hurriyetdailynews.com/erdogan-goes-to-prison.aspx?pageID=438&n=erd ogan-goes-to-prison-1999-03-27.

[34] *Id.*

[35] Rubin, *supra* note 1.

[36] Aslaneli, *supra* note 33.

[37] Rubin, *supra* note 1.

[38] FINKEL, *supra* note 3, at 73.

[39] Michael Rubin, *Ten Years Later, Turkey's Islamist Political Revolution Bearing Bitter Fruit*, AEI (2 Nov. 2012, 11:09 AM), http://www.aei.org/publication/ten-years-later-turkeys-islamist-political-revolution-bearing-bitter-fruit.

[40] Michael Rubin, *Erdoğan's Comments about Muslims Discovering America Says a Lot about His State of Mind*, AEI (24 Nov. 2014), http://www.aei.org/ publication/erdogans-comments-muslims-discovering-america-says-lot-state-mind.

[41] *Id.*

the seats in parliament with just 34 percent of the vote[42]), it did so with a message centred on the flailing economy[43]. Initially, AKP's governing focus seemed to match that message, as "it stabilized Turkey's currency, tackled inflation, and catalyzed growth"[44]. These early successes fueled the West's infatuation with Erdoğan and laid the groundwork for President Obama's glowing praise for the emerging "bond of trust". These successes, along with Erdoğan's skill as a politician, propelled the AKP to reelection in 2007 and 2011 with progressively larger shares of the vote[45]. In a country that has had a multiparty system since 1950[46], the AKP has had near absolute power for more than thirteen years.

Erdoğan's inclination to embrace Islamic authoritarianism also began immediately, but initially went largely unnoticed because of its subtlety. Initially, rather than proposing dramatic policy change, Erdoğan's transformation focused on slowly but surely changing the personnel manning the levers of government. He replaced all of the members of Turkey's banking board with alumni of Islamic finance, adjusted university admission formulas to admit more religious students, and altered the interview process for civil service to allow entry of more political allies[47]. The most impactful change may have been the dramatic Islamisation of the education system. Under the guidance of Erdoğan's son, Bilal, eleven hours of the school week are now dedicated to Sunni religious instruction, and the number of students in imam-hatip schools has risen from 70,000 in 2002 to one million today[48], which is more than a 28-fold increase.

The early warning signs of these trends did not go completely un-

---

[42] Rubin, *supra* note 39.
[43] *Id.*
[44] *Id.*
[45] FINKEL, *supra* note 3, at 73.
[46] *Id.* at 8.
[47] Rubin, *supra* note 39.
[48] Safak Pavey, *The Rise of Political Islam in Turkey: How the West Got It Wrong*, OPENDEMOCRACY (3 Nov. 2014), https://www.opendemocracy.net/5050/safak-pavey/rise-of-political-islam-in-turkey-how-west-got-it-wrong.

noticed by U.S. officials. In January 2004, U.S. Ambassador to Turkey Eric Edelman wrote:

> Erdoğan has traits which render him seriously vulnerable to miscalculating the political dynamic, especially in foreign affairs . . . [his] authoritarian loner streak . . . prevents growth of a circle of strong and skillful advisers, a broad flow of fresh information to him, or development of effective communications among the party headquarters, government, and parliamentary group[49].

While Erdoğan's steady Islamisation of Turkey raised some eyebrows in the West, it is Erdoğan's march toward authoritarianism that has been the most unmistakable. It is almost unimaginable, but the country that President Obama called a "model" partner "now imprisons more journalists than Iran and China and, according to Reporters without Frontiers, ranks below Russia, Venezuela, and Zimbabwe in press freedom"[50]. Further, "one in every five Turkish generals is now in prison on charges that, at best, are dubious"[51]. Perhaps the most blatant use of authoritarian power occurred in March 2014, when Turkey banned the popular social media website Twitter, a move that the U.S. State Department described as a "21st century book burning"[52]. Although reports suggest that this policy has ended, this conduct is a reminder of the fact that Turkey is increasingly inclined to repression[53].

The drive for authoritarian control reached its crescendo when Erdoğan began exerting his influence toward the goal of converting

---

[49] Okan Altiparmak & Claire Berlinski, *The Wikileaks Cables on Turkey: 20/20 Tunnel Vision*, MERIA J., VOL. 15, 21 Aug. 2011.

[50] Rubin, *supra* note 39.

[51] *Id.*

[52] Douglas Frantz, *21st Century Book Burning*, U.S. DEP'T OF STATE OFFICIAL BLOG (21 Mar. 2014), https://blogs.state.gov/stories/2014/03/21/21st-century-book-burning.

[53] Julian Hattem, *Turkey Ends Twitter Ban*, THE HILL (14 Apr. 2014), http://thehill.com/policy/technology/202579-turkey-ends-twitter-ban.

Turkey's political system into a presidential system[54]. This occurred, of course, as Erdoğan was himself moving into the position of President. Today, these changes no longer occur subtly, but instead in grand fashion. For example, Erdoğan now resides in the largest residential palace in the world, a 3.1 million square foot monstrosity that contains more than 1,000 rooms[55]. It was into this palace that Erdoğan, surrounded by guards dressed as Ottoman era soldiers, welcomed Palestinian President Mahmoud Abbas in January 2015[56]. The palace was also the chosen location for several of Erdoğan's cabinet meetings, including those that occurred on 9 March 2015[57], 20 April 2015[58], 14 December 2015[59], and 22 February 2016[60]. The cabinet meetings are simply another indication that Erdoğan has taken his push for a presidential system to a very public level. On 5 May 2016, Turkey's Prime Minister Ahmet Davutoğlu resigned his post as a direct result of this power struggle[61].

[54] Emre Peker, *Turkey President Erdoğan Defends Detentions, Dismisses EU Criticism*, Wall St. J. (15 Dec. 2014, 4:17 PM), http://www.wsj.com/articles/turkey-president-erdogan-defends-detentions-dismisses-eu-criticism-1418664422.

[55] David Blair, *Turkey's President Moves into World's Biggest Palace Costing £384 Million*, The Telegraph (5 Nov. 2014, 11:48 AM), http://www.telegraph.co.uk/ news/worldnews/europe/turkey/11210083/Turkeys-president-moves-into-worlds-biggest-palace-costing-384-million.html.

56Neil Munro, *New Ottoman Emperor Rejects Obama's Strategy*, Daily Caller (14 Jan. 2015, 10:26 PM), http://dailycaller.com/2015/01/14/new-ottoman-emperor-rejects-obamas-strategy.

[57] *President Erdoğan Chairs Cabinet Meeting for Second Time*, Today's Zaman (9 Mar. 2015, 12:57 PM), http://www.todayszaman.com/anasayfa_president-erdogan-chairs-cabinet-meeting-for-second-time_374710.html.

[58] *President Erdoğan Convenes Cabinet for Third Time*, Today's Zaman (20 Apr. 2015, 2:06 PM), http://www.todayszaman.com/anasayfa_president-erdogan-convenes -cabinet-for-third-time_378461.html.

[59] Erdinç Çelikkan, *President Erdoğan to Chair Cabinet Meeting on Feb. 22*, Hurriyet Daily News (22 Feb. 2016), http://www.hurriyetdailynews.com/president -erdogan-to-chair-cabinet-meeting-on-feb-22.aspx?pageID=238&nID=95489&News CatID=338.

[60] *Id.*

[61] Erin Cunningham, *Turkey's Prime Minister Resigns Amid High-Level Rifts and Deepening Crises*, Wash. Post (5 May 2016), https://www.washingtonpost.com / world/turkeys-prime-minister-is-expected-to-resign-amid-rifts-with-erdogan-reports/ 2016/05/05/5eaff339-67f3-49f1-a96a-a163354bd4ff_story.html.

In a September 2014 speech at the Council on Foreign Relations, Erdoğan opened his remarks by referencing the Ottoman State that preceded Turkey's establishment as an independent state in 1923. Erdoğan spoke longingly about the Ottoman Empire and implied that many of the current problems in the region are a result of the breakup of that empire:

> The Ottoman State had a very successful administration system, and for centuries, these areas of crisis today had maintained their existence without problem. The Palestinian issue, the problems in Iraq and Syria, Crimea, Balkans, are all issues that came about after the dissolution of the Ottoman Empire. Therefore, they date back to about 100 years ago[62].

This sentiment, coupled with the increasingly suppressive tactics deployed by the AKP, is highly inconsistent with the notion of a "model" democracy that is to be emulated. This conduct has led the U.S. to question whether its once-solid ally is now a friend or foe.

III. TURKEY, ISRAEL, AND HAMAS

Turkey's relationship with the State of Israel got off to a positive start when Turkey was quick to acknowledge Israel's statehood on 28 March 1949[63], becoming the first Muslim-majority nation to do so[64]. Relations between the two nations were fairly limited and uneventful until the 1990s, when they flourished[65]. This high point in relations lasted only about a decade, however, and began to deteriorate rapidly

---

[62] *Turkish President Erdoğan on ISIS, supra* note 30.

[63] *Turkey's Political Relations with the State of Israel*, REPUBLIC OF TURK. MINISTRY OF FOREIGN AFFAIRS, http://www.mfa.gov.tr/relations-between-turkey-and-israel%20.en.mfa (last visited on 8 Feb. 2015).

[64] Omer Zarpli, *The Old Turkey-Israel Relationship Isn't Coming Back*, THE NAT'L INTEREST (2 Oct. 2013), http://nationalinterest.org/commentary/the-old-turkey-israel-relationship-isnt-coming-back-9163.

[65] Jay Alan Sekulow, *Turkey-Israel Relations*, 1 J. THE CENTRE FOR STUDY L. & PUB. POL'Y AT OXFORD 1, 8–9 (2015).

when Erdoğan rose to power in Turkey[66]. Even during the period of relatively strong relations, fissures began to be visible as Islamist political parties in Turkey fought to weaken the military's support for Israel[67].

Many will point to the Gaza flotilla incident in 2010 as the main reason for the strained relations. On 31 May 2010, six ships attempting to breach the Israeli naval blockade of Gaza (which had been established in response to the Hamas kidnapping of an Israeli soldier, Gilad Shalit, in 2006) were boarded by Israeli commandos[68]. On only one vessel—the Comoros-flagged, Turkish-crewed *Mavi Marmara*—was there armed resistance to the Israeli landing. The ensuing fight on the *Mavi Marmara* left nine Turkish citizens dead and ten Israeli commandos wounded[69]. The incident made international headlines and continued to fester to the point that President Obama worked to broker an Israeli apology in 2013[70]. Even so, the incident triggered the *in absentia* prosecution of four senior Israeli military officers in the 7th High Criminal Court in Istanbul[71]. Observers have noted that the prosecution of the Israeli officers, as well as the failure to prosecute the Turkish Master of the *Mavi Marmara*, suggests that the flotilla—and the ensuing prosecution—was always more politically motivated than humanitarian[72].

While the *Mavi Marmara* incident was certainly a flashpoint of hostility between Turkey and Israel, a closer examination makes it clear that the relationship between the two countries deteriorated long before the flotilla incident made headlines. The most significant hurdle to positive relations between Turkey and Israel is Erdoğan's sup-

---

[66] Zarpli, *supra* note 64.

[67] Sekulow, *supra* note 65, at 10.

[68] Robert Weston Ash, *The Mavi Marmara Trial: Politicising the Turkish Justice System*, 1 J. The Centre for Study L. & Pub. Pol'y at Oxford 49, 53–54 (2015).

[69] *Gaza Flotilla Raid: No Israel Charges over Mavi Marmara*, BBC (6 Nov. 2014), http://www.bbc.com/news/world-middle-east-29934002.

[70] Zarpli, *supra* note 64.

[71] Ash, *supra* note 68, at 50.

[72] *Id.* at 83–85.

port for Hamas, a group that many of Turkey's allies—including the U.S.—deem to be a terrorist organisation[73]. This support was on full display in 2006 after Hamas' victory in the Palestinian elections. Just weeks after the election, and "less than a week after [Erdoğan] had told European officials that he would honour the international community's decision to isolate Hamas until it renounced terrorism and recognised the Jewish state's right to exist, Turkey received a Hamas delegation in Ankara"[74]. Further, in January 2015, Turkey welcomed Hamas leader Khaled Meshaal to Turkey after Meshaal's banishment from Qatar[75].

The juxtaposition between how Erdoğan views Hamas and Israel is alarming. Despite recent evidence that Israel-Turkey relations have experienced a warming trend[76], it has become fairly common for Erdoğan to compare Israeli actions to those of the Nazis. After the U.S. State Department condemned this habit on 19 July 2014, Erdoğan retorted, "What do Americans know about Hitler"[77]? On the other hand, Erdoğan appears to wholly accept the legitimacy of Hamas and, in fact, has gone out of his way to strengthen Turkey's ties with Hamas leadership, while completely dismissing the atrocities it commits[78]. This is not surprising given Erdoğan's own words after he hosted Sudanese President Omar al-Bashir in November 2009: "It is not possible for a Muslim to commit genocide"[79].

---

[73] *Foreign Terrorist Organizations*, U.S. DEP'T OF STATE, http://www.state.gov/j/ct/rls/other/des/123085.htm (last visited 18 May 2016).

[74] Rubin, *supra* note 1.

[75] Barak Ravid & Reuters, *Report: Qatar Expels Hamas Leader to Turkey*, HAARETZ (6 Jan. 2015, 4:31 PM), http://www.haaretz.com/news/middle-east/1.635602.

[76] *Israeli, Turkish Presidents Talk in Sign of Warming Ties*, PRESSTV (24 Mar. 2016), http://www.presstv.ir/Detail/2016/03/24/457322/Israel-Turkey-Erdogan-Rivlin-Istanb ul.

[77] Steven A. Cook, *What a Turkey!*, COUNCIL ON FOREIGN REL. (5 AUG. 2014), http://www.cfr.org/turkey/turkey/p33322.

[78] Sekulow, *supra* note 65, at 17–24.

[79] Mustafa Küçük, *Erdoğan Says America was Discovered by Muslims, Not Columbus*, HURRIYET DAILY NEWS (15 Nov. 2014), http://www.hurriyetdailynews.com/erdogan-says-america-was-discovered-by-muslims-not-columbus.aspx?PageID= 238&NID=74371&NewsCatID=338.

In November 2014, Israel uncovered a Hamas cell that was taking orders from Saleh al-Arouri, who lives freely in Turkey. The cell was planning numerous attacks in Israel, and al-Arouri claimed responsibility for the 2014 murder of three Israeli teenagers that set off a 40-day war. Still, Erdoğan and the Turkish government chose the side of al-Arouri and Hamas[80]. Even after al-Arouri eventually left Turkey, Hamas claimed that it was on his own volition, and the Turkish Foreign Ministry did not dispute the claim[81].

When asked whether Turkey risks being labeled a state sponsor of terrorism because of its support for Hamas, a U.S. State Department official stated that they do not "jump to that conclusion"[82]. Another official responded: "Hamas is a designated foreign terrorist organization. Hamas continues to engage in terrorist activity and . . . we continue to raise our concerns about the relationship between Hamas and Turkey with senior Turkish officials, including after learning of Khaled Mashaal's recent visit there"[83].

Erdoğan, for his part, has shown no remorse for the relationship with Hamas, and in fact insists that Turkey will "continue to have close contacts with all of the parties"[84]. To the charge of anti-Semitism, Erdoğan responds:

There are times when I personally am labeled as an anti-Semitic person. Criticizing Israel's massacres that defy international law, trample on human rights and life is not anti-Semi-

---

[80] Lee Smith, *Turkey's Erdoğan Builds Himself an Opulent Palace, Part of a 20-year Mess That is U.S. Middle East Policy,* Hudson Inst. (4 Dec. 2014), http://www.hudson.org/research/10857-turkey-s-erdogan-builds-himself-an-opulent-palace-part-of-a-20-year-mess-that-is-u-s-middle-east-policy.

[81] Sekulow, *supra* note 65, at 20.

[82] Jen Psaki, *Daily Press Briefing,* U.S. Dep't. of State (8 Jan. 2015), http://www.state.gov/r/pa/prs/dpb/2015/01/235672.htm.

[83] Jeff Rathke, *Daily Press Briefing,* U.S. Dep't. of State (30 Dec. 2014), http://translations.state.gov/st/english/texttrans/2014/12/20141230312625.html#axzz-3RfCAJGot.

[84] *Turkish President Erdoğan on ISIS, supra* note 30.

tism. Holding a state that massacres ten people by stopping an international ship taking aid to Gaza isn't anti-Semitism.

And it isn't anti-Semitism to criticize an administration that massacres, kills babies, children, innocent babies, children, in their homes, mosques, hospitals, schools, beaches, parks, without any discrimination.

Our criticism is not directed to the Jews. It is only and solely directed at the Israeli administration and its policies, and no one should distort this. There is a distinction here.

Whenever we criticize the massacring of innocent women in Palestine, some circles engage in a campaign to distort the perceptions about Turkey. Whenever we criticize the killing of innocent children, babies, in the Middle East, some media organizations target us[85].

Nowhere in this sweeping criticism of Israel did Erdoğan mention the atrocities committed by Hamas toward the Israeli people.

On one hand, it would seem like Erdoğan's allegiance to Hamas and animosity toward Israel would cause an enormous wedge between Turkey and the U.S. On the other hand, it would be fairly hypocritical of the Obama Administration to be too critical of Turkey for its position on Hamas when the U.S. has made a very similar decision to acknowledge and accept Hamas' legitimacy[86]. The George W. Bush Administration may have been similarly misguided when it chose Erdoğan to negotiate between Israel and Syria[87].

---

[85] *Id.*

[86] Lee Smith, *After Hamas-Fatah Deal, American Taxpayers Now Paying the Salaries of Palestinian Terrorists,* HUDSON INST. (3 June 2014), http://hudson.org/research/ 10343-after-hamas-fatah-deal-american-taxpayers-now-paying-the-salaries-of-palesti nian-terrorists.

[87] Richard Boudreaux, *Turkey Mediating Israel-Syria Talks,* L.A. TIMES (25 Apr. 2008), http://articles.latimes.com/2008/apr/25/world/fg-golan25.

IV. Choosing Sides in the world

Despite signs of improvement, Turkey's relationship with Israel represents the starkest challenge to U.S./Turkey relations (because of the strength of the U.S./Israel alliance and the tenacity of Erdoğan's disdain for Israel). Still, it is not the only place in the world where the U.S. and Turkey do not see eye to eye. In fact, if a country's friends are any indication of the true character of that nation, Turkey may never have been further from the U.S. than it is today.

Iran may be the most troubling of Turkey's friends. Erdoğan has hosted both former President Mahmoud Ahmadinejad[88] and President Hassan Rouhani[89] in Turkey and has traveled to Tehran himself in January 2014 with a goal of deepening ties between the two countries[90]. The result of these efforts was the signing of "nearly two dozen cooperative agreements, on everything from finance to tourism to communications"[91]. These deepening ties with Iran were also evident in 2010 when Turkey joined Brazil as the only two members of the United Nations Security Council to vote against sanctions on Iran[92]. This vote occurred just days after the Obama Administration criticised a deal that Turkey and Brazil negotiated with Iran (in talks encouraged by the U.S.) on its nuclear program[93]. After this initial criticism, the Obama Administration opened direct dialogue with Iran and also conceded that Iran has a right to enrich uranium[94]. Eventually, these U.S.-led talks resulted in

[88] Mike Brownfield, *Turkey's Dangerous Turn against the West*, The Daily Signal (8 June 2010), http://dailysignal.com/2010/06/08/turkeys-dangerous-turn-against-the-west.

[89] Ilan Berman & Nika Madyoon, *An Iranian-Turkish Reset*, Wash. Times (21 July 2014), http://www.washingtontimes.com/news/2014/jul/21/berman-madyoon-an-iran ian-turkish-reset.

[90] *Id.*

[91] *Id.*

[92] Press Release, Security Council, Security Council Imposes Additional Sanctions on Iran, Voting 12 in Favour to 2 Against, with 1 Abstention, U.N. Press Release SC/9948 (9 June 2010).

[93] Smith, *supra* note 80.

[94] Paul Richter, *Iran is Pushing Limits on Nuclear Deal, Former Obama Advisor Warns*, L.A. Times (20 July 2014), http://www.latimes.com/world/middleeast/la-

an historic, but controversial, agreement that afforded Iran significant relief from both U.S. and U.N. sanctions[95]. Turkey lauded the agreement, but expressed significant skepticism about both Russia's and Iran's motives in the region[96].

It should be noted that Turkey and Iran find themselves on different sides in the ongoing conflict in Syria[97]. Further, Iran's efforts to exert dominion in the region along sectarian lines have caused some disruption in its relationship with Turkey[98]. Even so, Turkey's desire for a close relationship with Iran (which long pre-dates the increase in diplomatic interaction between the U.S. and Iran) suggests that the U.S. and Turkey may not see eye to eye on Iran.

Even after considering Turkey's relations with Israel and Iran, there are numerous places in the world where the U.S. and Turkey take conflicting positions:

- ✦ Erdoğan "enthusiastically" hosted Sudanese President Omar al-Bashir in Turkey[99].
- ✦ In 2010, Turkey held secret war games with China without informing the U.S.[100]
- ✦ There is strong evidence that state-owned Turkish Airlines smuggled arms into Nigeria for the terrorist group, Boko Haram[101].

---

fg-obama-advisor-iran-nuclear-20140720-story.html.

[95] Michael R. Gordon & David E. Sanger, *Deal Reached on Iran Nuclear Program; Limits on Fuel Would Lessen With Time*, N.Y. TIMES (14 July 2015), http://www.nytimes.com/2015/07/15/world/middleeast/iran-nuclear-deal-is-reached-after-long-negotiations.html.

[96] Emre Peker, *Turkey Hails Iran Nuclear Deal*, WALL ST. J. (17 Jan. 2016, 10:41 AM), http://www.wsj.com/articles/turkey-hails-iran-nuclear-deal-1453045276.

[97] Tiffany N. Barrans, *Turkey-Iran Relations: Pragmatic Economics & the Ideological Ceiling to Strategic Relations*, 1 J. THE CENTRE FOR STUDY L. & PUB. POL'Y AT OXFORD 27, 40–43 (2015).

[98] *Id.* at 43.

[99] Brownfield, *supra* note 88.

[100] Rubin, *supra* note 1.

[101] Michael Rubin, *Did Turkey arm Boko Haram?*, AEI (13 May 2014, 3:42 PM),

- ✦ A Turkish ambassador tweeted support for al Qaeda after part of Mali was overtaken by terrorists[102].
- ✦ Even the U.S. offensive in Fallujah was deemed "genocide" by the Chairman of the Human Rights Committee in Turkey's parliament. Erdoğan himself said that "hundreds were martyred"[103].

So while many leaders in the U.S. may continue to insist that the alliance with Turkey is strong, a cursory look around the world suggests that the two countries take opposing sides more often than they stand together. With this backdrop, it becomes less surprising that, according to the Pew Global Attitudes Project Poll, Turkey has, for a considerable period of time, remained one of the most anti-American countries surveyed[104].

V. The War on Terror

When Osama bin Laden issued his on-camera justifications for the September 11, 2001, terrorist attacks on the World Trade Center and the Pentagon, he said he was avenging "eight decades of pain, humiliation and shame"[105]. As explained by Andrew Finkel, this is an unmistakable reference to the abolition of the Ottoman Empire (and hence the Islamic Caliphate) and the corresponding establishment of Turkey:

> [Osama bin Laden's] reference, Turks grasped at once, was to the creation of their own Republic in 1923 and to the decision of [Kemal] Atatürk to plow salt into the notion of a religiously empowered state. The 1924 abolition of the Caliphate—the leader of the Islamic community and a role enjoyed by the Ottoman sultan—was a renunciation of an authority that

---

http://www.aei.org/publication/the-trouble-with-turkey.
[102] *Id.*
[103] Vick, *supra* note 25.
[104] Wike, *supra* note 23.
[105] Finkel, *supra* note 3, at 139.

could transcend the border of the nation-state[106].

This deep-seated linkage between the origins of the War on Terror and the origins of Turkey makes Turkey's role in the War on Terror a crucially significant one. Add to that the geographic location of Turkey and the fact that it is a Muslim-majority member of NATO, and Turkey becomes one of the most important potential partners for the U.S.-led coalition in the War on Terror. However, in reality, Turkey's engagement in this international effort has been less than seamless.

Turkey's formal entrance into the War on Terror occurred on 1 November 2001, less than a month after the beginning of Operation Enduring Freedom on 7 October 2001[107]. This made Turkey one of the very first coalition partners of the U.S., and took place in spite of significant opposition from the Turkish population (at the outset, polling indicated that approximately 80% of the Turkish people opposed the war)[108].

Strong opposition from the Turkish people and divergent priorities in Washington and Ankara have created numerous fissures in this alliance. Even the most basic U.S. requests to use Turkish military bases have proven difficult. The aforementioned refusal in 2003 was simply a sign of what was to come. Prior to July 2015, even U.S. requests that search-and-rescue assets be stationed on Turkish bases were rejected[109]. This was particularly problematic in December of 2014 when the Islamic State shot down a Jordanian pilot, Lieutenant Muath al-Kaseasbeh, and a search-and-rescue effort failed. After negotiations for a prisoner swap were unsuccessful, the Islamic State burned Kaseasbeh

---

[106] *Id.* at 139–140.

[107] *Operation Enduring Freedom Fast Facts*, CNN (31 Dec. 2014, 2:15 PM), http://www.cnn.com/2013/10/28/world/operation-enduring-freedom-fast-facts.

[108] Ertugrul Kurkcu, *Desperately but Deliberately, Turkey Joins Bush's War*, MIDDLE EAST RES. INFO. PROJECT (8 Nov. 2001), http://www.merip.org/mero/mero110801.

[109] *Report: Turkey Balked at US Permission to Use Base for Rescue Aircraft*, TODAY'S ZAMAN (5 Feb. 2015), http://www.todayszaman.com/diplomacy_report-turkey-balked-at-us-permission-to-use-base-for-rescue-aircraft_371836.html.

alive in a cage, and a video recording of the horrific massacre was posted online[110]. Even this disregard for humanity did not change the Turkish government's mind on the matter of making its bases available to
the U.S. In July 2015, Turkey finally agreed to open Inçirlik Air Force
Base to the U.S. and coalition partners for the purpose of conducting
strikes against the Islamic State[111].

The U.S. and Turkey also differ frequently on the definition of
what constitutes a terrorist. In addition to the relationships with
Hamas, Iran, and Boko Haram that were previously discussed, a 2007
train derailment in Turkey revealed arms apparently bound for Hezbollah among the freight[112]. In addition to these ties to terrorist groups,
Turkey appears ambivalent at best about known terrorists residing or
transiting through Turkey. At other times, the Turkish government
openly embraces these terrorists.

For example, from 12 October 2001[113] until 26 November 2014[114],
Yasin al-Qadi appeared on the U.S. Specially Designated Terrorist
List (SDTL) for alleged financial ties to al-Qaeda. However, Erdoğan
met frequently with al-Qadi during his time on the SDTL[115]. In fact,
Erdoğan's personal security detail was known to escort al-Qadi, and

---

[110] Michael Wilner, *ISIS Releases Video Purporting to Show Jordanian Pilot
Being Burned Alive*, Jerusalem Post (3 Feb. 2015, 18:47), http://www.jpost.
com/Middle-East/ISIS-releases-pictures-purporting-to-show-Jordanian-pilot-be-
ing-burned-alive-389880.
[111] Patrick Tucker & Marcus Weisgerber, *Turkey Opens Key Air Base for U.S.
Strikes on ISIS*, The Nat'l J. (23 July 2015), https://www.nationaljournal.
com/s/71423/ turkey-opens-key-air-base-u-s-strikes-isis.
[112] Rubin, *supra* note 1.
[113] *Comprehensive List of Terrorists and Groups Identified Under Executive Order
13224*, U.S. Dep't of State (31 Dec. 2001), http://2001-2009.state.gov/s/ct/rls/fs/
2001/6531.htm.
[114] Scott Lanman & Ian Katz, *U.S. Drops Terrorism Finance Sanctions on Saudi
al-Qadi*, Bloomberg Bus. (26 Nov. 2014, 12:31 PM), http://www.bloomberg.com/
news/articles/2014-11-26/u-s-drops-terrorism-finance-sanctions-on-saudi-al-qadi.
[115] *New Evidence of Erdoğan's Secret Meeting with al-Qadi Emerges*, Today's
Zaman (15 Aug. 2014), http://www.todayszaman.com/national_new-evidence-of-
erdogans-secret-meeting-with-al-qadi-emerges_355836.html.

he "was reportedly allowed to enter Turkey illegally at least four times without using a passport or visa through a VIP section of an airport that had its security cameras blacked out"[116]. When asked about this association with al-Qadi in 2006, Erdoğan said: "I know Mr Qadi. I believe in him as I believe in myself. For Mr Qadi to associate with a terrorist organization, or support one, is impossible"[117]. The dismissal was eerily similar to his assurance that it is not possible for any Muslim to commit genocide.

An additional source of friction between the U.S. and Turkey is the frequency, and apparent ease, with which terrorist fighters are transiting into and out of Turkey. Erdoğan frequently claims (often with an air of personal offence) that Turkey is doing everything it can to prevent the free flow of fighters over its borders into and out of Iraq and Syria[118]. However, the evidence strongly indicates that very little has been done. One example of just how lax these efforts are is a YouTube video of what appears to be Islamic State terrorists casually riding the Istanbul metro[119]. The terrorist fighters are openly wearing Islamic State clothing and are at complete ease with no fear of being detained. It certainly appears as if Erdoğan has placed his desire to oust Syrian President Bashar al-Assad ahead of any other security objective and is, therefore, permitting any individuals who will oppose Assad a free pass through Turkey[120].

Tragically, the success these fighters have had in Syria is playing a significant role in the Islamic State's growth and its increasing threat

---

[116] James Phillips, *Erdoğan's Turkey Goes Soft on Terrorism*, THE DAILY SIGNAL (11 Feb. 2014), http://dailysignal.com/print/?post_id=137081.

[117] *Id.*

[118] *Turkish President Erdoğan on ISIS*, supra note 30.

[119] SyrianGirlpartisan, *#ISIS Rides Istanbul Metro Turkey*, YOUTUBE (27 Sept. 2014), https://www.youtube.com/watch?v=XGIT32I6Kgw.

[120] Doug Bandow, *Well-Armed Turkey Aided Rise of Islamic State: Yet NATO Promises to Defend Ankara from Extremists*, FORBES (8 Sept. 2014), http://www.forbes.com/sites/dougbandow/2014/09/08/well-armed-turkey-aided-rise-of-islamic-state-yet-nato-promises-to-defend-ankara-from-extremists.

to the rest of the world. Specifically, the Islamic State has carried out terror attacks in Turkey on at least three occasions: 12 January 2016[121], 17 February 2016[122], and 13 March 2016[123]. It is likely that these attacks will cause at least some continuation of the uptick in support for the U.S. among the Turkish population.

Conversely, for months, Erdoğan prevented Turkish Kurds from crossing into Syria to help save the Syrian Kurdish city of Kobane, which was under heavy assault from the Islamic State[124]. The motive was transparent: Erdoğan fears a unified Kurdish coalition more than he desires to defeat the Islamic State. In Erdoğan's opinion, Assad and the Kurds are both more loathsome than the Islamic State. Arguably, Erdoğan's fears were fortified when the PKK claimed responsibility for a 1 April 2016 car bombing that killed seven police officers and wounded twenty-seven others in Diyarbakir, Turkey[125].

Turkey's hesitancy to engage the Islamic State cannot be attributed to a lack of skin in the game. For one, as previously noted, Turkey shares a border with both Iraq and Syria. Even beyond that, Turkey holds a sovereign claim to a 2.47 acre enclave just inside Syrian territory that, until recently, contained the tomb of Suleyman Shah, the grandfather of the Ottoman Empire's founder, Osman Bey[126]. The

---

[121] *United States Condemns Terrorist Attack in Istanbul, Turkey*, U.S. Dept. of State, http://www.state.gov/r/pa/prs/ps/2016/01/251124.htm (last visited 18 May 2016).

[122] *United States Condemns Terrorist Attack in Ankara, Turkey*, U.S. Dep't of State, http://www.state.gov/r/pa/prs/ps/2016/02/252587.htm (last visited 18 May 2016).

[123] *The United States Condemns Terrorist Attack in Ankara, Turkey*, U.S. Dep't of State, http://www.state.gov/r/pa/prs/ps/2016/03/254645.htm (last visited 12 May 2016).

[124] James Phillips, *Turkey: Pressures U.S. to Crack Down in Syria-and Sits on the Sideline*, The Daily Signal (14 Oct. 2014), http://dailysignal.com/print/?post_id=161122.

[125] *PKK Claims Responsibility for Turkey Police Car Bombing*, Aljazeera (1 April 2016), http://www.aljazeera.com/news/2016/04/160401132738910.html.

[126] Sonar Cagaptay, *Fear, Loathing, and an Ottoman Shrine in the Cold War Between ISIS and Turkey*, The Wash. Inst. for Near East Pol'y (27 Oct 2014), http://www.washingtoninstitute.org/policy-analysis/view/fear-loathing-and-an-ottoman-shrine-in-the-cold-war-between-isis-and-turkey.

shrine was guarded by Turkish troops, but had been isolated by the Islamic State for several months, preventing the rotation of these troops since April 2014[127]. The shrine has enormous sentimental value for Turks, and its destruction would have been extremely demoralizing.

On 21 February 2015, Erdoğan dispatched nearly 600 Turkish troops, along with "39 tanks, 57 armoured vehicles, and 100 other military vehicles" into Syria to relocate the tomb[128]. After securing the tomb and related items of historic or sentimental value, Erdoğan's "troops blew up the building that housed the tomb so it could not be used later by the jihadists", and relocated the shrine to a location within yards of the Turkish border[129].

The mission to relocate the tomb is understandable, especially as it pertains to the rescue of Turkish soldiers. However, it will be difficult for Erdoğan to convincingly explain why this type of operation was not conducted sooner and in response to the pleas from the people of Kobane. After all, in order to reach the tomb of Suleyman Shah, the Turkish troops passed directly through the devastated streets of Kobane[130].

Predictably, the steady flow of terrorist fighters into and out of Turkey has also allowed the Islamic State to get a foothold in Turkey itself. While there has not been any effort by the Islamic State to claim territory in Turkey, their presence has certainly been felt. For example, in addition to the aforementioned terror attacks in Turkey, the Islamic State used a Turkish gang to attempt to kidnap a Syrian rebel

---

[127] Metin Gurcan, *Are Turkish Troops Guardians or Accidental Hostages at Syrian Tomb?*, AL MONITOR (5 Feb. 2015), http://www.al-monitor.com/pulse/originals/2015/02/turkey-syria-tomb-guardians-or-accidental-hostages.html#.

[128] Louisa Loveluck, *Turkish Military Enters Syria to Evacuate Soldiers from Enclave*, THE TELEGRAPH (22 Feb. 2015, 6:30 PM), http://www.telegraph.co.uk/news/world news/europe/turkey/11427714/Turkish-military-enters-Syria-to-evacuate-soldiers-from-enclave.html.

[129] *Id.*

[130] Luke Coffey, *Turkish Troops Pass Smouldering Kobane to Save Shrine*, ALJAZEERA (22 Feb. 2015), http://www.aljazeera.com/indepth/opinion/2015/02/turkish-troops-pass-smouldering-kobane-save-shrine-150222134326067.html.

commander who had left the battle zone and crossed into Turkey. The commander managed to escape after being shot in the stomach[131].

There have been incidents threatening the security of American personnel in Turkey, as well. On 12 November 2014, three U.S. Navy sailors were mobbed by members of the Turkish Youth Union. The attackers shoved bags over the sailors' heads and verbally and physically assaulted them before the sailors escaped[132]. While this attack does not appear to have been orchestrated by the Islamic State, it is a strong indication of just how rampant the anti-American sentiment is among the Turkish population.

Officials in Washington are certainly starting to take note of Turkey's weak efforts in the War on Terror. Congressman Ileana Ros-Lehtinen, an influential member of the U.S. House Foreign Affairs Committee, said: "[Turkey] has done so little. It has been a player, not for the solution, but part of the problem. Because of their internal political issues, they've let that get in the way of truly defeating [the Islamic State]"[133].

In October 2004, U.S. Vice President Joe Biden probably did not help matters when he claimed that Erdoğan had admitted to him in private that Turkey's policy in Syria had failed. Erdoğan fiercely denied the claim and demanded an apology[134]. Regardless of what was truly said between the two leaders behind closed doors, the incident served only to further disrupt the relationship between the U.S. and Turkey.

---

[131] Jeff Schogol, *Turkey Kidnap Plot Raises Doubt About U.S. Troop Safety*, USA TODAY (23 Oct. 2014), http://www.usatoday.com/story/news/nation/2014/10/22/kidnapping-plot-in-turkey/17756353.

[132] Jamie Crawford, *U.S. Sailors Attacked in Turkey; Bags Placed over Their Heads*, CNN (12 Nov. 2014, 2:19 PM), http://www.cnn.com/2014/11/12/politics/turkey-navy-sailors-bags-over-heards/.

[133] Martin Matishak, *Ros-Lehtinen Blasts Turkey as Slow to Act on ISIS*, THE HILL (21 Oct 2014), http://thehill.com/policy/defense/221393-ros-lehtinen-blasts-turkey-as-slow-to-act-on-isis.

[134] Kirisci, *supra* note 27.

The road ahead in Syria may indeed prove to be a bellwether for the future of the U.S.–Turkey alliance. This is especially true given the agreement to arm and train Syrian opposition forces that was signed on 19 February 2015 by U.S. Ambassador John Bass and a "senior Turkish foreign ministry official"[135]. Implementation of this agreement was fraught with challenges, not the least of which is the fact that the U.S. views the Islamic State as the primary threat in Syria, while Turkey views the Assad regime as the more dangerous threat. There is also significant disagreement internally in Washington about whether there are any trustworthy Syrian opposition forces, and even if so, how to accurately identify them without inadvertently arming additional extremists. As one expert on the region put it: "If U.S. officials could not figure out what two Chechen brothers in Boston were up to, how can they realistically claim to have the ability to vet those speaking no English and living in a war zone"[136]? These fears were realised when the first batch of trainees were summarily routed by an al-Qaeda affiliated group[137]. To make matters worse, the U.S.-backed rebels also surrendered multiple vehicles along with ammunition to the terrorists[138]. U.S. officials testified that only "four or five" U.S.-trained rebels were still in the fight, despite $500 million that was dedicated to the effort[139]. With these results in mind, the U.S. suspended the effort to train rebels on 9 October 2015[140].

---

[135] *US, Turkey to Arm and Train Syrian Rebels*, N.Y. POST (19 Feb. 2015), http://nypost.com/2015/02/19/us-turkey-to-arm-and-train-syrian-rebels.

[136] Michael Rubin, *Arming Rebels Wasn't the Only Option*, AEI (14 Aug. 2014), http://www.aei.org/publication/arming-rebels-wasnt-the-only-option.

[137] *Syria Crisis: US-Trained Rebels Give Equipment to al-Qaeda Affiliate*, BBC (26 Sept. 2015), http://www.bbc.com/news/world-middle-east-34368073.

[138] *Id.*

[139] *Id.*

[140] Michael D. Shear, Helene Cooper & Eric Schmitt, *Obama Administration Ends Effort to Train Syrians to Combat ISIS*, N.Y. TIMES (9 Oct. 2015), http://www.ny-times.com/2015/10/10/world/middleeast/pentagon-program-islamic-state-syria.html?_r=1.

The difficulty of training rebel forces was undoubtedly a contributing factor to the U.S. decision in October 2015 to send approximately fifty Special Operation Forces to Syria for the purpose of coordinating local coalition ground forces[141]. An additional 250 military personnel were deployed on 24 April 2016 as part of the shift in strategy away from training rebel forces[142]. The U.S. is also reportedly considering a backup plan that would provide existing rebel forces with additional high-powered weapons in the event the cease-fire collapses[143].

Complicating all of these dynamics is Turkey's deteriorating relationship with Russia. Much of the current tension between the two countries stems from the fact that Erdoğan and Turkey want to remove Assad from power[144], while Putin and Russia support the Assad government[145]. The tensions reached a boiling point, however, when Turkey shot down a Russian plane that crossed into Turkish airspace on 24 November 2015[146]. The two Russian pilots ejected, but one of them was shot and killed by Syrian opposition forces as he parachuted to the ground[147]. The incident prompted an animated exchange between Presidents Putin and Erdoğan, with Putin promising retaliation if there were additional incidents[148]. While U.S. interests in Syria at least

---

[141] *U.S. to Send Special Ops Troops to Syria*, The Nat'l J. (30 Oct. 2015), https://www.nationaljournal.com/s/91738/u-s-send-special-ops-troops-syria.

[142] Gordon Lubold & Adam Entous, *U.S. to Send 250 Additional Military Personnel to Syria*, Wall St. J. (24 Apr. 2016), http://www.wsj.com/articles/u-s-to-send-250-additional-military-personnel-to-syria-1461531600.

[143] Adam Entous, *U.S. Readies 'Plan B' to Arm Syria Rebels*, Wall St. J. (12 Apr. 2016), http://www.wsj.com/articles/u-s-readies-plan-b-to-arm-syria-rebels-1460509 400.

[144] Barrans, *supra* note 97, at 40.

[145] Nikolay Kozhanov, *Why Putin is Backing Assad in Syria*, Newsweek (18 Sept. 2015), http://www.newsweek.com/why-putin-backing-assad-syria-373477.

[146] Dion Nissenbaum, Emre Peker & James Marson, *Turkey Shoots Down Russian Military Jet*, Wall St. J. (24 Nov. 2015), http://www.wsj.com/articles/turkey-shoots-down-jet-near-syria-border-1448356509.

[147] Paul Sonne, *Russian Pilot Denies Turkey Issued Warning Before Firing on Warplane*, Wall St. J. (25 Nov. 2015), http://www.wsj.com/articles/russia-honors-pilot-killed-after-turkey-downs-aircraft-1448463406.

[148] *Id.*

somewhat overlap with Turkish interests, the emergence of a muscular Russia adds a very delicate complication to the mix, and the frosty relationship between Turkey and Russia makes it all the more tenuous.

Russia's influence in the region became even more complicated on 30 September 2015 when Russian planes launched airstrikes in Syria at the request of Assad[149]. Russian officials claimed the attacks were aimed at Islamic State strongholds, but the U.S. protested that anti-Assad rebel forces were targeted instead[150]. Russia continued to provide Assad with significant military support until 15 March 2016, when Putin ordered at least a portion of the Russian forces to withdraw[151]. According to Putin, Russian planes flew more than 10,000 combat missions in Syria, striking more than 30,000 targets, and aiding Assad's military in retaking 500 towns and villages[152]. While the specifics of Putin's assertions may be disputed, it is clear that Russia's intervention significantly bolstered the Assad regime.

The U.S. expressed repeated concern that the Russian intervention was counter-productive to the fight against the Islamic State and eventually brokered a cease-fire on 22 February 2016[153]. While the cease-fire has reduced the intensity of Russia's military involvement in Syria, it has not resulted in a large-scale drawdown of Russian assets in

---

[149] Andrew Roth, Brian Murphy, & Missy Ryan, *Russia Begins Airstrikes in Syria; U.S. Warns of New Concerns in Conflict*, WASH. POST (30 Sept. 2015), https://www.washingtonpost.com/world/russias-legislature-authorizes-putin-to-use-military-force-in-syria/2015/09/30/f069f752-6749-11e5-9ef3-fde182507eac_story.html.

[150] Patrick J. McDonnell, W.J. Hennigan, & Nabih Bulos, *Russia Launches Airstrikes in Syria Amid U.S. Concern About Targets*, L.A. TIMES (30 Sept. 2015), http://www.latimes.com/world/europe/la-fg-kremlin-oks-troops-20150930-story. html.

[151] *Syria Conflict: Russia's Putin Orders 'Main Part' of Forces Out*, BBC (14 Mar. 2016), http://www.bbc.com/news/world-middle-east-35807689.

[152] *Putin: Syria War Shows "Quality" of Russia's New Weapons*, CBS NEWS (10 May 2016), http://www.cbsnews.com/news/vladimir-putin-syria-war-russian-cruise-missil es-weapons-quality.

[153] *U.S. and Russia Agree on Syria Cease-Fire Terms*, CBS NEWS (22 Feb. 2016), http://www.cbsnews.com/news/us-and-russia-agree-on-syria-cease-fire-terms-offici als-say.

the region[154]. Putin remains eager to demonstrate his commitment to the Assad regime, and recently directed his military to escort more than a hundred journalists on a show-and-tell tour of the Russian presence in the region[155].

It is clear that Putin desires to exert influence throughout the Middle East, including in Syria and Turkey. This fact creates challenges for the U.S., but might also present an opportunity for the U.S. and Turkey to again recognise the common bonds that drew them into the NATO alliance together.

Ultimately, there is a large role for Turkey to play in the War on Terror, should it choose to accept it. The tragic irony, however, is that on several fronts, Turkey seems conflicted about which side it supports. In many ways, it seems as if Turkey does not understand that it must choose a side. The recent agreement to arm opposition forces in Syria is the latest attempt by the U.S. and Turkey to work together, but only time will tell whether it is anything more than Erdoğan taking advantage of an opportunity to damage Assad. The fact remains that the Islamic State is a killing entity bent on global dominance, and Turkey must either work to eradicate it or, by default, enable it.

VI. FETHULAH GÜLEN

Another burr in relations between the U.S. and Turkey is the spat between Erdoğan and Fethullah Gülen. According to his own website, "Fethullah Gülen is an authoritative mainstream Turkish Muslim scholar, thinker, author, poet, opinion leader and educational activist who supports interfaith and intercultural dialogue, science, democracy and spirituality and opposes violence and turning religion into a

---

[154] Frederik Pleitgen, *Russia's Military in Syria: Bigger than you Think and Not Going Anywhere*, CNN (9 May 2016), http://www.cnn.com/2016/05/09/middle east/russia-military-syria/index.html.

[155] *Id.*

political ideology"[156]. While Gülen is a devout Muslim, he also strongly favours a more Western-styled democracy. This frequently causes him to be sharply critical of Erdoğan and the AKP. Given that these clashes often revolve around Erdoğan's authoritarian streak (including his suppression of social media access and harassment of journalists), Gülen has established a significant following among the Turkish people.

In October 2014, in a move that is consistent with Erdoğan's behaviour towards those critical of his policies, Turkey's Security Council—with Erdoğan chairing—labeled the Gülen Movement as a national security threat[157]. The situation is further complicated for the U.S. by virtue of the fact that Gülen lives in Pennsylvania, and Erdoğan believes that he should be extradited[158]. In his September 2014 appearance at the Council on Foreign Relations in New York, Erdoğan described the situation:

> And we have expressed and explained this organisation to President Obama and others in the United States, because if we are model partners, if we have a strategic partnership, then—and since we deliver terrorists or anyone that the U.S. would want from us, we would expect the same in return. Somebody who is threatening national security in our country resides in Pennsylvania, and so, we ask that he be deported and that he be given to us. That's what befits a model partnership. I hope that the Turkish and the U.S. administrations will cooperate in fighting against this organisation, which constitutes a threat to both countries[159].

---

[156] *Introducing Fethullah Gülen*, FETHULLAH GÜLEN (8 Apr. 2010), http://fgulen. com/ en/fethullah-gulens-life/about-fethullah-gulen/introducing-fethullah-gulen.
[157] Ted Galen Carpenter, *Turkey: NATO's Loose Cannon*, CATO (18 Dec. 2014), http://www.cato.org/publications/commentary/turkey-natos-loose-cannon.
[158] Ilan Berman, *U.S.-Turkey Ties in Danger*, USA TODAY (13 May 2014), http:// www.usatoday.com/story/opinion/2014/05/13/us-turkey-obama-istanbul-forei gn-policy-column/8974009/.
[159] *Turkish President Erdoğan on ISIS*, *supra* note 30.

Of course, because Gülen operates out of Pennsylvania, the First Amendment protects his right to be critical of the Turkish government, and there are no grounds for his extradition. Even so, this disagreement over the right to criticise one's own government highlights just how far Erdoğan and the AKP have moved Turkey.

CONCLUSION

On paper, the U.S. and Turkey are allies in the War on Terror and through NATO. Leaders of both countries will publicly state that the alliance is of immense importance and as strong as ever. But, reality suggests something different. The Turkish people remain overwhelmingly cool to the U.S.[160] and evenly divided on the direction that Erdoğan has charted for their country[161]. Erdoğan's government seems to only be interested in an alliance with the U.S. if and when it is convenient. While this is fairly common within alliances, it leads one to question the future of the strategic relationship between the two countries.

If left wholly to their own preferences, many signs indicate that Erdoğan and the AKP would choose an Islamic authoritarian form of government. This preference presents a clear challenge to the future of the alliance between the U.S. and Turkey. The direction that Turkey ultimately chooses will not only have a significant impact on the future of the alliance, but also on the U.S.-led fight to quell and defeat Islamic terrorism.

---

[160] *Chapter 1: The American Brand*, PEW RESEARCH CTR. (14 July 2014), http://www. pewglobal.org/2014/07/14/chapter-1-the-american-brand.
[161] *Turks Divided on Erdoğan and the Country's Direction*, PEW RESEARCH CTR. (30 July 2014), http://www.pewglobal.org/2014/07/30/turks-divided-on-erdo-gan-and-the-countrys-direction.

TURKEY, CYPRUS, AND THE TURKISH REPUBLIC OF NORTHERN CYPRUS

MARSHALL H. GOLDMAN*

INTRODUCTION

Over the last one hundred years, extensive political changes have occurred, altering the territorial landscape in many parts of the world. Such changes have often been the result of civil wars, world wars, coups, or attempted coups. Turkey, Greece, and Cyprus faced such challenges, particularly with respect to their struggle over control of the northern and southern portions of the island of Cyprus. This struggle led to the self-declared state of the Turkish Republic of Northern Cyprus (TRNC) in the northern territory of the island.

*Mr Goldman is a Senior Research Associate of the Centre for the Study of Law & Public Policy at Oxford. He is also Senior Associate Counsel at the American Center for Law & Justice. Mr Goldman received his Bachelor of Arts (B.A.) degree (*cum laude*) from Oral Roberts University in Tulsa, Oklahoma; his Master of Arts in Public Policy (M.A.) degree from the Robertson School of Government at Regent University, Virginia Beach, Virginia (where he was the recipient of the Outstanding Research Award for distinction in scholarship); and his Juris Doctor (J.D.) degree from Regent University School of Law, Virginia Beach, Virginia.

The purpose of this paper is to provide the relevant context to the Cyprus question as well as to apply the Montevideo Convention criteria for statehood to determine whether the TRNC, at the time of its "inception", constituted a state under international law. Section I includes a brief history of Turkey following World Wars I and II. Section II discusses the recent history of Cyprus leading up to the creation of the TRNC in 1983. Section III examines the Montevideo Convention criteria for statehood as applied to the TRNC.

I. Turkey and Its National Interests

The Ottoman Empire was decisively defeated by the Allies in World War I. The 1920 Treaty of Sèvres was negotiated to end the conflict with the Ottoman Empire. This treaty "contained Allied wishes first, the wishes of Greece and Armenia second. Neither the needs of Turks nor the political and demographic realities of Turkey were considered. . ."[1]. The Treaty of Sèvres has been compared to the Treaty of Versailles as both "were punitive treaties, imposed by victors who adopted a high moral tone to hide self-interest. Both treaties contained economic clauses intended to ensure that the vanquished would never rise again. Both limited the military strength and territory of the loser. However, the Sèvres treaty was the harsher"[2]. Turkish leader Mustafa Kemal Atatürk strongly denounced the terms of this treaty[3].

---

[1] Justin McCarthy, The Ottoman Turks: An Introductory History to 1923, at 374 (1997).

[2] Id.

[3] See, e.g., A.E. Montgomery, The Making of the Treaty of Sèvres of 10 August 1920, 15 Hist. J. 775, 775 (1972) (explaining that the treaty was signed on 10 August 1920 but was never ratified. The success of Atatürk over the next two years rendered the projected peace terms obsolete, leading to the negotiation of an entirely new treaty: Lausanne).

The Treaty of Sèvres was negotiated with representatives of Farid Pasha, who was installed as vizier by Britain in March 1919. Atatürk mocked him as a "prisoner of the allies, rejecting his authority to negotiate on behalf of Turkey." Sèvres was signed by Pasha's proxies, Minister Resid Halis, Ambassador Hadi Pasha, Riza Tevfik, and Dama Ferid Pasha. Atatürk immediately denounced Sevres [because of its harsh terms], and

Atatürk did, however, agree to the terms of the 1923 Treaty of Lausanne which, in his view, was a great victory[4]. This treaty, which was signed by Great Britain, France, Italy, Japan, Greece, Romania, and the Serb-Croat-Slovene State on one side and Turkey on the other[5], delineated the boundaries of the modern state of Turkey[6]. For the Turks, the Treaty of Lausanne stood "as a milestone and validation of their continued national existence"[7].

Moreover, the establishment of Turkey as a state "crystallized the ideological orientation of the republican elite aimed at reshaping the state and its institutions on the basis of a secular model inspired by the West"[8]. Atatürk, the first President of modern Turkey, "introduced sweeping changes in Turkish society"[9].

used it to animate the War of Independence.
DAVID L. PHILLIPS, THE KURDISH SPRING: A NEW MAP OF THE MIDDLE EAST 7–8 (2015). In the Turkish War of Independence, Atatürk "mobilized his nation around a politico-military strategy of war that, in the final analysis, achieved an astounding success. Under his leadership, the Turkish people thwarted Britain, France, Italy, and Greece in their designs to impose a harsh treaty [i.e., the Treaty of Sèvres] on the defeated Ottoman Empire. . .". George W. Gawrych, *Kemal Atatürk's Politico-Military Strategy in the Turkish War of Independence, 1919–1922: From Guerrilla Warfare to the Decisive Battle*, 11 J. STRATEGIC STUD. 318, 318 (1988).
[4] Atatürk stated, "I don't think it is necessary any further to compare the principles underlying the Lausanne Peace Treaty with other proposals for peace. This treaty, is a document declaring that all efforts, prepared over centuries, and thought to have been accomplished through the SEVRES [sic] Treaty to crush the Turkish nation have been in vain. It is a diplomatic victory unheard of in the Ottoman history!" *Lausanne Peace Treaty*, REPUBLIC TURK. MINISTRY FOREIGN AFF., http://www.mfa. gov.tr/lausanne-peace-treaty.en.mfa (last visited 30 Mar. 2016).
[5] Treaty of Peace with Turkey, and Other Instruments, signed at Lausanne, pmbl., 24 July 1923, 28 L.N.T.S. 11, http://www.mfa.gov.tr/lausanne-peace-treaty----preamble.en.mfa.
[6] Helen Chapin Metz, ed., *Atatürk and the Turkish Nation*, in *Turkey: A Country Study*, U.S. LIBR. CONGRESS (1995), http://countrystudies.us/turkey/13.htm.
[7] TANER AKÇAM, FROM EMPIRE TO REPUBLIC: TURKISH NATIONALISM & THE ARMENIAN GENOCIDE 180 (2004).
[8] Talip Kucukcan, *State, Islam, and Religious Liberty in Modern Turkey: Reconfiguration of Religion in the Public Sphere*, 2003 BYU L. REV. 475, 485 (2003), http://digitalcommons.law.byu.edu/cgi/viewcontent.cgi?article=2156&context=lawreview.
[9] *Id.*

Atatürk's main aim in the process of modernization during the early years of the Turkish Republic was to change the basic structure of Turkish society and to redefine the political community. He tried to remove society from an Islamic framework and introduce society to a sense of belonging to a newly defined "Turkish nation." To achieve this goal, Atatürk launched a movement of cultural westernization to provide the Turkish nation with a new worldview that would replace its religious worldview and culture. Atatürk viewed the separation of religion and politics as a prerequisite to opening the doors to Western values[10].

Specifically, Atatürk sought to "establish an inherently capitalist nation-state based on the principle of popular sovereignty"; he also sought to encourage "loyalty to country—which was already beginning to overcome traditional loyalty to the sultanate during the National Struggle—into an intense Turkish nationalism, whether combined with the traditional bond of Muslim society or, preferably, replacing it; nationalism would be the Turks' rediscovery and reassertion of their Turkishness"; and he "aimed to educate individuals to undertake control of their own affairs, to stimulate a nationalist economy free from foreign dominance, and, significantly, to secularize the polity. . ."[11]. Further, "[i]n an ambitious drive to import European civilization, the republic disposed of the governing caliphate, the Arabic alphabet, [and] Islamic education. . ."[12]. Also, Turkey joined the League of Nations in 1932[13]; and in the late 1930s, for pragmatic reasons, Turkey "maintain[ed] a fully mobilised army"[14].

---

[10] *Id.* at 485–86 (citations omitted).

[11] M. Naim Turfan, *Atatürk, Mustafa Kemal*, OXFORD ISLAMIC STUDIES ONLINE, http://www.oxfordislamicstudies.com/article/opr/t236/e0083 (last visited 30 Mar. 2016).

[12] Ömer Taşpınar, *Turkey: the New Model?*, BROOKINGS INST. (Apr. 2012), http://www.brookings.edu/research/papers/2012/04/24-turkey-new-model-taspinar.

[13] DILEK BARLAS, ETATISM & DIPLOMACY IN TURKEY 127 (1998).

[14] JACOB M. LANDAU, ATATÜRK AND THE MODERNIZATION OF TURKEY 113 (1984).

During this period, Turkey's international policies were changing as well. With respect to Turkey's relationship with Greece, for example, the two states

> have rarely enjoyed good relations, and current tensions are fueled by historical grievances. Nevertheless, there was a brief period of cooperation between World Wars I and II. After the consolidation of Turkey's independence, Greece under President [sic] Venizelos and Turkey under Atatürk negotiated population transfers and property issues in an agreement that was further solidified with the signing of the Friendship Treaty in 1930. The treaty guaranteed the inviolability of their borders, marking what is considered the high point in Greek–Turkish relations. The situation soured at the time of World War II, however, when Greece became angered over Turkey's refusal to enter the conflict on the allied side, opting instead to remain neutral. Relations went downhill from there and have yet to recover[15].

The following provides further insight into Turkey's evolving strategic diplomatic relations. First, Turkey's exceptional geographic location enabled "her to have an influential voice in the foreign affairs arena, it also enable[d] her to attract strong friends"[16]. For example, "Turkey managed to manoeuvre herself into a position where she had a formal and explicit Treaty of Mutual Assistance with Great Britain as well as a Friendship and Non-Aggression Pact with Germany"[17]. Second, Turkey's strategic location was also a disadvantage because it made "it more difficult for Turkey to avoid confrontation with major powers"[18]. Third, and perhaps, most important for purposes of this paper, Turkey rec-

---

[15] Patricia Carley, *U.S. Foreign Policy and the Future of Greek-Turkish Relations*, 17 PEACEWORKS 1, 1 (1997), http://www.usip.org/sites/default/files/pwks17.pdf.

[16] SELIM DERINGIL, TURKISH FOREIGN POLICY DURING THE SECOND WORLD WAR: AN 'ACTIVE' NEUTRALITY 3 (1989).

[17] *Id.* at 1.

[18] *Id.* at 3.

ognised that a "small power ultimately stands or falls only according to the efficiency of its own resources"[19]. Turkey would "always be prepared to fight for the defence of her rights and territory"[20]. This third reality would eventually apply to Cyprus, as will be discussed below.

Following World War II, "Turkey took a resolutely pro-Western stance as the Cold War developed in the late 1940s. . ."[21]. In 1945, Turkey joined the United Nations[22], and in 1952, Turkey joined the North Atlantic Treaty Organization[23]. Also during the 1950s, the Cyprus question intensified primarily because of Greece's efforts to end British rule and unify the island with the Greek mainland[24].

In sum, the geopolitical climate in the twentieth century was changing, and Turkey was attempting to navigate its way through such changes. The next section focuses on similar issues with respect to Cyprus, beginning around World War I and concluding in 1983, the year in which the TRNC proclaimed itself to be a state. Both of these sections lead into Section III which looks at the Montevideo Convention criteria for statehood as applied to the TRNC.

II. The Cyprus Question

In this section, Cyprus's recent history is examined with special emphasis on how it relates to Turkey. Though this paper focuses primarily on Turkey's relationship with Cyprus, aspects of British and Greek history are interwoven in this article's analysis as well. With this in mind, the strategic location of Cyprus must first be addressed.

---

[19] *Id.* at 4.

[20] *Id.*

[21] Helen Chapin Metz, ed., *Turkey after Atatürk*, in *Turkey: A Country Study*, U.S. Libr. Congress (1995), http://countrystudies.us/turkey/15.htm.

[22] *Member States of the United Nations*, United Nations, http://www.un. org/en/members/index.shtml (last visited 30 Mar. 2016).

[23] Lawrence S. Kaplan, The United States and NATO: The Formative Years 219 (1984).

[24] Carter Vaughn Findley, Turkey, Islam, Nationalism, and Modernity: A History (2010).

Cyprus "is on the sea lane of the great maritime highway connecting the Mediterranean Sea through two sea gates–the Suez and Bab al-Mandab–with the Indian Ocean"[25]. It links to "the Strait of Hormuz, leading to the Persian Gulf, and the Strait of Malacca, connecting to the Pacific"[26]. Cyprus is only 3,572 square miles in size[27]. Turkey "lies just forty miles from its northern coast. To the east, Syria is only seventy-five miles away. . . . Mainland Greece lies approximately five hundred miles west"[28]. Cyprus "has been regarded as vital territory by almost every empire that has wished to assert control over the wider Eastern Mediterranean region"[29]. A brief recent history of Cyprus follows.

In 1878, Great Britain took administrative control of Cyprus from Turkey[30]. In 1914, Great Britain completely annexed Cyprus[31]. In 1915, Great Britain offered to cede Cyprus to Greece "if Greece were to join her in the war, but as Greece did not join until 1917, Britain did not grant Greece's request, made at the Versailles negotiations in 1919. . ."[32]. In fact, under the terms of the 1923 Treaty of Lausanne, Turkey "formally ceded Cyprus to Britain, which declared it a Crown Colony in 1925"[33]. Turkey "supported British rule of the island as the best guarantee that the position of the Turkish Cypriots would be secure from the Greek threat of Enosis"[34]. Enosis refers to Greece's desire

---

[25] James Leigh & Predrag Vukovic, *A Geopolitics of Cyprus*, 15 MERIA J., no. 4 (Dec. 2011), http:// www.gloria-center.org/2011/12/a-geopolitics-of-cyprus/. Bāb al-Mandab is the name of the straight between Arabia and Africa that connects the Red Sea with the Gulf of Aden and the Indian Ocean.

[26] *Id.*

[27] James Ker-Lindsay, Britain and the Cyprus Crisis, 1963–1964, at 8 (2004), http://www.academia.edu/199221/Britain_and_the_Cyprus_Crisis_1963–1964.

[28] *Id.*

[29] *Id.*

[30] Ian Hendry & Susan Dickson, British Overseas Territories Law 340 (2011).

[31] *Id.*

[32] William Mallinson, Cyprus: A Modern History 11 (2005) (footnote omitted).

[33] *Id.*

[34] Bestami Sadi Bilgiç, *The Cyprus Crisis of October 1931 and Greece's Reaction: The Place of Turkey and Turkish Cypriots in the Eyes of Greek and Greek Cypriot Leadership*, 1 Rev. Int'l L. & Pol., Ankara, no 2, 91, 92 (2005), http://www.usak.

for "the union of Cyprus with Greece"[35].

Greek and Turkish Cypriots[36] were not satisfied with the arrangement with Britain as Greek Cypriots wanted Enosis and Turkish Cypriots were considering partition[37]. In 1931, "riots broke out on the island against the British regime"[38] following (and, perhaps, as a consequence of) the Metropolitan of Kytion's Proclamation which emphasised the Greek Cypriot desire for Enosis[39]. By the end of October 1931, "order was restored almost completely over the island. The leaders of the rebellion were arrested and deported"[40].

The Metropolitan's proclamation and the resulting riots revealed that "the Cyprus question was seen in Greece as a matter among Greece, Greek Cypriots and Britain. There was almost no mention about Turkey or Turkish interests on the island"[41]. But the fact that the Turkish Cypriots did not support the British position did not mean that they supported the union of the island with Greece. "Every time the Greek Cypriot dignitaries submitted to the British authorities their demands for *enosis*, petitions by the leaders of the Turkish Cypriot

---

org.tr/dosyalar/dergi/pBh18Jh1jTQkEneYC2XdYTOmpbnIzk.pdf (footnote omitted).

[35] *Cyprus in the Period 1571–1959*, REPUBLIC TURK. MINISTRY FOREIGN AFF., http://www.mfa.gov.tr/cyprus-in-the-period-1571---1959.en.mfa (last visited 30 Mar. 2016).

[36] Turkish Cypriots are ethnic Turks living in or originating from Cyprus. *See Policy Towards Turkish Cypriots*, EMBASSY REPUBLIC CYPRUS WASH. D.C., http://www.cyprusembassy.net/home/index.php?module=page&pid=23 (last visited 30 Mar. 2016). Greek Cypriots are a separate ethnicity. *See Cyprus Ethnicity*, LIBR. CONGRESS COUNTRY STUD. (Jan. 1991), http://lcweb2.loc.gov/ cgi-bin/query/r?frd/cstdy:@field(DOCID+cy0053).

[37] *Independence*, BBC NEWS, http://news.bbc.co.uk/2/shared/spl/hi/europe/04/cyprus/html/independence.stm (last visited 30 Mar. 2016).

[38] Bilgiç, *supra* note 34, at 95.

[39] *Id.* at 96 (Ambassador Skinner wrote: "During this dark period of fifty years we have let no opportunity pass of proclaiming our sacred desire to be united to Mother Greece, an inspiration which England was the first to recognize as just and sacred when in 1915 she offered Cyprus to the Hellenic Government of that time".).

[40] *Id.* at 97.

[41] *Id.* at 100.

community countered these"[42].

The years leading up to World War II "were quieter, with the British and Greeks in Cyprus retreating into their respective social and mental compartments"[43]. The end of World War II, however, "brought renewed and more widespread demands for enosis, in Greece . . ."[44]. Also, in 1946, "the British government announced plans to liberalize the colonial administration of Cyprus and to invite Cypriots to form a Consultative Assembly for the purpose of discussing a new constitution"[45]. The Church of Cyprus was not satisfied, "and twenty-two Greek Cypriots declined to appear, stating that enosis was their sole political aim"[46]. The British proposals "did not come near fulfilling the expectations and aspirations of the Greek Cypriots. The idea of 'enosis and only enosis' became even more attractive to the general population"[47].

Matters in Cyprus became even more strained in the 1950s. In 1950, "more than 95% of the indigenous Greek population voted in favour of the Union (Enosis) of the island with Greece, demanding that the people of Cyprus be allowed to exercise their right to self-determination; however, the British colonial Government rejected the Greek position"[48]. In August of 1954, "Greece's UN representative formally requested that self-determination for the people of Cyprus be included on the agenda of the General Assembly's next session. That request was seconded by a petition to the secretary general from Archbishop Ma-

---

[42] *Id.* at 101.

[43] MALLINSON, *supra* note 32, at 11 (footnote omitted).

[44] *Id.*

[45] Eric Solsten, ed. *World War II and Postwar Nationalism*, in *Cyprus: A Country Study*, U.S. LIBR. CONGRESS (1991) [hereinafter Solsten, *World War II*], http://countrystudies.us/cyprus/10.htm.

[46] *Id.*

[47] *Id.*

[48] Achilles C. Emilianides, *The Cyprus Questions before the House of Commons: 1954-1955*, in GREAT POWER POLITICS IN CYPRUS: FOREIGN INTERVENTIONS AND DOMESTIC PERCEPTIONS 11, 13 (Michalis Kontos, et al., eds. 2014), http://www.cambridgescholars.com/download/sample/58990 (footnote omitted).

karios"[49]. Turkey, however, "rejected the idea of the union of Cyprus and Greece; its UN representative maintained that 'the people of Cyprus were no more Greek than the territory itself'"[50].

In 1955, when their demands for self-determination were not addressed[51], the Greek Cypriots "embarked upon a militant struggle to free the country from colonial rule. . . . Turkey's declared policy toward Cyprus, which had until the early fifties been one of support toward the colonial status quo, began to shift toward a policy of partition of the island along ethnic lines"[52]. In November 1956, Professor Nihad Erim submitted a confidential memo to Turkish Prime Minister Menderes, "proposing the geographical division of the island coupled with the transfer of populations. This straightforward proposal for ethnic cleansing would result in the formation of two separate political entities, one Greek and one Turkish, each of which would then proceed to political union with Greece and Turkey respectively"[53]. This memo "formed the basis of Ankara's policy for the next twenty years"[54]. Erim believed that partition was "the 'second best solution', provided that, in his assessment, Turkey could not achieve, through political means, repossession of the whole of Cyprus"[55].

Such rising tensions between Turkey, Greece, and Great Britain are further explained in the following way:

> The shift of events toward partition was the outcome of a
> complex, multifaceted process. It was connected with Turkey's
> 'pre-emptive defence' strategy aimed at preventing *enosis*, in

---

[49] Solsten, *World War II*, *supra* note 45.

[50] *Id.*

[51] *Historical Review*, Ministry Foreign Aff. Republic Cyprus, http://www. mfa. gov.cy/mfa/mfa2006.nsf/ cyprus01_en/cyprus01_en?OpenDocument (last updated 15 Jan. 2008).

[52] *Id.*

[53] *Id.*

[54] *Id.*

[55] Chrysostomos Pericleous, The Cyprus Referendum: A Divided Island and the Challenge of the Annan Plan 147 (2009) (footnote omitted).

some respects an undercover of expansionist ambitions to take control of Cyprus in the event of Britain's withdrawal. It was also connected with an internal nationalist pressure in Turkey and the demagogic exploitation of nationalism by the Menderes government. It was also further connected with Britain's tactical manoeuvring intended as a counterweight to the *enosis* movement. It was finally, and perhaps more significantly, the ultimate outcome of unyielding *enosis* targeting by the Greek Cypriot leadership, which tended to ignore the existence of the Turkish Cypriot community and failed to realize and realistically assess the dangers posed by Turkey's determination to foil *enosis*[56].

These tensions led to a meeting in Zurich, Switzerland, on 11 February 1959 with representatives from Great Britain, Greece, and Turkey to discuss a plan for Cyprus's independence[57]. Following the Zurich meeting, various leaders met on 19 February 1959 in London, England, where a final agreement was reached with Turkey, Greece, Great Britain, and the Greek and Turkish Cypriots[58]. The London Agreement "essentially incorporated and finalized the Zurich Agreement of 1959 [and] created the Republic of Cyprus as an independent state. . ."[59]. These agreements "provided for a presidential republic with a Greek president and a Turkish vice president. . ."[60]. The newly elected president was Archbishop Makarios, and the newly elected vice-president was Dr Fazil Küçük[61].

---

[56] *Id.* at 148–49 (footnote omitted).

[57] John Milios & Tasos Kypriandis, *Greek and Greek-Cypriot Political Strategies on Independence: Class, Nation, and Statehood, in* BEYOND A DIVIDED CYPRUS: A STATE AND SOCIETY IN TRANSFORMATION 99, 112 (Nicos Trimikliniotis & Umut Bozkurt eds., 2012).

[58] *Id.*

[59] HARALAMBOS ATHANASOPULOS, GREECE, TURKEY, AND THE AEGEAN SEA 19 (2001).

[60] Milios & Kypriandis, *supra* note 57.

[61] Eric Solsten, ed. *The Republic of Cyprus, in Cyprus: A Country Study*, U.S. LIBR. CONGRESS (1991) [hereinafter Solsten, *Republic*], http://countrystudies.us/ cyprus/12.htm.

Three important treaties, the Treaty of Establishment[62], the Treaty of Guarantee[63], and the Treaty of Alliance[64], were also negotiated. The Treaty of Establishment designated Cyprus's sovereign territory, among other rights and protections[65]. In the Treaty of Guarantee, Greece, Turkey, and the United Kingdom agreed to "recognise and guarantee the independence" of Cyprus, but continued to hold the authority to consult and take action to restore the *status quo*[66]. In this respect, Article II reads, in part, "Greece, Turkey and the United Kingdom likewise undertake to prohibit, so far as concerns them, any activity aimed at promoting, directly or indirectly, either union of Cyprus with any other State or partition of the Island"[67]. The Treaty of Alliance provided for the defence of Cyprus in the event of an attack or aggression[68]. Within this treaty, Article II reads, "[t]he High Contracting Parties undertake to resist any attack or aggression, direct or indirect, directed against the independence or the territorial integrity of the Republic of Cyprus"[69].

Despite the adoption of the three treaties, on November 30, 1963, "Makarios advanced a thirteen-point proposal designed, in his view, to eliminate impediments to the functioning of the government. The thirteen points involved constitutional revisions, including the aban-

[62] Treaty Concerning the Establishment of the Republic of Cyprus (Treaty of Nicosia), 16 Aug. 1960, 382 U.N.T.S. 8, No. 5476, http://peacemaker. un.org/sites/peacemaker.un.org/files/CY_600816_Treaty Nicosia.pdf [hereinafter Treaty of Establishment].

[63] Treaty of Guarantee, 16 Aug. 1960, 382 U.N.T.S. 3, No. 5475, http:// peacemaker.un.org/sites/peacemaker.un.org/files/CY%20GR%20TR_600816_Treaty%20of%20Guarantee.pdf.

[64] Treaty of Alliance (with Additional Protocols), 16 Aug. 1960, 397 U.N.T.S. 289, No. 5712, http://peacemaker.un.org/sites/peacemaker.un.org/files/CY%20 GR%20TR_600816_Treaty%20of%20Allianc%20(with%20additionnal%20protocols).pdf [hereinafter Treaty of Alliance].

[65] Treaty of Establishment, *supra* note 62.

[66] Treaty of Guarantee, *supra* note 63, art. 2, 4 (The clause reads in pertinent part, "In so far as common or concerted action may not prove possible, each of the three guaranteeing powers reserves the right to take action with the sole aim of re-establishing the state of affairs created by the present Treaty".).

[67] *Id.* art. 2.

[68] *See* Treaty of Alliance, *supra* note 64, art. 2.

[69] *Id.*

donment of the veto power by both the president and the vice president. . ."[70]. On December 16, Turkey rejected it, "declaring the proposal an attempt to undermine the constitution"[71]. As a "consequence of the ensuing standoff, the Turkish Cypriot ministers withdrew from the Council of Ministers, and Turkish Cypriot civil servants ceased attending their offices"[72]. Immediately following such action by the Turkish Cypriots, "there was a marked heightening of tensions on the island. . . . Two days later, fighting finally broke out between the Greek and Turkish Cypriots"[73].

It quickly became clear that outside peacekeeping assistance was necessary. In January of 1964, UN Secretary General U Thant "sent a special representative to the island. After receiving a firsthand report in February, the Security Council authorized a peace-keeping force under the direction of the secretary general. Advance units reached Cyprus in March, and by May the United Nations Peace-keeping Force in Cyprus (UNFICYP) totaled about 6,500 troops"[74]. Also in March of 1964, the UN Security Council (UNSC) adopted Resolution 186, which requested that the Cypriot government "take all additional measures necessary to stop violence and bloodshed in Cyprus"[75].

The Greek Cypriots and Turkish Cypriots responded in different ways to the presence of the UN forces and UNSC Resolution 186. The Greek Cypriot leaders set forth that the "establishment of UNFICYP by the UN Security Council had set aside the rights of intervention

---

[70] Solsten, *Republic, supra* note 61.

[71] *Id.*

[72] *History of Cyprus*, HIGH COMMISSION REPUBLIC CYPRUS CANBERRA, http://www. mfa.gov.cy/mfa/highcom/highcomcanberra.nsf/cyprus02_en/cyprus02_en?OpenDocument (last visited 30 Mar. 2016).

[73] KER-LINDSAY, *supra* note 27, at 23.

[74] Eric Solsten, ed., *Intercommunal Violence*, in *Cyprus: A Country Study*, U.S. LIBR. CONGRESS (1991) [hereinafter Solsten, *Intercommunal Violence*], http://countrystudies. us/cyprus/13.htm.

[75] S.C. Res. 186, para. 2, U.N. SCOR, 19th Year, U.N. Doc. S/INF/19, at 2–4 (4 Mar. 1964), http://www.un.org/en/ga/search/view_doc.asp?symbol=S/RES/186 (1964).

granted to the guarantor powers—Britain, Greece, and Turkey—by the Treaty of Guarantee. The Turkish leadership, on the other hand, contended that the Security Council action had reinforced the provisions of the treaty"[76].

Problems in the region continued when, in April of 1967, "a military junta seized power in Greece"[77] due to the "failure of both the Monarch and the caretaker governments. . ."[78]. President Makarios' relationship with Greece's new regime "was tense from the outset and became increasingly strained. President Makarios made it known that he was convinced that the Athens junta was involved in efforts to undermine his authority and policies through extremist underground organizations in Cyprus conspiring against his government and against his life"[79]. His instincts proved to be correct.

On 15 July 1974, "the Greek military junta and its Greek Cypriot collaborators carried out a coup against" President Makarios in Cyprus[80]. In response, Turkish Prime Minister Ecevit declared that Turkey would not "permit anyone to intervene in the rights of the Cypriot Turks"[81] and issued the following statement: "The coup in Cyprus is a Greek intervention in Cyprus. The constitutional system in Cyprus was destroyed and an illegal military government was established. Turkey considers this act a violation of international agreements and guarantees on Cyprus"[82].

---

[76] Solsten, *Intercommunal Violence, supra* note 74.

[77] Tom Housden, *Cyprus: How the Crisis Unfolded*, BBC News (1 Apr. 2004, 10:06 AM), http://news.bbc.co.uk/2/hi/europe/1760565.stm.

[78] Christos Kassimeris, *Causes of the 1967 Greek Coup*, 3, Routledge, https://www.researchgate.net/publication/250893576_Causes_of_the_1967_Greek_Coup (originally published in 2 Democracy & Security 1 (2006)).

[79] *The 1974 Turkish Invasion and its Consequences*, Press and Info. Off., Republic of Cyprus (Dec. 2010), http://www.moi.gov.cy/moi/pio/pio.nsf/All/6F5DD418DD053ED1C2256D6D001E7571?OpenDocument.

[80] *Id.*

[81] Nasuh Uslu, The Cyprus Question as an Issue of Turkish Foreign Policy and Turkish-American Relations 1959-2003, at 124 (2003) (footnote omitted).

[82] *Id.* at 124–25 (footnote omitted).

On 20 July 1974 and 14 August 1974, the Turkish military intervened relying on "Article IV of the Treaty of Guarantee of 1960"[83]. Greece believed that the Turkish intervention, particularly the intervention in August of 1974, exceeded the scope of the Treaty of Guarantee in that it "was undertaken when the Greek junta, which had engineered the coup in Cyprus, had collapsed, the Cyprus constitutional order had been re-established and negotiations were pending in Geneva between Greece, Turkey, and the United Kingdom"[84]. The UNSC was similarly concerned as evidenced by Resolution 353, adopted on 20 July 1974, which called "upon all States to respect the sovereignty, independence and territorial integrity of Cyprus"[85].

On 16 August 1974, Turkish forces declared a ceasefire after "they had secured 37 percent of the island"[86]. They also decided to maintain about "35,000 Turkish troops . . . in the north"[87]. A comprehensive agreement between the Greek and Turkish Cypriots could not be reached[88]. As such, *"in the absence of a formal cease-fire agreement,* the military *status quo,* as recorded by UNFICYP at the time, became the standard by which it was judged whether any changes constituted

---

[83] *Historical Background*, TURKISH REPUBLIC N. CYPRUS MINISTRY FOREIGN AFF., http://mfa.gov.ct.tr/cyprus-negotiation-process/historical-background/ (last visited 30 Mar. 2016); *see also* Treaty of Guarantee, *supra* note 63, art. 4 ("In so far as common or concerted action may not prove possible, each the three guaranteeing Powers reserves the right to take action with the sole aim of re-establishing the state of affairs created by the present Treaty".).

[84] Gillian M. White, *The Turkish Federated State of Cyprus: A Lawyer's View*, 37 WORLD TODAY 135, 137 (1981), http://www.jstor.org/stable/40395280.

[85] S.C. Res. 353, para. 1, U.N. SCOR, 29th Year, U.N. Doc. S/INF/30, at 7 (20 July 1974), http://www.un.org/en/ga/search/view_doc.asp?symbol=S/RES/353 (1974).

[86] *Special Research Report No. 3: Cyprus: New Hope after 45 Years on the Security Council Agenda*, SECURITY COUNCIL REPORT (4 Sept. 2008), http://www.security-councilreport.org/special-research-report/lookup-c-glKWLeMTIsG-b-4474149. php [hereinafter *Cyprus: New Hope*]; *see also UNFICYP Background*, UNFICYP UNITED NATIONS PEACEKEEPING FORCE IN CYPRUS, http://www.un.org/en/peacekeeping/missions/unficyp/background.shtml (last visited 30 Mar. 2016); SATISH CHANDRA & MALA CHANDRA, INTERNATIONAL CONFLICTS AND PEACE MAKING PROCESS: ROLE OF THE UNITED NATIONS 284 (2006).

[87] *Cyprus: New Hope, supra* note 86.

[88] *Id.*

violations of the cease-fire"[89].

On 13 February 1975, the Turkish Federated State of Cyprus (TFSC) was "proclaimed . . . by the Council of Ministers and the Legislative Assembly of the Turkish Cypriot Administration"[90]. This proclamation "was intended to serve as a bargaining chip in negotiating a higher degree of autonomy for the Turkish Cypriot community, but subsequent negotiations under UN auspices were unsuccessful"[91]. The TFSC "failed to secure even a limited degree of international acceptance and [was] consequentially hampered in its efforts to promote the economic and political interests of the Turkish Cypriot community"[92].

Following several years of minimal progress, on 15 November 1983, Turkish Cypriot leaders issued a unilateral declaration of independence and "the TFSC was dissolved and replaced by the Turkish Republic of Northern Cyprus (TRNC)"[93]. The declaration was issued by the Turkish Cypriot parliament and described why the Turkish Cypriot leaders made such a decision[94]. The 1983 Turkish Cypriot declaration of independence was the culmination of decades of conflict from external as well as internal forces (and is a contributing factor to the conflict even at the time of this article)[95]. With this background

---

[89] *See* Chandra & Chandra, *supra* note 86, at 286 (emphasis added). This is relevant with respect to whether the TRNC has a defined territory under the Montevideo Convention criteria to be discussed in the following section.

[90] White, *supra* note 84, at 135.

[91] Yaël Ronen, Transition from Illegal Regimes under International Law 63 (2011).

[92] White, *supra* note 84, at 139.

[93] Ronen, *supra* note 91.

[94] *Id.* Such reasons included the following: "the usurpation of the legislature, executive and judiciary by Greek Cypriots; the domination and exploitation of Turkish Cypriots by their Greek Cypriot compatriots; and the discrimination to which Turkish Cypriots were subject". *Id.*

[95] The 1983 Turkish Cypriot declaration of independence complicated long-term peace efforts.

> [S]uccessive initiatives throughout the 1980s and 1990s failed to produce any results. This was largely due to the intransigence of the Turkish Cypriot leadership and successive Turkish governments. . . . However, towards the end of the 1990s, the situation changed dramatically after the

in mind, Section III addresses whether the TRNC satisfied the four Montevideo Convention criteria for statehood when it proclaimed itself to be a state in 1983.

III. THE MONTEVIDEO CONVENTION CRITERIA AS APPLIED TO THE TRNC

The Montevideo Convention on the Rights and Duties of States (1933) contains the "best known formulation of the basic criteria for statehood"[96], and these criteria are considered to reflect the requirements for statehood under customary international law[97]. Article 1 of

European Union decided to open accession talks with the Cypriot government. . . . Realizing that any decision to accept Cyprus would inevitably harm its own accession process, Turkey threatened to annex northern Cyprus. Undeterred, the EU insisted that it would not give Ankara a veto over who could and could not become a member. . . . [F]ollowing a general election in Turkey in November 2002, which brought to power a more moderate government, attitudes in Ankara began to change. . . . On 24 April, 2004, the two communities voted on the proposals. . . . [I]t was rejected by three-quarters of the Greek Cypriot community. Just one week later, on 1 May 2004, Cyprus joined the EU as a divided island. In 2008, the UN launched a fresh initiative. . . . [but] they failed to make an early breakthrough. . . . [A]t the end of 2011, [Turkey] called for a 'Taiwan-style' diplomatic arrangement for Northern Cyprus to help ends it isolation and further the ailing talks.

JAMES KER-LINDSAY, THE FOREIGN POLICY OF COUNTER SECESSION: PREVENTING THE RECOGNITION OF CONTESTED STATES 42–43 (2012) (citation omitted). More strongly stated, the "breakaway state in northern Cyprus not only is not an independent State founded as an expression of the right of self-determination of the Turkish Cypriot People, but rather it is the result of a secessionist act that has created a Turkish local administration in northern Cyprus". NIKOS SKOUTARIS, THE CYPRUS ISSUE: THE FOUR FREEDOMS IN A MEMBER STATE UNDER SIEGE 29–30 (2011).

[96] James Crawford, *The Criteria for Statehood in International Law*, 48 BRIT. Y.B. INT'L L. 93, 111 (1976–1977); *see also* Convention on Rights and Duties of States art. 1, 26 Dec. 1933, 49 Stat. 3097, http://avalon.law.yale.edu/ 20th_century/intam03.asp.

[97] *See, e.g.*, JOSHUA CASTELLINO, INTERNATIONAL LAW AND SELF-DETERMINATION 77 (2000) (citing D.J. HARRIS, CASES AND MATERIALS OF INTERNATIONAL LAW 102 (5th ed. 1997)) ("The Montevideo Convention is considered to be reflecting, in general terms, the requirements of statehood in customary international law".); Tzu-wen Lee, *The International Legal Status of the Republic of China on Taiwan*, 1 UCLA J. INT'L L. & FOREIGN AFF. 351, 387 n.70 (1996–1997) ("[The Montevideo] Con-

the Montevideo Convention established the following four prerequisites to statehood: "(a) a permanent population; (b) a defined territory; (c) government; and (d) capacity to enter into relations with other states"[98]. "At the crux of the Montevideo criteria lay the concepts of effectiveness, population, and territoriality"[99].

The four criteria focus on whether "an entity [becomes] a state, not with how an entity might cease to be a state"[100]. These criteria "only matter at the initial stage, when a self-determination-seeking entity is seeking to attain statehood. . ."[101]. If non-state entities "became states and then lost their label of statehood due to a territorial dispute, the lack of government, a migratory shift in population, or the inability to conduct foreign relations in some manner, the end result would consist of endless chaos and violence"[102]. Clearly then, "statehood matters at the time of state *creation*; it no longer matters during state *existence*, absent

vention is regarded as representing in general terms the criteria of statehood under customary international law").

Customary international law is made up of rules that come from "a general practice accepted as law" and that exist independent of treaty law. Customary international humanitarian law (IHL) is of crucial importance in today's armed conflicts because it fills gaps left by treaty law in both international and non-international conflicts and so strengthens the protection offered to victims.

International law comes from both treaty law and rules of what is known as customary international law. Treaties are written conventions in which States formally establish certain rules. Customary international law, on the other hand, is not written but derives from "a general practice accepted as law". To prove that a certain rule is customary, one has to show that it is reflected in state practice and that the international community believes that such practice is required as a matter of law.

Customary International Humanitarian Law, INT'L COMMITTEE RED CROSS (29 Dec. 2010), https://www.icrc.org/eng/war-and-law/treaties-customary-law/ customary -law/overview-customary-law.htm.

[98] Crawford, *supra* note 96, at 111 (citation omitted).

[99] Thomas D. Grant, *Defining Statehood: the Montevideo Convention and its Discontents*, 37 COLUM. J. TRANSNAT'L L. 403, 416 (1999).

[100] *Id.* at 435.

[101] MILENA STERIO, THE RIGHT TO SELF-DETERMINATION UNDER INTERNATIONAL LAW: "SELFISTANS," SECESSION, AND THE RULE OF THE GREAT POWERS 47 (2013).

[102] *Id.*

truly exceptional circumstances"[103]. Also, these criteria "are found not to prescribe specific rights, powers or liberties which all States must, to be States, possess; rather they are presumptions as to the existence of such rights, powers or liberties. . ."[104].

Lastly, as the *In re Citizenship of X* case demonstrates, "artificially creating the Montevideo factors" is not sufficient for statehood[105]. In this case, a British army officer took possession of a former anti-aircraft platform, proclaimed it the "Duchy of Sealand"[106], and designated himself as the "Roy of Sealand"[107]. The plaintiff, who was a German citizen by birth and who held the positions of "Foreign Secretary and Chairman of the Council of State of the 'Duchy'"[108], sought a determination on his citizenship. In this regard, he "was notified that he had not lost his German citizenship because the 'Duchy of Sealand' *did not constitute a State within the meaning of international law*"[109]. He then challenged this decision arguing that the Duchy of Sealand was, in fact, a state[110]. The Administrative Court of Cologne did not agree and held that "to constitute a state under international law three essential attributes had to be present: territory, population, and government [and] [t]he Duchy of Sealand lacked at least two of these"[111].

With respect to territory, the Administrative Court reasoned that the former anti-aircraft platform was "not situated on any fixed point of the surface of the earth. . . . The preponderant view of legal writers is that only a part of the surface of the earth can be regarded as State territory"[112]. Therefore, the man-made artificial platform (i.e., the "Duchy

---

[103] *Id.*

[104] Crawford, *supra* note 96, at 110.

[105] Christopher L. Blakesley et. al., The International Legal System: Cases and Materials 188 (2001).

[106] Monroe Leigh, *Judicial Decisions*, 77 Am. J. Int'l L. 144, 160 (1983).

[107] VG, 3 May 1978, 9 K 2565/77, http://www.uniset.ca/naty/80ILR683.htm.

[108] *Id.*

[109] *Id.* (emphasis added).

[110] *Id.*

[111] Leigh, *supra* note 106, at 161.

[112] VG, 3 May 1978, 9 K 2565/77, http://www.uniset.ca/naty/80ILR683.htm.

of Sealand"), "cannot be called either a 'part of the earth's surface' or 'land territory' because it does not constitute a segment of the earth's surface"[113].

With respect to a State's people, the Administrative Court explained that the State "complements the family . . . and has the duty to promote community life"[114]. This duty "must be aimed at the maintenance of an essentially permanent form of communal life in the sense of sharing a common destiny"[115]. The court further reasoned that a community "must play a more decisive role in serving the other vital human needs of people . . . includ[ing] education and professional training, assistance in all the eventualities of life and the provision of subsistence allowances where necessary"[116]. In the court's view, the "nationals" of the "Duchy of Sealand" failed to satisfy the population requirement necessary for statehood as well[117]. As such, this case demonstrates that statehood criteria analysis must be legally and factually based and not based on artificial creations of the law. With these background points in mind, a look at the Montevideo Convention criteria as applied to the TRNC follows.

A.   DID THE TRNC POSSESS A PERMANENT POPULATION?

Arguably, there was a permanent population in northern Cyprus and the fact that there were fewer than 100,000 Turkish Cypriots in 1983 would not have changed this[118]. Some states "exist with rather few inhabitants, e.g., Tuvalu and Nauru (about 12,000 and 10,000 inhabitants, respectively). So far, in no case has statehood been denied on the

---

[113] *Id.*

[114] *Id.*

[115] *Id.*

[116] *Id.*

[117] *Id.*

[118] FRANK HOFFMEISTER, LEGAL ASPECTS OF THE CYPRUS PROBLEM: ANNAN PLAN AND EU ACCESSION 50 (2006).

grounds of the small number of people"[119]. Also, the population "does not have to be homogeneous racially, ethnically, tribally, religiously, linguistically, or otherwise. But, it must be a settled population . . ."[120], and it should be "more or less stable"[121].

In the instant matter, following Turkey's 1974 Cyprus intervention, more than 200,000 Greek and Turkish Cypriots were transferred to the north and south of the island respectively which "resulted in the all-but-complete separation of the two rival communities"[122]. "By mid-1975, the bulk of the Turkish Cypriot population scattered throughout Cyprus had been transferred north. . ."[123]. By 1983, the Turkish Cypriot population was relatively stable. The TRNC, therefore, likely would have satisfied the first Montevideo Convention criterion for statehood.

Despite this reasoning, one could argue that there was not a permanent population in the TRNC because of the questionable way in which the population transfers were handled following Turkey's 1974 intervention[124]. Greek leaders "regularly complained that the Turkish military intervention in 1974 caused the displacement of 200,000 Greek Cypriots and resulted in 1,600 Greek Cypriot missing"[125] (though the validity of such numbers has been questioned[126]). Greeks and Greek Cypriots alike claimed that the Turkish intervention "resulted in ethnic cleansing and eventually de facto partition"[127]. None-

---

[119] Ruth Lapidoth, *When Is an Entity Entitled to Statehood?*, 6 ISR. J. FOREIGN AFF. 77, 78 (2012), http://www.israelcfr.com/documents/6-3/6-3-5-Ruth Lapidoth.pdf.

[120] ANTHONY AUST, HANDBOOK OF INTERNATIONAL LAW 15–16 (2d ed. 2010).

[121] Lapidoth, *supra* note 119, at 78.

[122] EYAL BENVENISTI, THE INTERNATIONAL LAW OF OCCUPATION 192 (2d ed. 2012).

[123] ANDREW BOROWIEC, CYPRUS: A TROUBLED ISLAND 2 (2000).

[124] "Both the displacement of Greek Cypriot inhabitants of the area of Cyprus occupied by Turkey and the transfer into this area of Turks from Turkey are acts which are forbidden by" Article 49, par. 6 of the Geneva Conventions. LOUKIS G. LOUCAIDES, ESSAYS ON THE DEVELOPING LAW OF HUMAN RIGHTS 118 (1995).

[125] ADEL SAFTY, THE CYPRUS QUESTION: DIPLOMACY AND INTERNATIONAL LAW 246 (2011).

[126] *Id.*

[127] Barry Bartmann, *Political Realities and Legal Anomalies: Revisiting the Politics of International Recognition, in* DE FACTO STATES: THE QUEST FOR SOVEREIGNTY

theless, the TRNC likely still would have satisfied the first Montevideo Convention criterion for the initial reasons set forth[128].

B. Did the TRNC Have a Defined Territory?

The TRNC likely would have satisfied the second criterion for statehood, which is that the state must have a defined territory. In the *Island of Palmas* case, the Permanent Court of Arbitration noted that, "[t]erritorial sovereignty involves the exclusive right to display the activities of a State"[129]. In another sense, the "potential state has to have

---

12, 25 (Tozun Bahcheli et al. eds., 2004).

[128] As a brief aside, the question of implantation of settlers is an ongoing issue for the TRNC, Turkey, and Greece. A December 2013 article, for example, commented that the TRNC "has been accused of artificially increasing the number of TRNC citizens by readily granting citizenship to mainly peasant Turkish mainlanders, thus altering the demographics in the North". *No repatriation of TRNC citizens: Eroglu*, LGC News (12 Dec. 2013), http:// www.lgcnews.com/repatriation-trnc-citizens-eroglu/. Tied to this issue is the issue of repatriation. Though these two issues are beyond the scope of this paper, the following question is included for further discussion:

> The question arises, whether the process of Turkish settlement may finally result in *faits accomplis*, which may confer legal rights on the settlers and their recognition as part of the Cypriot population; or alternatively, whether these *faits accomplis* may constitute legal grounds which will prevent compulsory repatriation of the settlers. In this respect it may be argued that the stay of the settlers in Cyprus for a long time, their intermingling with the Cypriot population, the creation by them of families and descendants, possibly also through marriages between them and the local Cypriot population, their settlement in houses and properties and their professional and family stabilization in Cyprus will on humanitarian grounds prevent their expulsion. The argument may also be put forward that the settlers' stay in Cyprus for many years and the factual situations that such stay entails may result in their acquiring certain human rights that would prevent their expulsion in spite of the fact that their original entry and the continuation of their stay was against the will of the lawful Government of Cyprus and contrary to the Laws of the Republic of Cyprus.

Loucaides, *supra* note 124, at 113.

[129] The Island of Palmas (U.S. v. Neth.), Hague Ct. Rep. 2d (Scott) 83 (Perm. Ct. Arb. 1928), *reprinted in Judicial Decisions Involving Questions of International Law*, 22 Am. J. Int'l L. 867, 867 (1928); Crawford, *supra* note 96, at 111.

a more or less defined area—'a consistent band of territory'"[130]. The size of the territory should not matter[131].

The following three points must also be noted. First, the definitive "establishment of a new State on certain territory defeats claims by other States which relate to the whole of the territory so occupied; and where the claims relate to part only of the territory, makes them dependent for settlement on the consent of the new State"[132]. Second, a new "State may exist despite claims to its territory, just as an existing State continues despite such claims"[133]. Third, "the State must consist of a certain coherent territory *effectively governed*"[134].

With respect to the Cyprus matter, if the 1974 Turkish intervention was viewed as illegal, then the resulting self-proclaimed TRNC could similarly be viewed as illegal. One could argue that no "territorial acquisition or special advantages obtained by the illicit use of force" should be recognised as legal[135]. Other states would, therefore, be under a duty not to recognise the TRNC as a state[136]. But this conclusion depends, in part, on the premise that "the Turkish action was illegal, a matter which is less clear than some have admitted. . ."[137].

Northern and southern Cyprus is currently divided by the 'Green Line' which "was first established in 1964, when Major-General Peter Young was the commander of a 'peace force', a predecessor of the

---

[130] Lapidoth, *supra* note 119 (citations omitted).

[131] AUST, *supra* note 120, at 16.

[132] Crawford, *supra* note 96, at 112 (footnote omitted).

[133] *Id.* (footnote omitted).

[134] *Id.* at 114 (emphasis added).

[135] Stefan Talmon, *The Duty Not to 'Recognize as Lawful' a Situation Created by the Illegal Use of Force or Other Serious Breaches of a Jus Cogens Obligation: An Obligation without Real Substance?*, *in* THE FUNDAMENTAL RULES OF THE INTERNATIONAL LEGAL ORDER: JUS COGENS AND OBLIGATIONS ERGA OMNES 99, 109 (Christian Tomuschat & Jean Marc Thouvenin eds., 2006) (citing U.N. Doc. A/7326, p. 41, para. 111, item 7), http://users.ox.ac.uk/~sann2029/6.% 20Talmon%2099-126.pdf.

[136] White, *supra* note 84, at 138.

[137] *Id.*

present UNFICYP"[138]. Since 1974, "Cyprus has been divided into a Turkish-Cypriot northern region and a Greek-Cypriot southern region. . . . UNFICYP is responsible for [the area] that separates the two sides. . ."[139]. The zone (i.e., the Green Line), "extends approximately 180 [kilometers] across the island. In some parts of old Nicosia it is only a few meters wide. In other places it is a few kilometers wide. . . . Its northern and southern limits are the lines where the belligerents stood following the ceasefire of 16 August 1974. . ."[140]. "UNFICYP maintains the *status quo* (including innocent civilian activity and the exercise of property rights) without prejudice to an eventual political settlement concerning the disposition of the area"[141]. Despite several unsuccessful attempts by the UN to resolve such issues within Cyprus[142], UNFICYP essentially became a "*de facto* partition"[143].

In this regard,

> the Turkish Cypriot territorial claim, although not strong from a legal perspective, is based on two main factors. One of them is the belief that since the Greek and Turkish Cypriots cannot live together peacefully, in order to ensure their communal safety, the Turkish Cypriots require a separate territory of their own. The second claim, which is more logical, is that the Turkish Cypriots, although illegitimate and not recognized [by any state except Turkey], have had their own separate territory in the northern part of the island since 1974. Thus, the extent of territory that they control has remained constant for more

---

[138] *Green Line - Crossing Points Regulations*, Republic Cyprus Customs & Excise Dep't, http://www.mof.gov.cy/mof/customs/customs.nsf/All/05AEEF 243C9BFC-8BC22572BF002D0A28?OpenDocument (last updated 15 Apr. 2014).

[139] *About the Buffer Zone*, United Nations Peacekeeping Force Cyprus, http://unficyp.unmissions.org/about-buffer-zone (last visited 30 Mar. 2016).

[140] *Id.*

[141] Chandra & Chandra, *supra* note 86, at 286 (emphasis added).

[142] Etain Tannam, International Intervention in Ethnic Conflict: A Comparison of the European Union and the United Nations 88 (2014).

[143] *Id.* (citing Oliver P. Richmond, Mediating in Cyprus: The Cypriot Communities and the United Nations 103 (1998)).

than [40] years now. Similarly, its existence in this sense was recognized with the 1974 Geneva Agreement, signed by the Foreign Ministers of Greece, Turkey and the UK in the period between the two Turkish invasions, which noted the *"existence in practice in the Republic of Cyprus of two autonomous administrations, that of the Greek Cypriot community and that of the Turkish Cypriot community"*[144].

The question then is whether the 'Green Line' was a sufficient boundary such that the TRNC would have satisfied the territorial requirement for statehood.

Not surprisingly, each interested party offers a different perspective. Turkey, for example, is the only state to recognise the TRNC[145], and, as such, "has shown continuous support for the autonomous existence of the Turkish Cypriots"[146]. In 2002, former Turkish leader Mesut Yilmaz reconfirmed Turkey's view that "there exist[s] two different nations and two sovereign states in the island. . ."[147]. Turkey and the Turkish Cypriots contend that the 1974 Turkish military response was necessary and lawful to protect the Turkish Cypriot community in response to the unstable political climate in both Greece and Cyprus at the time:

> From the perspective of the Turkish Cypriot community, the Turkish intervention of 1974, coming after the crisis that erupted in the island, was not an illegal intervention because it is based on Article 4 of the Treaty of Guarantee under

---

[144] Cansu Akgün, *The Case of TRNC in the Context of Recognition of States Under International Law*, 3 ANKARA BAR REV. 7, 14 (2010), http://www. ankarabarosu. org.tr/siteler/AnkaraBarReview/tekmakale/2010-1/1.pdf (emphasis added) (footnotes omitted).

[145] DAVID RAIČ, STATEHOOD AND THE LAW OF SELF-DETERMINATION 122 (2002).

[146] George Kyris, *The European Union, Turkey, and the Cyprus Problem: the Failure of a Catalyst, in* TURKEY AND THE EUROPEAN UNION: FACING NEW CHALLENGES AND OPPORTUNITIES 11, 14 (Firat Cengiz & Lars Hoffmann eds., 2013).

[147] *Id.* at 15.

which Turkey, as one of the guarantor powers, had a right and obligation to intervene, reestablish the *status quo* and protect the Turkish Cypriots. Therefore, they argue that the Turkish intervention was in response to prior Greek interventions[148].

The TRNC would likely submit that it had territorial sovereignty in northern Cyprus, at least to the extent necessary to satisfy this aspect of the Montevideo Convention criteria.

Greece, in contrast to the Turkish position, argues that,

as [to] the illegal Turkish invasion in July 1974 and the occupation, since then, of some 37% of the territory of the Republic of Cyprus, it is a classic case of an international problem of the invasion and occupation by foreign forces of territory of a UN and EU member-state, in direct violation of the UN Charter and a plethora of UN Security Council resolutions.

Turkey refuses to withdraw its illegal occupation force from Cyprus; a force which, according to Turkish statements, consist[s] of some 43,000 Turkish troops[149].

The Greek Cypriot view aligns with Greece with respect to the territorial question as evident by the following governmental statement: "The political situation in the occupied area of Cyprus, which is not under the effective control of the Government of the Republic of Cyprus, is dominated by the presence of the Turkish occupation forces, the Turkish mainland settlers and the overwhelming influence of Ankara"[150].

Also, the international community, in 1983, did not and still has

---

[148] Akgün, *supra* note 144, at 16 (footnote omitted).

[149] *The Cyprus Issue*, HELLENIC REPUBLIC MINISTRY FOREIGN AFF., http:// www.mfa. gr/en/the-cyprus-issue/ (last visited 30 Mar. 2016).

[150] *Political Situation in the Occupied Areas*, MINISTRY FOREIGN AFF. REPUBLIC CYPRUS (Aug. 2007), http://www.mfa.gov.cy/mfa/mfa2006.nsf/cyprus08_en/ cyprus08_en?OpenDocument (last updated 11 Feb. 2011).

not recognised the TRNC as an independent state. Nevertheless, since the 'Green Line' has acted as a *de facto* partition of the island since at least 1974, the TRNC could have satisfied the second criterion for statehood.

C. DID THE TRNC HAVE AN EFFECTIVE GOVERNMENT?

The TRNC likely would have satisfied the third Montevideo Convention criterion for statehood which is that a state must have an effective government. Interestingly, "international law defines 'territory' . . . by reference to the extent of governmental power exercised, or capable of being exercised, with respect to some territory and population"[151]. The "point about 'government' is that it has two aspects: the actual exercise of authority, and the right or title to exercise that authority"[152]. Though this second aspect may not have helped the TRNC with respect to satisfying the third criterion, it should not be definitive either, as the analysis seems to focus on a government's *effectiveness*. Also, "the existence of a system of government, in and referable to, a specific territory indicates without more a certain legal status, and is in general a precondition for statehood. Continuity of government in a territory is one factor determining continuity of the State concerned. . ."[153] (to this point, the Palestinian Authority, for example, has lacked actual and consistent rule for decades)[154].

The effectiveness of the TRNC government must, therefore, be examined. As set forth in the TRNC constitution, the government is a "secular republic based on the principles of democracy" and sovereignty is vested in the TRNC citizens[155]. The legislative power is vested in the

---

[151] Crawford, *supra* note 96, at 116.

[152] *Id.* at 117.

[153] *Id.* at 118–19.

[154] Israel retains responsibilities and jurisdiction over Israeli settlements that are within what is widely referred to as "Palestinian territories", although Israel insists that such territories are "disputed". Israel retains control over external security. The parties agreed that they still must negotiate Palestinian borders.

[155] Constitution of the Turkish Republic of Northern Cyprus, 5 May 1985, pt. I, arts.

"Assembly of the Republic on behalf of" the TRNC people, executive powers are "carried out and exercised by the President of the Republic and the Council of Ministers . . .", and the judicial powers are "exercised on behalf of the people of the Turkish Republic of Northern Cyprus by independent courts"[156]. Such a framework would seem to indicate that the TRNC government is effective.

> [F]rom an internal perspective, the TRNC has a government which in practice is able to exercise effective and exclusive control of its own territory and has a constitution which grants its citizens an extensive range of civil and political liberties. According to Article 1 of the TRNC Constitution, the state is a secular republic based on the principles of democracy and the supremacy of law. In terms of its governing capability, the TRNC clearly meets or exceeds any plausible criteria for effective governance. Although the TRNC officials who are active in the decision-making process consult closely with their Turkish counterparts on a number of matters, and despite the fact that the TRNC has kept adapting economic policies in its history in line with Turkish direction or control in important matters, in broader terms it does maintain effective territorial control of a given area over which it provides governance services and has sovereign authority with democratic structures[157].

However, the extent of Turkish control over the northern portion of the island must also be considered. In 1984, for example, "Turkey provided two-thirds of its budget. Militarily it had full control since 1974, with some 40,000 troops stationed there, while in terms of communication it has been the only route to the outside world for northern Cyprus because of the international boycott of the TRNC"[158].

1, 3, http://www1.umn.edu/humanrts/research/cyprus-constitution.html.

[156] *Id.* arts. 4, 5, 6.

[157] Akgün, *supra* note 144, at 14–15 (footnotes omitted).

[158] Farid Mirbagheri, Cyprus and International Peacemaking 141 (1998)

The *Loizidou* case[159], though a dispute about property rights, offers an insightful discussion about whether Turkey or the TRNC control northern Cyprus. In this case, the Cypriot government (i.e., the Republic of Cyprus) set forth that "Turkey is in effective military and political control of northern Cyprus"[160]. In contrast to the Greek Cypriot position, Turkey emphasised that the TRNC

> is a democratic and constitutional State which is politically independent of all other sovereign States including Turkey. The administration in northern Cyprus has been set up by the Turkish Cypriot people in the exercise of its right to self-determination and not by Turkey. Moreover, the Turkish forces in northern Cyprus are there for the protection of the Turkish Cypriots and with the consent of the ruling authority of the

(footnote omitted). As recently as 2008, Turkey provided about one-third of the TRNC's budget. CENT. INTELLIGENCE AGENCY, THE CIA WORLD FACTBOOK 2010 184 (2009). Though this would indicate that Turkey now has less control over the TRNC's budget, control in this context (i.e., whether an entity has an effective government) is determined at the initial stage when an entity is seeking to be recognised as a state. With respect to current troop levels, as recently as December 2015, about 35,000 Turkish troops were stationed on the island. Ben Wright, *Cyprus May Be Small, But Its Reunification Could Have Huge Global Ramifications*, THE TELEGRAPH (Dec. 14, 2015), http://www. telegraph.co.uk/finance/economics/12050149/Cyprus-may-be-small-but-its-reunification-could-have-huge-global-ramifications.html.

[159] Loizidou v. Turkey, 1996-VI Eur. Ct. H.R. 2216, http://hudoc.echr.coe. int/sites/eng/pages/search.aspx?i=001-58007. The applicant, Mrs Titina Loizidou, was a Cypriot national. *Id.* at para. 11. She grew up in Kyrenia in northern Cyprus, where she claimed to own certain plots of land. *Id.* at paras. 11–12. In 1972, she got married and moved to Nicosia. *Id.* at para. 11. She also claimed that she was no longer able to return to her property due to the Turkish forces on the island following the 1974 Turkish intervention. *Id.* at para. 12. According to the Turkish Government, she had lost ownership on or about 7 May 1985 as a result of the operation of Article 159 of the TRNC Constitution. *Id.* at para. 18, 30. The Court held that because the international community does not regard the TRNC as a State under international law, the Court could not "attribute legal validity for purposes of the Convention to such provisions as Article 159" of the TRNC Constitution. *Id.* at paras. 36, 44. Therefore, Mrs Loizidou could not be "deemed to have lost title to her property as a result of Article 159 . . .". *Id.* at para. 46.

[160] *Id.* at para. 50; *see also* OLIVIER DE SCHUTTER, INTERNATIONAL HUMAN RIGHTS LAW: CASES, MATERIALS, COMMENTARY 151 (2d ed., 2014).

"TRNC". Neither the Turkish forces nor the Turkish government in any way exercise governmental authority in northern Cyprus. Furthermore, in assessing the independence of the "TRNC" it must also be borne in mind that there are political parties as well as democratic elections in northern Cyprus and that the Constitution was drafted by a constituent assembly and adopted by way of referendum[161].

The European Court of Human Rights, the court before which the *Loizidou* case was brought, ultimately decided that the property at issue in northern Cyprus was a matter which fell "within Turkey's 'jurisdiction'"[162]. Though the facts and outcome of this case exceed the scope of this paper, the arguments presented, particularly by Turkey, are worth considering with respect to whether the TRNC had an effective government.

Despite the question of the TRNC's right to exercise its authority, and despite the *Loizidou* court's decision, the TRNC, arguably, would have satisfied the third Montevideo Convention criterion for statehood since the TRNC had an operational constitution and a functioning and *effective* government.

D. Did the TRNC Have the Capacity to Enter Relations with Other States?

The TRNC would not have satisfied the fourth criterion for statehood as the following discussion will show. With respect to the capacity to enter relations with other states, capacity "depends partly

---

[161] Loizidou v. Turkey, 1996-VI Eur. Ct. H.R. 2216, at para. 51.
[162] *Id.* at para. 57.
> It is obvious from the large number of troops engaged in active duties in northern Cyprus . . . that her army exercises effective overall control over that part of the island. Such control, according to the relevant test and in the circumstances of the case, entails her responsibility for the policies and actions of the "TRNC". . . .

Id. at para. 56.

on the power of internal government of a territory, without which
international obligations may not be carried into effect, and partly on
the entity concerned being separate for the purpose of international
relations so that no other entity both carries out and accepts responsibility for them"[163].

Turkey's relationship with the TRNC will be addressed first. Turkey is the only state that recognises the TRNC's sovereignty[164], and, as
such, "is with no doubt the most important supporter of the TRNC in
every field. . ."[165]. For example,

> [t]he Embassy of the Republic of Turkey in Lefkoşa and the
> Embassy of the TRNC in Ankara, together with its Consul-
> ate-General in İstanbul and the Consulates in İzmir and Mer-
> sin undertake the usual diplomatic and bureaucratic relations
> of their countries. . . .

> Many protocols have been signed between the TRNC and the
> Republic of Turkey to regulate the existing trade and economic
> relations. The Trade and Payment Protocol was the first to be
> signed among these documents in 1975. This Protocol was
> signed with the aim of strenghtening [sic] the economic and
> trade relations between the two countries. The Protocol also
> aimed at solving the import and export problems faced by the
> TRNC in cooperation with Turkey. . . .

> In 1997, the formation of a Partnership Council between the
> TRNC and Turkey on economic and financial matters was
> decided. The Council also aimed to work on cooperation in
> the fields of security, defence and foreign policy[166].

---

[163] JAMES R. CRAWFORD, THE CREATION OF STATES IN INTERNATIONAL LAW 62 (2007).
[164] RAIČ, *supra* note 145, at 25.
[165] *Relations with Turkey*, TURKISH REPUBLIC N. CYPRUS MINISTRY FOREIGN AFF., http://mfa.gov.ct.tr/foreign-policy/relations-with-turkey/ (last visited 30 Mar. 2016).
[166] *Id.*

Therefore, the TRNC had the capacity to and does, in fact, engage in international relations with Turkey.

Britain's relationship with the TRNC is not nearly as strong.

One may take into account that the British Government in parliamentary statements regularly refers to 'Turkish Cypriot authorities'. The British Government's opinion on the legal status of the Turkish Cypriot authorities may also be manifested in the nature of the relations with these authorities. For example, . . . [t]he British Government has presented claims for compensating for loss and damage suffered by British citizens during the fighting in 1974 to the Turkish Cypriot authorities, has maintained a general informal dialogue with them through the British High Commission in Nicosia, and has maintained a 'residual presence' of the British High Commission in the Turkish sector of Nicosia. . . . On the other hand, the British Government does not recognize travel documents issued by the Turkish Cypriot authorities and does not endorse them with entrance clearances[167].

Such acts are likely not sufficient to conclude that the TRNC and the British engage in foreign relations.

The TRNC's *inability* to engage in foreign relations is more pronounced with respect to most other states.

States regard northern Cyprus as either a territory occupied by Turkey and/or a territory under the control of a Turkish Cypriot local *de facto* government. As a consequence of the nonrecognition of their state, Turkish Cypriots are to a large extent politically and economically isolated. There are no direct flight connections or postal links with northern Cyprus,

---

[167] STEFAN TALMON, RECOGNITION OF GOVERNMENTS IN INTERNATIONAL LAW: WITH PARTICULAR REFERENCE TO GOVERNMENTS IN EXILE 31–32 (1998) (citations omitted).

Turkish Cypriots are banned from taking part in international sporting events, they are denied access to the international financial markets, they cannot export agricultural products to the European Union and even some divorce decrees by Turkish Cypriot courts are not recognised[168].

Moreover, the TRNC's Foreign Ministry

is a relatively unimportant ministry, primarily because the TRNC lacks international recognition. Likewise, its various 'diplomatic missions' abroad are of limited value. In fact, many of the TRNC 'embassies' are registered as companies, and 'diplomats' are often provided temporary business related visas by host countries. . . . The Foreign Ministry was also sidelined because the Cyprus Problem has been formally negotiated through the President's office. Thus, the ministry does not play an autonomous role in policy development or implementation[169].

Clearly, the TRNC's capacity to engage in international relations has been stifled by most states.

Also, three days after the Turkish Cypriots unanimously proclaimed the TRNC to be an independent state, the UNSC adopted Resolution 541, which stated that "the attempt to create a 'Turkish Republic of Northern Cyprus' [was] invalid"[170]. In May of 1984, in UNSC Resolution 550, the Council repeated its earlier call in Resolution 541 for all states not to recognise the "purported State of the

---

[168] Stefan Talmon, *Air Traffic with Non-Recognised States: the Case of Northern Cyprus*, U. Oxford, 1 http://users.ox.ac.uk/~sann2029/FCO_Paper% 20by%20 Dr%20Stefan%20Talmon.pdf (citation omitted) (last visited 30 Mar. 2016).

[169] Erol Kaymak, *The Development of Turkish Cypriot Politics*, *in* The Government and Politics of Cyprus 231, 239 (James Ker-Lindsay & Hubert Faustmann eds., 2008) (footnotes omitted).

[170] S.C. Res. 541, U.N. SCOR, 38th Year, U.N. Doc. S/INF/39, at 15–16 (18 Nov. 1983), http://www.un.org/en/ga/search/view_doc.asp?symbol=S/RES/541(1983).

Turkish Republic of Northern Cyprus"[171]. In addition to such UN resolutions, the independence of the TRNC was "rejected by the Committee of Ministers of the Council of Europe, the European Communities, and the Commonwealth Heads of Government"[172]. From a practical view, therefore, the TRNC's ability to engage in international relations was virtually non-existent. As such, the TRNC would have failed to satisfy the fourth Montevideo criterion for statehood.

CONCLUSION

In the twentieth century, extensive political changes occurred, altering the territorial landscape in various parts of the world. Turkey's relationship with Cyprus and Greece demonstrates how these changes are difficult to navigate. Despite such challenges, President Erdogan's recent victory in Turkey and the island's current unification efforts, led by Nicos Anastasiades, President of the Greek Cypriot community, and Mustafa Akinci, President of the Turkish Cypriot community, suggest that the north and south may be closer to settling these matters[173].

The way in which the Greek Cypriots are responding to Greece's fi-

---

[171] Raič, *supra* note 145, at 124; *see* S.C. Res. 550, para. 3, U.N. SCOR, 39th Year, U.N. Doc. S/INF/40, at 12–13 (11 May 1984), http://www.un.org/en/ ga/search/ view_doc.asp?symbol=S/RES/550(1984).

[172] Raič, *supra* note 145, at 124–25 (footnotes omitted).

[173] Though President Erdoğan may be considered authoritarian, his recent victory could benefit Cyprus since he has "repeatedly spoken of the need for a solution, expressing frustration over Turkish Cypriots' secular ways and the cost of bankrolling their mini-state". Helena Smith, *Time for Cyprus's Reunification Has Come – But Erdogan Holds the Key,* Guardian (30 Oct. 2015, 7:16 AM), http://www.theguardian.com/world/2015/oct/30/cyprus-reunification-erdogan-economic-gains-settlement-election-turkey. Moreover, because of Nicos Anastasiades, President of the Greek Cypriot community, and Mustafa Akinci, President of the Turkish Cypriot community, "Cyprus has politicians determined to end its ethnic partition". *Id.* The two sides have made progress, for example, "on how to share power in a future decentralized Cypriot state, on the nature of its legislative and judicial institutions and on the political equality of the two communities. . .". *See also* Tony Barber, *Cyprus: Crossing the Divide,* Financial Times (25 Jan. 2016, 7:09 PM), http://www.ft.com/cms/s/0/083fa076-bf91-11e5-846f-79b0e3d20eaf.html#axzz42zYyqXfx.

nancial problems may also demonstrate that Cyprus is learning from its past, at least regarding financial matters. "In early 2013, Cyprus's massively unbalanced banking sector collapsed, as foreign capital fled and left much of the financial sector insolvent. . . . In March 2013, Cyprus received a $13 billion bailout that required the country's largest bank, Laiki, to close, forcing heavy losses on wealthy depositors"[174]. Cyprus, though, "has been largely diligent in implementing reforms required in return for an international bailout it received in 2013", and "wants to reverse a perception that the two countries [Cyprus and Greece] are inextricably linked. . ."[175].

The TRNC is still navigating through challenging waters. As explained herein, in 1983, the TRNC would not have satisfied all four Montevideo Convention criteria necessary for statehood. With respect to a permanent population, there was a permanent population in northern Cyprus when the TRNC was declared due to the island's partition following the 1974 Turkish intervention. With respect to a defined territory, since the 'Green Line' has acted as a *de facto* partition of the island since 1974, the TRNC likely would have satisfied the second criterion for statehood. With respect to a government, the TRNC did have a government which operated effectively. Finally, though the TRNC may have had the *capacity* to enter relations with other states, the reality was that all states, other than Turkey, would not engage the TRNC. As such, the fourth criterion for statehood would not have been satisfied.

Currently, the TRNC is entangled in the Syrian refugee crisis and has been affected by fallout from the Arab Spring, as well.

---

[174] Christopher Alessi & James McBride, *The Eurozone in Crisis*, COUNCIL ON FOREIGN REL. (11 Feb. 2015), http://www.cfr.org/eu/eurozone-crisis/p22055.

[175] John O'Donnell & Michele Kambas, *Cyprus Seeks Distance from Greek Euro Drama*, REUTERS (11 Mar. 2015), http://www.reuters.com/article/eurozone-greece-cyprus-idUSL5N0WC44Q20150311; *see also* Holly Ellyatt, *That Was Quick! Cyprus Exits Bailout with Cash to Spare*, CNBC (8 Mar. 2016, 1:51 AM), http://www.cnbc.com/2016/03/08/that-was-quick-cyprus-exits-bailout-with-cash-to-spare.html.

While Lebanon and Turkey are often cited as nations hosting the maximum number of Syrian refugees from the ongoing civil war there, followed by Jordan, Iraq and Egypt in that order; the Turkish Republic of Northern Cyprus is playing a significant role in their transit to safety. . . . Northern Cyprus has also been hit hard by the widespread violence in the region from Libya to Iraq in the aftermath of the so-called Arab Spring and the advent of the Islamic State extremist group[176].

In sum, both internationally recognised and aspiring states face challenges that require a delicate balance between their self-interests and international engagement. In light of the foregoing, when one considers other states and entities struggling to resolve similar statehood issues, the Montevideo Convention criteria as applied to the TRNC offers a unique perspective and sheds light on this complex and fact-driven issue.

---

[176] Abhishek G. Bhaya, *Mideast Violence, Refugee Crisis Take a Toll on Northern Cyprus*, TURKISH REPUBLIC OF NORTHERN CYPRUS: MINISTRY OF FOREIGN AFF. (4 Mar. 2015), http://mfa.gov.ct.tr/mideast-violence-refugee-crisis-take-a-toll-on-northern-cyprus-2/. The TRNC is working closely with the United Nations High Commissioner for Refugees "to provide the necessary facilitation to the refugees who apply to seek refuge" there. *Regarding the Refugee Issue*, TURKISH REPUBLIC OF NORTHERN CYPRUS: MINISTRY OF FOREIGN AFF. (22 Sept. 2015), http://mfa.gov.ct.tr/press-statement-on-the-refugee-issue/.

L'Église catholique et l'Anatolie (The Catholic Church and Anatolia)

Abstract: The special relationship between the Catholic Church and Anatolia, now Turkey, can be explained by the common and turbulent history of these two entities. Rome and Constantinople were two capitals of the Roman Empire. Nonetheless, Anatolia has gradually moved away from Rome although the Catholic Church has strengthened its authority from the tomb of Peter. Wars, religious quarrels and invasions have created a difficult and unstable relationship. Efforts, however, have been made to re-establish a closer union with the Orthodox denominations, but no attempt has succeeded in completely healing the rifts. Relations between Catholic Rome and Anatolia have had—and continue to have—an undeniable international importance because of the location and power of Anatolia. This state relationship has also led to much suffering for Turkish Catholics, as they are still subject to local power, without the possibility of a real "appeal to the Pope". Beyond the situation of Christians and Catholics in Anatolia, relations between Rome and Anatolia still determine, to a large extent, the relationship between Turkey and Europe. The political process of re-Islamisation of Turkey and its current neo-Ottoman discourse tends to give fundamental importance to the religious dimension of the relationship between Turkey and Europe.

This article is being published in French in order to emphasize the international scope and influence of the Centre.

Grégor Puppinck is the director of the European Centre for Law & Justice, an international affiliate of the American Center for Law & Justice. His contribution represents the Centre's recognition that our understanding of international policy can only be advanced through cross-border collaboration with individuals who share our values.

L'ÉGLISE CATHOLIQUE ET L'ANATOLIE

GRÉGOR PUPPINCK
ANDREEA POPESCU
CHRISTOPHE FOLTZENLOGEL*

INTRODUCTION

L'Anatolie, avant d'être occupée par la République de Turquie fut autrefois le cœur de l'Empire romain d'orient puis de l'Empire byzantin et enfin de l'Empire ottoman.

Pour comprendre la situation actuelle de l'Église catholique en Turquie et de sa relation avec le Patriarcat Oecuménique de Constan-

*Grégor Puppinck est directeur du Centre européen pour le droit et la justice (ECLJ), une organisation non gouvernementale agissant auprès des institutions européennes, en particulier auprès de la Cour européenne des droits de l'homme et de l'Organisation des Nations-Unies. L'ECLJ a participé à de nombreuses affaires jugées par la Cour européenne en matière notamment de liberté de religion. Grégor Puppinck est également expert auprès du Conseil de l'Europe. Diplômé de l'Université de Paris II-Assas et de l'Institut des Hautes Etudes Internationales (IHEI), il est titulaire d'un doctorat en droit pour une thèse portant sur le processus de formation de la norme bioéthique. Il a enseigné aux facultés de droit de Mulhouse et de Strasbourg. Il est l'auteur de nombreux articles et de plusieurs ouvrages dans le domaine des droits de l'homme. Il est aussi Senior Fellow de l'Centre for the Study of Law & Public Policy at Oxford. Andreea Popescu est une avocate roumaine, ancienne juriste à la Cour européenne des droits de l'homme et à l'ECLJ. Christophe Foltzenlogel est diplômé de la Faculté de droit de Strasbourg où il s'est spécialisé en droit de l'humanitaire et en droits de l'homme, il est juriste en charge des recherches à l'ECLJ.

tinople, il faut faire un détour par l'histoire de ce que furent les deux moitiés d'un même Empire romain et d'une même Église.

Ces deux moitiés d'empire ont connu un destin opposé : la terre de l'Église d'Orient, avec le long maintien de l'Empire d'Orient, a été vaincue par les musulmans, tandis que l'Église d'Occident, avec la chute de l'Empire d'Occident, a bâti l'Europe et survit à la modernité.

En 1920 il y avait encore deux millions de chrétiens en Turquie ; ils ne sont plus que 68 600 aujourd'hui, à l'exclusion des migrants et représentent 0,1% de la population.

Depuis la seconde moitié du XXème siècle, les relations entre la Turquie et l'Église catholique sont entrées dans une nouvelle phase : après mille ans d'absence, les papes multiplient leurs visites en Anatolie à l'invitation du Patriarche Œcuménique de Constantinople et du gouvernement turque. Ces visites résultent, du côté catholique, d'une double orientation du Second Concile du Vatican en faveur d'un rapprochement avec les autres confessions chrétiennes et de l'ouverture d'un dialogue avec les religions non chrétiennes.

Du côté du Bosphore, ces invitations s'inscrivent d'une part dans un contexte de très grande faiblesse d'une Église de Constantinople réduite à quelques milliers de fidèles, et d'autre part dans le désir du gouvernement turc d'intégrer l'Union européenne. Enfin, l'OTAN a également intérêt à arrimer durablement la Turquie au bloc européen pour des motifs de sécurité, de même que l'Union européenne pour des motifs économiques. De nombreux intérêts convergent ainsi en faveur de la pacification des relations entre Rome et Istanbul ; la réunion de ces deux centres géopolitiques dans un même ensemble politique serait une tentative de refondation de l'ancien Empire. Bien qu'elle ait un fondement historique très ancien, constitué en réalité de plus d'inimitiés que d'amitiés, cette réunion se heurte néanmoins à la faiblesse de ses fondations culturelles. L'union autrefois entre Rome et Constantinople était religieuse et culturelle. A présent, malgré sa laïcité officielle, la société turque a rejeté le christianisme et son gouvernement se détourne de la culture occidentale.

Les relations entre les confessions chrétiennes revêtent un intérêt ecclésial et eschatologique, mais aussi géopolitique. Un intérêt ecclésial d'abord, car l'unité de l'Église est une demande du Christ et un témoignage. Ces relations ont aussi un intérêt géopolitique. Ainsi par exemple, le maintien de l'unité entre les patriarcats de Rome et de Constantinople aurait permis de mieux contrer l'invasion turque, de même que la division de l'Église sur la péninsule ibérique avait favorisé l'invasion maure. Actuellement encore, les relations entre églises et entre ces deux pôles géopolitiques continuent d'influencer la configuration politique du continent européen. Ainsi, la position du Saint Siège à l'égard de l'adhésion de la Turquie à l'Union européenne a une influence politique et symbolique, et donc fondamentale, sur cette question d'importance majeure.

Aujourd'hui, l'Europe est de nouveau confrontée à une question turque, pour plusieurs raisons : son poids démographique, sa puissance économique, l'importance et le nationalisme de sa population immigrée en Europe, sa résilience culturelle, sa réislamisation, sa prétention impériale. Le gouvernement de la Turquie actuelle prétend s'affirmer, une nouvelle fois, comme « une autre Rome », comme une Rome islamique, « leader » de l'espace musulman s'étendant des confins chinois turcophones à l'extrémité occidentale de la méditerranée. Ankara se prend à rêver de succéder à Byzance, à Constantinople et à Istanbul.

Alors que le destin des deux pôles de l'ancien Empire est définitivement lié, leurs orientations paraissent actuellement radicalement opposées.

I. DE LA DIVISION DE L'ÉGLISE À SA DOMINATION PAR LES OTTOMANS

A. Rome et Constantinople : une Lente Séparation

1. La lente préparation du schisme de 1054

Si le schisme a eu lieu en 1054 après Jésus-Christ, embrasant la relation entre Rome et Constantinople, cette séparation entérinait seulement une division grandissante depuis des siècles entre les évêques de l'Est et de l'Ouest[1].

Après la conquête de l'Anatolie par l'Empire romain, le règne de l'Empereur Auguste a été synonyme d'une relative période de paix et de prospérité, permettant au christianisme de se répandre. Des persécutions avaient lieu, mais d'après la Tradition, Saint Jean se retira à Ephèse pour écrire le quatrième Evangile, en présence de Marie, ce qui a donné une grande importance religieuse à la région.

A la fin du IIIème siècle, Dioclétien a séparé l'Empire en deux pour des raisons politiques et administratives, et d'après certains pour contenir le Christianisme[2]. De toute évidence, si tel était l'un de ses objectifs, il échoua puisque Constantin gagna la guerre civile qui avait été la conséquence de cette séparation en 284 et se convertit. L'ambition de Constantin était de construire une « Nouvelle Rome » sur l'ancienne citée grecque de Byzance, appelée par la suite Constantinople[3]. A la fin du IVème siècle, l'Empire était chrétien mais les deux villes de Rome et Constantinople étaient prêtes pour la compétition.

La déclaration de la primauté de l'évêque de Rome a rapidement posé problème. Alors que la liturgie orthodoxe reconnait la primauté de Saint Pierre, l'évêque de Constantinople la conteste[4]. D'après les or-

---

[1] Steven Runciman, *Le Schisme d'Orient, la papauté et les Églises d'Orient XI-XII*ème *siècles*, Les Belles Lettres, Paris, 2005.

[2] Paul Allard, *La persécution de Dioclétien et le triomphe de l'Église,* Librairie Victor Lecoffre, vol. 1, p.16. Affirmation basée principalement sur la grande persécution de 303 à 311 sous le règne de Dioclétien.

[3] Pierre Maraval, Le Christianisme de Constantin à la conquête arabe, Presses Universitaires de France, Paris, 1997, p. 9.

[4] Joseph de Maistre, Œuvres du Comte J. de Maistre, A. Montrouge, Du Pape, 1ère

thodoxes[5], aucun sens « excessif » ne devrait être donné à cette affirmation ni à la revendication de la prédominance de Saint-Pierre parmi les apôtres, parce que les cinq grands patriarcats de Rome, Constantinople, Alexandrie, Antioche et Jérusalem[6], devraient être dans l'unité et aucun ne serait supérieur aux autres.

Au Concile œcuménique de Constantinople, en 381 après J-C, les Pères du concile ont déclaré que « l'évêque *de Constantinople supplantera l'évêque de Rome, Constantinople étant la nouvelle Rome* ». Cependant, l'Empereur Théodose, qui a convoqué ce Concile n'a pas invité l'Evêque de Rome. Plus tard, le quatrième concile de Chalcédoine reconnaitra la primauté de Rome, mais le Canon était trop vague pour que le Pape puisse l'accepter. L'idée qu'un concile œcuménique était maintenant la seule autorité inspirée pour traiter de la doctrine et de la discipline prenait de l'importance à Byzance, alors qu'en Occident, le pape était de plus en plus considéré comme l'autorité suprême. Le Patriarche de Constantinople, Acacius, a essayé de convenir d'une doctrine avec l'empereur Zénon mais il a été excommunié par le Pape Simplicius en 484[7]. Après la chute de l'Empire romain, la rupture entre Rome et Constantinople a été totale de 484 à 518.

De plus, l'Empire romain étant déchu en occident, l'insécurité reprit dans l'Ouest. Les invasions arabes qui suivirent ont accru cette insécurité. Du fait de ces invasions et de ces guerres, la communication n'était plus assurée entre Rome et les patriarches d'Orient. De nombreuses nominations patriarcales n'ont jamais atteint Rome, accroissant la séparation entre les deux parties de l'ancien empire et de l'Église pendant des siècles. En outre, en 654, les Arabes conduits par le Calife Muawiya I, prirent Ankara puis firent le siège de Constantinople de

---

éd., 1841, p. 278.

[5] Philothée, Du Pape, Dentu éd., Paris, 1863, p. 213.

[6] John Meyendorff, *The Primacy of Peter: Essays in Ecclesiology and the Early Church*, St. Vladimir's Seminary Press, U.S., 1980.

[7] Hefele-Leclercq, Histoire *des Conciles d'après les documents originaux*, Letouzey & Ané éd., Paris, 2ème éd., 1908, deuxième partie, p. 924.

674 à 678, donnant lieu à la première grande confrontation de l'Empire romain d'Orient avec l'Islam[8].

La langue a également joué un rôle déterminant dans la séparation. Alors que l'Église catholique romaine s'exprimait en latin à l'ouest, le grec maintenait sa prééminence dans l'Empire byzantin et demeure la langue liturgique de l'Église orthodoxe. La langue a eu une importance dans les différends théologiques à travers les siècles. Le latin est très précis et clair alors que le grec est souvent plus subtile et flexible. Ainsi, alors que l'Église catholique romaine clarifiait et définissait ses dogmes, l'Église byzantine tenait d'innombrables disputes et débats sur la foi et la doctrine[9]. Le sentiment d'unité entre chrétiens commençait à décliner.

Suite à la chute de l'Empire romain, l'Église catholique romaine a « hérité » du pouvoir civil et juridique du fait de la disparition de l'administration romaine[10]. A Byzance, l'empereur maintint son pouvoir civil et judiciaire et conserva les patriarches dans une certaine soumission à son égard. De fait, l'empereur incarne la continuité de son empire et est toujours considéré comme prêtre[11]. Cette unité du pouvoir sera appelée *césaro-papisme*[12] au XIXème siècle.

Au cours de son règne, Constantin intervint fréquemment dans la vie de l'Église. Il a convoqué des conciles quand un dogme méritait d'être clarifié, il a aidé l'Église à imposer et à faire appliquer ses déci-

---

[8] Marius Canard, *Les expéditions des Arabes contre Constantinople dans l'histoire et dans la légende,* Journal Asiatique, 61-121, 1926, p. 208.

[9] Runciman, *supra* note 1, p. 21.

[10] Alain Ducellier, *L'Église byzantine, Entre Pouvoir et Esprit, 313-1024,* Desclée, Paris, 1990.

[11] Gilbert Dagron, *Empereur et prêtre,* Étude sur le *césaropapisme byzantin*, Gallimard, 1996.

[12] Richard Swedberg, *The Max Weber Dictionary : Key Words and Central Concepts,* Stanford University Press, 2005, p. 22. (Définition de Max Weber: « un dirigeant séculier, *césaropapiste...exerce l'autorité suprême dans les questions ecclésiastiques au nom de sa légitimité autonome" et implique "la subordination complète des prêtres au pouvoir séculier* » (traduction libre)).

sions. A la chute de l'Empire romain en occident, l'élite s'est effondrée contrairement à Byzance où l'élite municipale et sénatoriale s'est maintenue[13]. C'est seulement en 1059 qu'un décret romain établit que dorénavant l'élection du pape relèverait exclusivement la compétence des cardinaux de Rome et non plus celle de l'empereur. « *L'évêque de Rome, cessant d'être un jouet entre les mains de la noblesse romaine ou celle des princes transalpins, avait recouvré son indépendance* »[14]. Ceci représente un changement essentiel. L'évêque de Rome était alors en mesure d'affirmer sa supériorité à l'égard des rois et empereurs, comme il est écrit : « *Jésus vint, et leur parla, en disant: tout pouvoir m'a été donné dans le ciel et sur la terre. Allez donc, et enseignez toutes les nations* »[15]. A l'inverse, à Byzance l'empereur était encore considéré comme le Vicaire du Christ sur la terre, placé au-dessus des cinq patriarches historiques[16].

Ainsi, lorsque l'Église catholique romaine a essayé d'imposer des conciles, des définitions en latin et la soumission au pape au nom de sa primauté à l'église grecque, un débat théologique s'en suivit et l'affrontement fut inévitable[17]. Il s'est produit le 16 juillet 1054, lorsque le légat du Pape déposa à Sainte Sophie une bulle d'excommunication du Patriarche et de tous ses assistants[18]. Des siècles plus tard, un historien a décrit cette longue période du milieu du second millénaire comme étant : « *Violemment hostile aux* « *Latins* » *et à tout ce qui, de près ou de loin, rappelait Rome, il* [le Patriarche de Constantinople] *lui paraissait plus important de disputer les Lieux Saints aux catholiques, en des bagarres et des pugilats que les soldats turcs considéraient d'un œil narquois, que de creuser les problèmes théologiques.* »[19]

---

[13] Ducellier, *supra* note 10.

[14] Runciman, *supra* note 1, p.56.

[15] *Mathieu* 28:18-19.

[16] Dagron, *supra* note 11.

[17] Le patriarche de Constantinople Keroularios et les papes ont pris des directions opposées pour de nombreuses raisons. Le filioque est le point le plus important sur lequel l'évêque de Rome et les évêques d'Orient se sont battus.

[18] Ducellier, *supra* note 10, p. 214.

[19] Daniel Rops, *L'Église des temps classiques, L'ère des grands craquements*, Librairie Arthème Fayard, 1958, vol. 2, p. 247.

2. Les tentatives pour rétablir la communion avec Rome

Depuis le Vème siècle, les chrétiens de ces terres étaient séparés en trois branches : les Nestoriens de Perse, les Monophysites de Syrie et les églises fidèles au Concile de Chalcédoine (églises coptes, araméennes et grecques). Une telle situation n'était pas acceptable pour Rome, qui a tenté de restaurer l'unité de l'Église sous sa juridiction. Cette volonté prendra plus tard le nom d'uniatisme.

L'uniatisme est une doctrine de l'Église catholique visant à restaurer la pleine communion des communautés ayant quitté l'unité depuis une longue période. Elle permet aux communautés de conserver leurs rites et leur personnalité si elles reconnaissent le dogme et la primauté de Rome[20]. C'est l'Empereur byzantin Michel VII Doukas qui, à la fin du XIème siècle, a proposé un tel accord au Pape Grégoire VII en échange d'un soutien militaire après avoir perdu l'Anatolie[21]. Il avait promis une union entre l'Église grecque orthodoxe et Rome, mais il mourut ce qui empêcha que cette union soit entérinée, malgré l'accord du Pape. Une autre tentative eut lieu en 1112, menée par le Pape Pascal II, mais les discussions théologiques n'aboutirent pas[22]. Une émeute eut lieu à Constantinople contre les latins. Des membres du clergé grec y participèrent et le légat du Pape fut décapité. Ce fut l'une des raisons pour lesquelles la quatrième croisade, sous l'influence des Vénitiens[23], se tourna contre Constantinople en 1204 et mis à sac la ville

---

20   Raymond Le Coz, Histoire de l'Église d'Orient, Chrétiens d'Irak, d'Iran et de Turquie, Cerf, Paris, 1995, p. 336. (Benoît XIV, au milieu du XVIIIème siècle le rappellera très bien: « Le missionnaire ne doit pas persuader le schismatique oriental qui cherche à revenir à l'unité catholique qu'il doit embrasser le rituel latin, le rôle du missionnaire est de ramener l'oriental à la Foi Catholique, pas de lui apporter le rituel latin. »).

[21] Bernard Leib, Rome, Kiev et Byzance à la fin du XIe siècle, Ayer Publishing, 1968.

[22] Le type de pain utilisé pour la consécration, le filioque et la place du Pape dans l'Église sont resté non résolus.

[23] A. Frolow, « La déviation de la 4e Croisade vers Constantinople. Problème d'histoire et de doctrine », Revue de l'histoire des religions, 145-2, 1954, pp. 168-187.

pendant trois jours. Suite à la prise de Constantinople par les croisés, un évêque latin fut nommé à la place du patriarche grec.

En 1215, le quatrième Concile du Latran, dans son quatrième canon[24], exhortera les grecs à rejoindre l'Église catholique romaine et à accepter ses principes afin il n'y ait plus « *qu'un seul troupeau et un seul berger.* »[25]

En 1439, une importante bulle a été adoptée au cours du Concile de Bâle-Ferrare-Florence-Rome au sujet des Arméniens. Ils avaient accepté les vérités dogmatiques[26] et donc Rome les avaient acceptés en retour et avait reconnu la liturgie et les droits traditionnels de leur clergé. Cette bulle « *Exultate Deo* » du 22 novembre 1439[27], sera par conséquent la base des accords postérieurs avec les autres églises byzantines.

Le 4 février 1442, la bulle « *Cantate Domino* » unit Rome et les Jacobites d'Alexandrie et de Jérusalem[28]. Les Assyriens ont retrouvé la pleine communion avec Rome le 30 Novembre 1444 par la Bulle « *Venite et exultemus Domino* »[29]. Le Métropolite Nestorien Timothy de Tarse a conclu une union avec le pape Eugène IV le 7 Août 1445 au nom des fidèles de Chypre. De nombreux Chaldéens revinrent quelques années plus tard à l'hérésie nestorienne, mais en 1489 l'île de Chypre fut envahie par la République de Vénétie qui latinisa le pays.

Le 6 juillet 1439, l'union avec les grecs fut proclamée au cours du Concile de Bâle-Ferrare-Florence-Rome et proclamée en décembre

[24] Catholic Encyclopedia, *Fourth Lateran Council 1215*, Robert Appleton Co., New York, 1913.

[25] *Jean* 10:16.

[26] Le Credo de Nicée, les sept sacrements ainsi que les deux natures et deux volontés en la personne de Jésus-Christ.

[27] P. Guérin, *Les Conciles généraux et particuliers*, Victor Palmé, Paris, 1869, tome 3, p. 225.

[28] Abbé Rohrbacher, Histoire universelle de l'Église *Catholique,* Gaume Frères & J. Duprey éd., Paris, 3ème éd., 1861, tome 29, p. 158.

[29] Roger Gaïse, O.P., Les signes sacramentels de l'Eucharistie dans l'Église *latine*, Universitaires Fribourg Suisse éd., 2001, p. 221.

1452 dans la basilique Sainte Sophie. Les grecs avaient cependant attendu trop longtemps, car cinq mois plus tard Constantinople tombait aux mains de Mehmet II qui choisit de nommer un nouveau Patriarche opposé à l'union avec Rome.

Ces traités d'union expliquent la diversité des rites et des églises au sein de l'Église catholique.

B. L'Église Catholique au Cours de la Période Ottomane : Entre Persécution et Tolérance

Le 29 mai 1453, Mehmet II prit Constantinople qui devint Istanbul, capitale de l'Empire ottoman vers 1458. Par conséquent il n'y avait plus d'Empire byzantin, mais les « églises des empires » survécurent (ou églises byzantines, en grecques : Melkites). Les patriarches de Constantinople accrurent même leur pouvoir dans ce nouveau contexte.

Dans un premier temps, une grande tolérance est appliquée, comme Jean Bodin le révèle en 1576 dans les *Six livres de la République* : « *Mais le Roi des Turcs, qui tient une bonne partie de l'Europe, garde sa Religion aussi bien que* [tout autre] *Prince du Monde, et ne force personne,* [*mais*] *au contraire permet à chacun de vivre selon sa conscience ; et qui plus est, il entretient auprès de son sérail à Péra, quatre Religions toutes diverses, celle des juifs, des chrétiens à la romaine, et à la grecque, et celle des mahométistes.* »[30] Cette tolérance a facilité l'accueil des musulmans par les Grecs chrétiens, par comparaison avec le souvenir des latins.

1. Les tribulations des Chaldéens

La principale église d'Anatolie reconnaissant le Pape comme l'évêque universel est l'église chaldéenne. L'histoire de cette église révèle toutes les difficultés rencontrées par le Saint-Siège pendant des siècles pour maintenir l'unité des chrétiens dans ces territoires. Elle montre

---

[30] Jean Bodin, Les six livres de la République : un abrégé du texte de l'édition de Paris de 1583, Gérard Mairet éd., Université de Chicoutimi, Québec, 4ème éd., 1993, pp. 70-73.

les problèmes constants d'un pays multi-religieux: la diffusion des hérésies et des divisions, les conflits entre les communautés; l'éloignement de Rome et l'opposition conjuguée du Califat et du Patriarcat aux Catholiques.

L'église chaldéenne a d'abord été affaiblie par la règle de succession héréditaire établie au XVIème siècle. En effet, le patriarche Simon IV publie un décret en 1450 établissant l'hérédité du Patriarcat au profit du neveu du patriarche (le *népotisme* au sens littéral). Des divisions ont lieu, en particulier entre les Nestoriens et les fidèles à Rome. Diyarbakir, au sud-est de l'Anatolie, est resté une place forte des Chaldéens uniates. En 1681, les Catholiques créèrent un Patriarcat chaldéen et élisent Joseph I à sa tête. Mais les autorités ottomanes ne voulaient avoir affaire qu'à un seul interlocuteur, capable d'être obéi par les fidèles. Les autorités ottomanes concevaient la religion comme dépendante de la nationalité : les fidèles devaient être soumis à l'autorité religieuse de leur nation, et non pas à celle d'un chef « étranger » – le Pape – jouissant d'une juridiction universelle transnationale.

En 1667, les Chaldéens de Diyarbakir convertirent le Métropolite Nestorien de leur ville, Joseph, qui fut alors considéré comme un ennemi par la puissance ottomane. Il fut régulièrement convoqué devant les tribunaux pour justifier son indépendance, puisque l'uniatisme était illégal selon les lois ottomanes. La seule possibilité de survivre pour les Catholiques était alors de payer les autorités. Les Chaldéens ont donc versé beaucoup d'argent aux autorités ottomanes, comme en témoigne un évêque au Pape[31]. Avec Joseph III, la ville entière se convertit au Catholicisme. Joseph III alla jusqu'à Mossoul et y convertit 6 000 personnes, après avoir payé les autorités ottomanes pour son voyage. Ces conversions exaspérèrent les Nestoriens qui firent emprisonner Joseph III. Néanmoins, il obtint un ordre impérial (*firmân*) du gouvernement ottoman reconnaissant son autonomie par rapport au

---

[31] Le Coz, *supra* note 20, p. 330 (Monseigneur Picquet dans une lettre écrite à Diyarbakir: « Il a fallu nécessairement laisser ici une bonne partie de notre argent, sans cela on ne peut rien faire en ce pays en faveur de l'Église. »).

Patriarche Nestorien, Elias XII Denho. Les difficultés ont continué pour les successeurs, jusqu'à la mort en 1828 du dernier évêque catholique revendiquant le titre de Patriarche, son successeur ne prétendra plus à ce titre.

2. Le statut de non-musulman

a. Le système du « millet »

Le système du millet a été mis en place par l'Empire ottoman pour diriger les populations en fonction de leur religion ou nation, dont il nommait le chef. Le mot millet vient de l'arabe « *millah* » qui se traduit littéralement par nation. Un Millet était un système légal pour une communauté religieuse, qui permettait au groupe d'être gouverné selon ses propres lois dans le cadre et sous l'autorité ultime de l'Empire. Ainsi, le Sultan ottoman était le chef religieux de tous les musulmans, sans distinction de région ou pays d'origine. Il y avait un seul « Millet » pour les musulmans établissant une institution unique, autonome, qui faisait place à un seul chef, avec des règles, des tribunaux et des taxes spécifiques[32]. Les fidèles de l'Église orthodoxe faisaient quant à eux partie du « *Rum Millet* », malgré les différences de langues. Ce « *Rum Millet* » fut créé immédiatement après la chute de Constantinople en 1453 ; *Rum* faisant paradoxalement référence à Rome. De même, un millet était appliqué à tous les groupes ethniques arméniens, quelle que soit l'église dont ils faisaient partie : Église apostolique arménienne ou Église catholique arménienne. Aux yeux du pouvoir ottoman, une même loi s'appliquait à eux tous[33]. Dans le cadre de chaque millet, le Patriarche de la « nation » réunissait les pouvoirs religieux et administratifs dans certaines branches du droit[34]. Ce système ne faisait pas la différence, au sein de chaque nation, entre les fidèles attachés ou non à Rome, si

---

[32] Abdulaziz Abdulhussein Sachedina, *The Islamic Roots of Democratic Pluralism*, Oxford University Press, 2001.

[33] Oguzhan Tan, *State and Religious Diversity in Turkey, An Historical Overview from the Ottomans to the Republic Period*, Danubius, 2014, p. 32.

[34] Daniel G Bates & Amal Rassam, *Peoples and Cultures of the Middle East*, Upper Saddle River, NJ, Prentice-Hall Inc., 2001.

bien que des chrétiens unis à Rome étaient, du point de vue ottoman, soumis à la juridiction d'un Patriarche non uni à Rome. Ceci explique comment les Patriarches orthodoxes pouvaient contrôler, et même nuire aux chrétiens fidèles à Rome au sein de « sa » nation. Les problèmes liés au système des millets s'est conjugué avec la problématique de la territorialité de la juridiction ecclésiale. Le principe dans l'Église, tant catholique qu'orthodoxe, est celui de la compétence territoriale exclusive de l'ordinaire du lieu. Cela signifie, qu'en théorie, au sein de l'Église universelle, chaque évêque est l'unique chef religieux d'un territoire et de tous ceux s'y trouvant, indépendamment de leur nationalité. Par conséquent, deux évêques ne devraient pas être responsables d'un même territoire, et un évêque n'a aucun pouvoir sur un autre territoire, à l'exception de l'évêque de Rome selon l'Église catholique[35]. Ainsi, dans l'Empire ottoman, les Catholiques furent obligés d'obéir au Patriarche orthodoxe, non seulement parce qu'il pouvait revendiquer une compétence territoriale, mais également parce que la loi civile du millet le lui permettait. Or la caractéristique de l'Église catholique est précisément d'être transnationale, par conséquent elle n'entre pas en correspondance avec le système du millet, ni plus tard avec le futur traité de Lausanne.

Comme il n'y avait pas de système de millet pour les Catholiques dans l'Empire ottoman avant le XIXème siècle[36], le Sultan a permis que des souverains chrétiens d'Occident puissent être protecteurs de quelques églises. Cette protection a été assurée par des traités appelés des « capitulations ».

b. Les capitulations

---

[35] *Code de droit canon*, 1983, c.515 : « §1. En règle générale, une partie du peuple de Dieu qui constitue un diocèse ou une autre église particulière est limitée à un territoire défini de façon à inclure tous les fidèles vivant dans le territoire. §2. Néan*moins, si dans le jugement de l'autorité suprême de l'*Église, il semble avantageux après que les conférences des évêques concernés ont été entendus, les églises particulières distinctes *par le rite des fidèles ou d'une autre raison similaire peuvent être érigés sur le même territoire* ».
[36] Marie Carmen Smyrnelis, *Une société hors de soi, identités et relations sociales à Smyrne aux XVIIIe et XIXe siècles*, XX-376, Paris, Leuven, Peeters, 2005.

En 1517, le Califat fut institué, Sélim I Yavus conquit l'Egypte et devint ainsi Sultan de l'Empire ottoman et Calife de tous les musulmans. Dans ce contexte, et selon la loi islamique les populations « infidèles », juifs ou chrétiens, ont le statut juridique inférieur de « *dhimmi* »[37], qui leur garantit peu de droits[38].

Soliman I (1520-1566), son successeur souvent appelé le « Magnifique » par les Occidentaux et le « Législateur » en Orient, initia une « ouverture » politique avec certains pays européens, au moyen des Capitulations[39]. Les capitulations étaient des chartes par lesquelles le Sultan accordait quatre droits aux bénéficiaires : le droit de résidence, la liberté de religion, l'inviolabilité du domicile, et la transmission des propriétés par héritage. D'après Raymond Le Coz, « *outre leurs incidences politiques, les différentes Capitulations constituent un tremplin idéal pour permettre l'expansion en Orient de diverses confessions Chrétiennes de l'Europe.* »[40]

A l'époque des Capitulations et du Protectorat (1535-1923) les églises et sanctuaires de l'Église catholique ont pu être maintenus. Soliman I, sur la base d'un accord diplomatique aux enjeux tant politiques qu'économiques, donna en 1535 les premières Capitulations à la France qui devint alors la puissance protectrice des Catholiques dans l'Empire[41]. Alors que l'Empire ottoman était en guerre avec plusieurs

---

[37] Gilles Ferragu, Église *et diplomatie au Levant au temps des Capitulations*, Rives nord-méditerranéennes, 2000, p. 6.

[38] Juan Eduardo Campo, *Encyclopedia of Islam*, Infobase Publishing, 2010 éd., pp. 194-195. Traduction libre « dhimmi » : « *Les Dhimmis sont des non-Musulmans vivant au sein de communautés islamiques et ayant un statu régulé et protégé... A l'époque moderne, si ce terme a parfois été réutilisé, il est généralement obsolète* ».

[39] Félix Gaffiot, *Dictionnaire Latin-Français*, 1934, p. 260. Si le mot « Capitulation » utilisé par les dirigeants musulmans et chrétiens européens semble connoter une reddition, le mot vient en fait du latin « capitulum » qui signifie « articles » ou « titre de loi » : Cod. Just. 5, 37, 28. C'est un traité basé sur un modèle d'entreprise et d'établissement.

[40] Le Coz, *supra* note 20, p. 315.

[41] En 1790, Sélim III a signé avec Frédéric-Guillaume I un traité d'assistance mutuelle qui accorde aux Prussiens les avantages des capitulations dont bénéficient

puissances européennes, l'établissement d'une alliance avec la France au moyen des capitulations permit à Soliman de diviser et de fragiliser politiquement et militairement la chrétienté. En effet, à cette même époque, les papes essayaient d'unir tous les rois chrétiens de l'Occident contre l'expansion de l'Empire ottoman[42].

De nouveaux appels aux croisades furent lancés contre les Turcs au XVème siècle[43], elles manifestent la volonté constante des Papes[44] de limiter et de réduire l'expansion de l'Islam[45]. L'une d'entre elles aboutit à la fameuse et importante bataille de Lépante (1571) qui arrêta l'expansionnisme ottoman. Attaqué par la marine ottomane, le Pape Pie V appela pour la défense de la Chrétientés les flottes de toute l'Europe rassemblées sous le nom de la « Sainte-Ligue » et demanda à tous les Chrétiens de prier le rosaire. Malgré un rapport de force numérique favorable aux ottomans, ceux-ci subirent une véritable débâcle. L'Église catholique attribue la victoire à la Vierge Marie et la commémore

---

d'autres pays et un traité commercial avec les États-Unis est signé en 1830 permettant leur missionnaire de venir aussi dans ces régions.

[42] Stanford J. Shaw, *History of the Ottoman Empire and Modern Turkey: Volume 1. Empire of the Gazis: The Rise and Decline of the Ottoman Empire 1280–1808*, Cambridge University Press, 1976, pp. 97-98.

[43] Roberto Rusconi, "Public purity and discipline: states and religious renewal", *4 The Cambridge History of Christianity, Christianity in Western Europe c. 1100 - c. 1500*, Miri Rubin & Walter Simons éd., Cambridge University Press, p. 460.

[44] Pape Eugene IV, *Concile de Bâle*, 1434, http://www.papalencyclicals.net/Councils/ecum17.htm (*inter alia :* « On peut espérer que de très nombreux adeptes de l'abominable secte de Mahomet seront converti à la foi catholique ») ; Louis Pastor, *Histoire des Papes depuis la fin du Moyen-Age*, Plon, Paris, 1888, p. 321. Pape Callixte III : « Je jure [...] *d'exalter la vraie foi, et d'éradiquer de l'Orient la secte diabolique de Mahomet le réprouvé et l'infidèle [Islam]* ».

[45] David Nirenberg, "Christendom and Islam", *4 The Cambridge History of Christianity, Christianity in Western Europe c. 1100-c. 1500*, Miri Rubin & Walter Simons ed., Cambridge University Press, 2009, p. 160. A cette époque, les musulmans étaient considérés comme les ennemis de la Chrétienté : « Sarasin » n'est pas devenu une insulte banale chez les Chrétiens du Moyen-Age. On ne peut pourtant prétendre qu'en dehors de territoires comme la Péninsule Ibérique ou les éphémères États Latins on puisse détecter que l'Islam ai présenté une menace existentielle à l'ordre Chrétien en lui-même. Il faut pour cela attendre la toute fin de notre période, avec la chute de Constantinople (1453) et le début de l'expansion Ottomane vers l'est.

chaque année par la fête de Notre-Dame du Rosaire dans le calendrier liturgique romain.

La France ne participa pas à la Sainte Ligue et resta liée à l'Empire par les Capitulations françaises de 1535, qui furent prolongées en 1569[46].

Au cours du XIXème siècle, on a pu communément prétendre que le régime ottoman était devenu plus tolérant sous la pression de l'occident. En 1834, le Sultan ottoman Mahmoud II a nommé un prêtre araméen, Agop Tchoukourian, « Patrice » de tous les chrétiens uniates de l'Empire, incluant l'Église chaldéenne, ce qui lui a donné – enfin – une reconnaissance légale[47]. Le « Patrice » (Patricien) est considéré comme l'égal du Patriarche de Constantinople et du Patriarche arménien, ce qui « libère » les uniates de l'orthodoxie et de Rome.

De plus, le Sultan suivant, Abdoul Majid, a mené une importante réforme : le « *Tanzimat* » (« réorganisation », 1839-1876)[48] : une charte impériale reconnaissant l'égalité de tous les sujets de l'empire – sans considérer leur religion ou nationalité – et une égalité de droits et de taxes alors même que d'après la sharia les « *dhimmi* » ne sont pas égaux en droits et sont soumis à des impôts spéciaux : le *karaj* et le *jizya* (taxe foncière et capitation)[49].

3. Les Missions des "Latins" au Moyen-Orient

A la signature des Capitulations de 1604 entre le Roi de France Henri IV et le Sultan Ottoman Ahmet I, tous les religieux « Francs » gardiens de l'église du Saint Sépulcre et les pèlerins avaient un laisser-passer pour Jérusalem à travers l'Empire[50]. Sous Richelieu, cette

---

[46] Jean-Claude Roberti, *Les Uniates,* Cerf, Paris, 1992, p. 34.
[47] *Id.,* p. 65.
[48] William L. Cleveland & Martin Bunton, *A History of the Modern Middle East,* Westview Press, 4th ed., 2009, p. 82.
[49] Lewis Bernard, *The Jews of Islam,* Princeton University Press, 1984, pp. 17-18.
[50] Giuseppe Buffon, *Les Franciscains en terre sainte,* Cerf, Paris, 2005, p. 257.

faveur servira à faire revenir à l'Église catholique romaine des Chrétiens de rites orientaux.

La présence de communautés s'est révélée utile pour maintenir et développer l'évangélisation de la première Église chaldéenne au cours du XVIème siècle. Par exemple, les Franciscains institués comme gardiens de lieux saints par le Pape Clément VI en 1342, étaient très actifs dans les œuvres de charités comme les hospices pour pèlerins. En 1583, un groupe de jésuites a fondé une école à Istanbul, elle existe encore de nos jours. A Andrinople, les Assomptionnistes dirigèrent une école avec un certain succès[51]. Les Capucins sont présents également, grâce à Louis XIII et son successeur. Ainsi, en 1679, quelques communautés arméniennes retournèrent à la foi catholique romaine[52]. Cependant, la peste, l'Islam et les Nestoriens étaient les trois adversaires immuables du travail des Catholiques dans l'empire. On peut dire que chaque fois que les Catholiques ont été en mesure d'établir un hôpital, une école, une église ou de convertir des Turcs, l'action était à la merci des administrateurs, ou risquait d'échouer en raison des hérésies ou de maladies.

Des missionnaires étaient inlassablement envoyés pour évangéliser les provinces. En 1841, trente-deux prêtres Lazaristes, quatorze frères et vingt sœurs de la charité furent envoyés dans l'Empire ottoman[53]. Cependant, ils étaient si peu nombreux que les frères et les sœurs se réunissaient souvent dans la même ville et dans le même bâtiment, à proximité du Consulat[54]. A Salonique en 1882, le Consul comptait six Lazaristes et dix-huit sœurs de la charité[55], ce qui était décrit comme

---

[51] Alexis Vrignon, Les missions catholiques françaises en Turquie d'Europe *(des années 1840 à 1914)*, Mémoire, Université de Nantes, 2007, p. 85.

[52] Église arménienne catholique, *Biographie des anciens Patriarches de l'église arménienne catholique*, http://www.armeniancatholic.org/inside.php?lang=fr&page_id=231.

[53] Archives du Quai d'Orsay. Série Mémoires et Documents. Sous-série Turquie. 129. Feuillet 206. Lettre du procureur général des lazaristes au ministre des Affaires étrangères, 29 mars 1841. Vrignon, *supra* note 51, p. 85.

[54] *Id.*

[55] *Id.*

une « vague missionnaire »[56]. Ces chiffres donnent la mesure de la faiblesse et de la précarité de l'Église catholique romaine dans la région.

Après la guerre de Crimée (1854-1855) qui opposa la Russie et l'Empire ottoman au Royaume-Uni, la France et le Piémont, un traité fut signé le 30 mars 1856, dans lequel l'Empire ottoman proclamait la liberté religieuse sur tous ses territoires (*Hatti Hamayoun*)[57]. La guerre a fait la lumière sur la situation et elle a donné lieu à un mouvement de sympathie, contrôlé par l'Empire ottoman, pour les chrétiens dans ces régions. Ainsi, des intellectuels français[58] décidèrent de créer l'Œuvre *des* Écoles d'Orient, avec trois bus principaux : défendre la Foi en Jésus-Christ à travers les services, œuvrer à l'unité des Chrétiens, et apporter une aide matérielle. Le Pape Pie IX a approuvé l'Œuvre le 29 janvier 1858. « L'Œuvre a pris son envol deux ans plus tard [*1860*], *après les massacres du Mont-libyen, qui ont eu lieu dans une région de l'Empire ottoman particulièrement complexe et difficile à gérer en raison de sa diversité ethnique et religieuse. Surtout à cause du ressentiment de la population musulmane contre les lois sur l'égalité et les droits civils, qui* avaient été imposées par les autorités, *mais jamais vraiment accepté* »[59]. 22 000 chrétiens, surtout des maronites furent tués au cours de ce massacre, avec la complicité des autorités turques[60].

II. L'Église catholique et la Turquie moderne

En 1920 il y avait deux millions de chrétiens en Turquie[61], ils ne sont plus que 68 600, à l'exclusion des migrants[62]. Ils représentent

---

[56] *Id.*

[57] Hervé Legrand & Mgr Guiseppe Maria Croce, *L'œuvre d'Orient, solidarités anciennes et nouveaux défis*, Cerf, Paris, 2010, p.13.

[58] *Id.*

[59] *Id.* Traduction libre.

[60] François Renault, Le Cardinal Lavigerie *1825-1892*, Fayard, Paris, 1992, p. 55.

[61] Daniel Pipes, « La disparition des chrétiens au Moyen-Orient », *Middle East Quarterly*, Hiver 2001.

[62] *Louis Pelâtre & François Yakan présentent les églises de Turquie*, Radio Vatican, 13 Octobre 2010.

aujourd'hui 0,1% de la population. Les chrétiens en Turquie sont perçus comme nécessairement étrangers à la nation turque. Même s'ils sont titulaires de la nationalité turque, n'étant pas des musulmans sunnites, ils ne sont pas dans la même situation juridique que la majorité de la population[63].

En Turquie, les Catholiques représentent une petite minorité. Ils sont environ 25 000 : 15 000 Catholiques romains, 3 450 Catholiques arméniens, 2 000 Grecs catholiques, 4 000 chaldéens[64]. La majorité des Catholiques de rite latin sont des levantins, d'origine italienne ou française pour la plupart bien qu'il y ait quelques turcs d'origine (qui se sont généralement convertis au moment de leur mariage). Les autres sont des expatriés[65]. Les Catholiques turcs sont principalement concentrés à Istanbul. Depuis 2003, la Turquie accueille de nombreux réfugiés d'Irak, du Congo, du Cameroun, et du Nigéria ainsi que des Philippins catholiques[66].

A. Les Problèmes Rencontrés par les Catholiques en Turquie

Les Catholiques, comme les autres minorités religieuses, ont de grandes difficultés avec l'administration turque, qui les perçoit comme des citoyens de deuxième ordre[67].

1. L'absence de statut légal pour l'Église catholique.

Dans les années 1920, Atatürk a réformé le pays pour changer l'identité turque : il voulait créer une Turquie indépendante, compacte

---

[63] *Le témoignage du Père Balhan, curé de la paroisse d'Ankara*, Radio Vatican, 27 Novembre 2014 : http://fr.radiovaticana.va/news/2014/11/27/le_t%C3%A 9moignage_du_p%C3%A8re_balhan,_cur%C3%A9_de_la_paroisse_dankara/1112702.

[64] Vicariat Apostolique Catholique Latin : http://www.katolikkilisesi.org/fr/index. html.

[65] The Catholic Church in Turkey, *GCatholic.org* : http://www.gcatholic.org/dio ceses/country/TR.htm.

[66] Turquie : Vivre sa Foi dans un pays laïc où l'Etat est omniprésent, Œuvre d'Orient, 1er juillet 2011.

[67] Abdullah Kiran, "How a social engineering project affected Christians in Turkey", *International Journal for Religious Freedom: Researching Religious Freedom*, Issue 1 & 2 (2013), vol. 6, p. 51.

et homogène et éliminer l'influence religieuse sur l'État[68]. En 1932, la capitale a été déplacée à Ankara. Le 1er novembre 1922 il abolit le Sultanat, et après avoir été élu président le 3 mars 1924, il abolit le Califat, le plaçant sous la responsabilité du Directorat des Affaires Religieuses (*Diyanet*) et le subordonnant à l'autorité du Conseil des Ministres. Ce directorat devient un instrument du contrôle de l'État sur la religion. Il organisait hiérarchiquement, dirigeait et réglait toutes les questions religieuses musulmanes, y compris leurs institutions religieuses. Les imams devinrent des agents publics payés par l'État et ils n'étaient pas autorisés à écrire leurs propres prêches. L'instruction coranique fut placée sous la responsabilité du Ministère national de l'éducation. Ainsi la religion en Turquie fut-elle placée sous surveillance[69].

L'introduction du principe de laïcité en Turquie n'a pas signifié une séparation entre l'État et la religion mais le contrôle absolu de l'État sur la religion. Atatürk voulait priver les chefs religieux de toute possibilité d'intervention dans les affaires gouvernementales[70]. L'intégralité du système judiciaire fut réformée en 1924, supprimant les tribunaux religieux[71]. En 1938 une loi proscrit la création d'associations religieuses[72]. Toutes les religions étaient traitées avec suspicion. Sous la République turque, les églises n'étaient pas autorisées à posséder ou maintenir des propriétés, avoir des écoles ou des œuvres de charité, ni même à former un nouveau clergé dans les séminaires[73].

Le principe de laïcité en Turquie n'accordait pas de statut légal aux communautés religieuses. L'Église catholique ne pouvait donc pas jouir de droits qui n'étaient pas accordés aux institutions musulmanes[74].

---

[68] Annie Laurent, *L'Europe, malade de la Turquie*, François-Xavier de Guibert éd., 2005, p. 73 ; *Attaturk's reforms*, www.allabourtturkey.org.

[69] Laurent, *supra* note 68, p. 73.

[70] *Id.*, p. 80.

[71] *Id.*, p. 81.

[72] *Id.*

[73] Religious Freedom in Turkey, *American Hellenic Council*, 25 juin 2014, http://www.americanhellenic.org/index.php/news/issues/34-religious-freedom-in-turkey.

[74] *La Croix*, édition du 15 décembre 2004.

L'Église catholique n'avait pas de statut légal, pas même en tant que « communauté non-musulmane ». L'Église catholique étant considérée comme une entité « étrangère ». Reconnaître des droits aux minorités était perçu comme une menace pour l'unité du pays. Par ailleurs, si l'Église catholique avait été reconnue, elle aurait été placée sous le contrôle de l'État par le biais du Directorat des Affaires Religieuses[75].

Le traité de Lausanne du 24 juillet 1923, ratifié par la Turquie en août 1923, ne garantissait pas seulement aux minorités (« raciales, linguistiques et religieuses » d'après le droit international) une égalité de droit mais aussi un garantie de droits particuliers, tels ceux de pouvoir construire leurs propres écoles et parler leur propre langue. Cependant, la délégation turque à Lausanne ne reconnut que les « non-musulmans » comme minorité, et firent accepter cette définition par la Conférence[76]. De plus, en pratique, les turcs interprétèrent cette notion arbitrairement, ne considérant comme minorités que les millets connus sous l'Empire ottoman—les arméniens, les grecs et les juifs—bien qu'aucune mention n'ait été faite à cet égard dans le Traité[77]. L'interprétation du traité faite par l'État turc[78] a par conséquente exclu

---

[75] Laurent, *supra* note 68, p. 123.

[76] Baskin Oran, *Minority Concept and Rights in Turkey: The Lausanne Peace Treaty and Current Issues, in Human Rights in Turkey,* Zehra F. Kabasakal Arat. ed., University of Pennsylvania Press, avril 2007, pp. 35-52.

[77] Samim Akgönül, *The Minority Concept in the Turkish Context, Practices and Perceptions in Turkey, Greece and France,* Brill, 2013.

[78] 28 L.N.T.S. 11 (Les articles 37 à 45 du Traité énumèrent les droits des minorités. Ces dispositions sont égales aux dispositions constitutionnelles (article 37). Selon ce traité, les minorités jouissent d'une liberté de mouvement et de l'émigration (article 38 § 3), des mêmes droits civils et politiques que les musulmans (article 39 § 1), de l'égalité devant la loi (article 39 § 2) et de la non-discrimination dans la jouissance des droits civils et politiques (article 39 § 3), l'utilisation libre de toute langue, en privé, dans le commerce, la religion, dans la presse, dans une publication, à des réunions publiques ou à usage oral devant les tribunaux (article 39 § § 4 et 5), l'égalité de traitement et à la protection par la loi pour établir, gérer et contrôler toutes les institutions, les écoles ou les établissements de bienfaisance, religieuses et sociales pour l'enseignement et l'éducation, le droit d'utiliser leur propre langue et d'exercer librement leur propre religion (article 40). L'Etat doit fournir des installations adéquates pour veiller à ce que dans les écoles publiques dans les villes et les districts avec une majorité de la population non-musulmane l'instruction soit

de sa protection les autres groupes religieux ou nationaux, tels que les Syriaques, les Chaldéens, les Assyriens, les Nestoriens et les Catholiques.

Au regard de la loi turque, l'Église catholique n'existe pas en Turquie[79], elle n'a pas de personnalité juridique ni les droits qui en découlent[80]. L'Église catholique pourrait néanmoins justifier la légitimité de sa présence en Turquie par les lettres adressées par le Gouvernement turc aux autorités françaises, italiennes et britanniques en marge du traité de Lausanne, par lesquelles il garantit le maintien de leurs œuvres éducatives et hospitalières[81].

Encore en 2012, Monseigneur Lucibello, Nonce apostolique en Turquie, a rappelé combien il était urgent qu'Ankara reconnaisse légalement l'Église catholique romaine[82].

---

donnée dans leur propre langue (article 41 § 1). Il faut respecter les traditions et les coutumes des minorités non musulmanes en ce qui concerne leur statut familial ou personnel (article 42 § 1). Il doit également permettre une protection complète aux églises, synagogues, cimetières et autres établissements religieux, les installations et l'autorisation aux fondations pieuses et aux institutions religieuses et caritatives (article 42 § 3) et garantir le droit à l'objection de conscience et de religion. Néanmoins, les droits accordés aux citoyens non-musulmans ne sont pas pleinement mis en œuvre).

[79] Interview par l'Œuvre d'Orient d'Otmar Oehring, « *Reconnaissance légale de la communauté religieuse : un défi pour la nouvelle Turquie* », 14 juin 2011 : http://www.oeuvre-orient.fr/2011/06/14/reconnaissance-legale-de-la-communaute-religieuse-un-defi-pour-la-nouvelle-turquie/.

[80] Laurent, *supra* note 68, p. 122. (Ils n'ont pas la jouissance du droit de faire partie de démarches légales, ni le droit de propriété sur leur travail ou leurs bâtiments, le droit d'acheter ou de faire construire des bâtiments (la dernière église construite en Turquie est celle de St Antoine à Istanbul en 1906), le droit d'ouvrir un compte bancaire, le droit d'hériter, de conclure un contrat, d'embaucher, de diriger ou gérer des écoles).

[81] Rinaldo Marmara, *The State of Religious Equality – The View of Minority Communities*, The Archon 2nd International Conference on Religious Freedom, Berlin, 4 et 5 décembre 2013 ; Laurent, *supra* note 68, p. 122.

[82] L'Église catholique turque demande la restitution de 200 propriétés. Mieux vaut demander la reconnaissance juridique, *Asia News*, 23 avril 2012, http://www.asianews.it/news-en/Turkish-Catholic-Church-calls-for-a-return-of-200-properties.-Better-to-ask-for-legal-recognition-24576.html.

2. Violations du droit de propriété

En 1936, le gouvernement a exigé des minorités reconnues (grecs, arméniens et juifs) qu'elles fassent un inventaire de leurs propriétés et les lui déclarent. Ces propriétés ont été confiées à des fondations *ad hoc* et considérées comme des biens d'État, suivant en cela l'exemple donné par la République française quelques années auparavant. L'article 101 § 4 du Code Civil interdit aux communautés religieuses d'obtenir le statut légal de fondations[83] et donc de posséder des biens. Ces expropriations sont contraires aux articles 40 et 41 du traité de Lausanne qui prévoient que des communautés religieuses non musulmanes peuvent créer des fondations afin d'assurer l'exercice de leur foi et de mettre en place des organismes de bienfaisance et d'autres fondations. Elles s'opposent également à l'article 24 de la Constitution qui énonce le droit à la liberté de religion et à l'éducation.

Plus tard, par une décision de 1974, la Cour de cassation turque a interdit la vente de propriétés aux minorités chrétiennes, les considérant contraires à l'intérêt national. Cette même décision ordonnait de confisquer leurs écoles, orphelinats et hôpitaux s'il était constaté qu'ils avaient été obtenus après 1936[84].

Lorsque, l'État reconnait *de facto* que certains biens sont propriété de communautés religieuses, cette propriété demeure précaire car non établie légalement. Par exemple, l'Orphelinat de Buyukada, confisqué par l'État en 1964 a été restitué au Patriarche Œcuménique de Constantinople en 2010 suite à un arrêt de la Cour européenne des droits de l'homme. Le Patriarcat en est de nouveau propriétaire sans que cette propriété soit formellement établie[85].

Le 28 août 2011, le Premier Ministre turc Recep Tayyip Erdogan,

---

[83] Interview par l'Œuvre d'Orient d'Otmar Oehring, *supra* note 79.

[84] Mine Yıldırım, Åbo Akademi Uni et Otmar Oehring, Chef du Bureau des droits de l'Homme de la Mission, Turquie, Que signifie le décret de restitution Turc ? 6 octobre 2011, *disponible sur* http://www.forum18.org/archive.php?article_id=1621.

[85] *Id.*

a annoncé la restitution des propriétés qui appartenaient aux minorités religieuses confisquées après 1936[86] : un millier appartenant aux Grecs orthodoxes, une centaine appartenant aux Arméniens, et plusieurs appartenant aux Catholiques chaldéens et aux juifs ; pour la plupart il s'agissait d'hôpitaux, d'écoles, de cimetières, et d'orphelinats. Pour les Catholiques romains, aucune restitution n'était prévue puisqu'ils ne sont pas considérés comme étant bénéficiaires du traité de Lausanne[87]. Les Catholiques demandent toujours la restitution de 200 propriétés saisies pas le gouvernement turc[88].

3. Les limitations abusives du droit de culte

Les Catholiques ne sont pas libres non plus de construire de nouveaux lieux de culte, et sont limités à l'utilisation des bâtiments historiques de l'Église encore en état et accessible, le gouvernement ayant transformé beaucoup de ces églises en musées, surtout en Cappadoce, où se trouvent des centaines d'églises-musées dans lesquelles le culte est interdit[89]. L'exemple de l'église St Paul de Tarse est significatif : il s'agit d'une Église catholique construite dans les années 1800. Elle a été confisquée par le gouvernement en 1943 et déclarée musée en 1990. Par la suite les turcs ont autorisé des Catholiques à y célébrer occasionnellement la messe, mais contre le paiement d'un droit d'entrée et à la

---

[86] « La Turquie va restituer des biens saisis à des minorités religieuses », Œuvre d'Orient, Communiqué de presse, 1er septembre 2011.

[87] Turquie, Erdogan rend les propriétés foncières confisquées aux minorités religieuses, *Vatican Insider*, 29 août 2011, *disponible sur :* http://www.lastampa. it/2011/08/29/vaticaninsider/eng/world-news/turkey-erdogan-returns-real-estate-properties-seized-from-religious-minoritiesFg3yxJEHgbZgGc2uJ6RdcP/pagina. html.

[88] L'Église catholique turque demande la restitution de 200 propriétés. Mieux vaut demander la reconnaissance juridique, *Asia News*, 23 avril 2012, http:// www. asianews.it/news-en/Turkish-Catholic-Church-calls-for-a-return-of-200-properties.-Better-to-ask-for-legal-recognition-24576.html.

[89] Mine Yıldırım, *The Right to Establish and Maintain Places of Worship in Turkey (Le droit d'établir et d'entretenir des lieux de culte en Turquie)*, 8 Religion & Human Rights, Issue 3, 2013, pp. 203-222.

condition que les instruments liturgiques soient à chaque fois apportés par les fidèles et enlevés immédiatement après chaque célébration[90].

4. Les Catholiques et leurs églises cibles d'attaques

Comme tout chrétien en Turquie, les Catholiques sont victimes de violences. Le 5 février 2006, le Père Andréa Santoro a été tué par balle au cours de la messe dans l'église de Trazbon[91]. Un an plus tard, en 2007, le Père Adriano Franchini a été poignardé au ventre à Izmir[92]. Le 3 juin 2010, le vicaire apostolique d'Anatolie, Mgr Luigi Padovese, a été tué au cours d'un assassinat « rituel » par Murat Altun, son assistant et chauffeur âgé de 26 ans. Il a été poignardé 25 fois alors qu'il se préparait à rencontrer le Pape Benoît XVI le jour suivant sur l'île de Chypre[93]. Tous ont été frappés en raison de leur foi. En avril 2011, l'Église catholique d'Adana a été attaquée. Même si quelques coupables ont été punis, l'État turc ne protège pas de manière effective la vie et l'intégrité physique des victimes[94]. En 2009, le Pape Benoît XVI a conforté les évêques de Turquie avec les mots de Saint Jean aux églises d'Ephèse et Smyrne dans le livre de l'Apocalypse: « Je sais *que tu as de la persévérance, que tu as souffert à cause de mon nom, et que*

[90] Turkish Government Denies Request for Church in Tarsus (Le gouvernement turc refuse la demande d'église à Tarse), *Catholic News Service*, 5 août 2009 ; Peter Wensierski, *Tolerance in Turkey: Catholics Want to Reclaim St. Paul's Birthplace (Tolérance en Turquie: les Catholiques veulent réclamer le lieu de naissance de Saint Paul)*, *Spiegel online International*, 20 mars 2008.

[91] Priest's Killing Shocks Christians in Turkey (Le meurtre d'un prêtre choque les chrétiens en Turquie), *Catholic World News*, 6 février 2006 ; "Blessed are the meek: the life and martyrdom of a priest on mission in Turkey," (Heureux les doux : la vie et le martyre d'un prêtre en mission en Turquie) *Sandro Magister*, 7 février 2006.

[92] Priest stabbed in Turkey (Un prêtre poignardé en Turquie), *Catholic News Agency*, 17 décembre 2007, http://www.catholicnewsagency.com/news/priest_stabbed_in_turkey/.

[93] Catholic bishop stabbed to death in southern Turkey, (Un évêque catholique poignardé à mort dans le sud de la Turquie), *CNN News*, 3 juin 2010, http://news.blogs.cnn.com/2010/06/03/catholic-bishop-stabbed-to-death-in-southern-turkey/.

[94] *Turkey Progress Report*, Eur. Comm'n, 50, octobre 2014. Discours de Sa Sainteté Benoît XVI aux évêques de Turquie lors de leur visite « ad limina », petite salle du Trône, 2 février 2009.

*tu ne t'es point lassé. ... ne crains pas ce que tu vas souffrir ... Sois fidèle jusqu'*à la mort, et je te donnerai la couronne de vie » (Ap 2, 3, 10)[95].

B. Les Relations Diplomatiques Entre la République de Turquie et le Saint-Siège

Le Saint-Siège et l'Empire ottoman ont établi des relations diplomatiques en 1868, plus de 100 ans avant le Royaume Uni (1982), les États-Unis (1984), et le Mexique (1992)[96]. Jusqu'en 1959, le Saint-Siège était représenté en Turquie par les délégués apostoliques[97]. Le 26 février 1960, le Saint-Siège et la Turquie ont convenu de l'installation d'une nonciature apostolique à Ankara. Mgr Angelo Giuseppe Roncalli, qui fut délégué apostolique en Turquie de 1935 à 1944, devenu le Pape Jean XXIII en 1958 (« Le Pape Turc »)[98], reçut la visite de Celal Bayar, président de la Turquie, le 11 juin 1959, établissant alors des relations diplomatiques.

1. Les voyages apostoliques des papes en Turquie

Pour tous les papes, la Turquie est une « terre sainte de l'Église »[99] : un pays doté d'un glorieux passé chrétien et d'un héritage commun à tous les chrétiens[100]. Elle est le lieu où l'Église catholique romaine rencontre sa sœur, l'Église orthodoxe, et travaille pour l'unité des chrétiens[101]. Pour les papes, la Turquie est aussi un lieu de dialogue

---

[95] *Id.*

[96] Victor Gaetan, "The Pope, Erdogan, Syria, and Ukraine", (Le Pape, Erdogan, la Syrie et l'Ukraine) *Foreign Affairs*, 28 novembre 2014, http://www. foreignaffairs. com/articles/142400/victor-gaetan/catholic-geopolitics.

[97] *Id.*

[98] Père Tom, "The Holy Land of the Church" (La Terre Sainte de l'Église), *Church of the Good Shepherd*, 4 novembre 2012, http://www.goodshepherdbh. org/2012/11/04/the-holy-land-of-the-church/.

[99] Pape Benoît XVI.

[100] Père Tom, *supra* note 98.

[101] Pape Jean-Paul II à S.E. Altan Güven, Ambassadeur de la République de Turquie au Saint-Siège (6 décembre 1997) disponible à l'adresse suivante http://w2.vatican.va/content/john-paul-ii/fr/speeches/1997/december/documents/ hf_jp-ii_spe_19971206_ambassador-turkey.html.

avec la foi islamique. Suivant la *Déclaration Nostra AÉtate*, le Concile exhorte les chrétiens et musulmans « à oublier le passé et à travailler sincèrement à la compréhension mutuelle et à préserver ainsi que promouvoir ensem*ble pour le bénéfice de toute l'humanité, la justice sociale et le bien-être moral, ainsi que la paix et la liberté* ».[102]

Paul VI s'est rendu en Turquie en juillet 1967. C'était le premier voyage officiel d'un pape en Turquie depuis plus de mille ans[103]. Dans son discours au cours de la cérémonie d'accueil il a exprimé son désir de contribuer à la réalisation de la paix et de la fraternité et sa gratitude envers les minorités catholiques de Turquie, qui par leur travail contribuent à cet idéal ; rappelant le travail des nombreux ordres catholiques dans les domaines de la culture, de l'éducation, du social et des soins médicaux. Dans l'église orthodoxe patriarcale de Saint George, le pape a rappelé ce qui pourrait rassembler les Orthodoxes et les Catholiques : le même amour pour le Christ et l'Église, la recherche commune du Christ et la fidélité au Christ, la même foi exprimée par les Pères de l'Église, et la charité fraternelle.

Jean-Paul II fit à son tour le pèlerinage à Constantinople (Istanbul) et Ephèse, les 29 et 30 novembre 1979. Avec le Patriarche Œcuménique Dimitrios I, il a annoncé l'ouverture d'un « *dialogue théologique* » entre les deux Églises qui identifierait, confronterait et pourrait peut-être résoudre les difficultés empêchant l'unité ; une déclaration commune fut publiée. De même, Benoît XVI rendit une visite apostolique à Ankara, Ephèse et Istanbul du 28 novembre au 1er décembre 2006. Elle intervint peu après son discours de Ratisbonne qui provoqua une violente critique dans le monde islamique car le Pape y citait un ancien empereur byzantin soulignant le lien entre l'Islam et la violence. 25 000 personnes protestèrent contre la venue du pape. Le Pape

---

[102] *Nostra Aetate*, § 3.

[103] Victor Gaetan, Pope Francis' Pilgrimage in Turkey Reflects Past and Future (Le pèlerinage du Pape François en Turquie, reflet du passé et de l'avenir), *National Catholic Register*, 30 novembre 2014, http://www.ncregister.com/daily-news/past-and-future-reflected-in-pope-francis-pilgrimage-to-turkey.

rencontra les personnalités officielles de la République, mais le cœur de sa visite fut la fête de Saint André, célébrée le 30 novembre au *Phanar*, siège du Patriarcat[104]. À l'issue de la liturgie, le Pape et le Patriarche Œcuménique Bartholomé I ont renouvelé leur engagement réciproque à persévérer dans le rétablissement de la pleine unité.

Confirmant cette nouvelle tradition, le Pape François vint à son tour en Turquie, du 28 au 30 novembre 2014, à Ankara et Constantinople, dans un contexte accru d'hostilité contre les chrétiens, tant en Turquie que dans son voisinage immédiat. Le Pape a déclaré qu'il est « *essentiel que tous les citoyens, Musulmans, Juifs et Chrétiens – jouissent des mêmes droits et respectent les même devoirs tant dans les dispositions que dans l'exercice de la loi* »[105].

Durant son voyage, le Pape a visité la Mosquée Bleue d'Istanbul[106] et a rencontré les réfugiés aidés par l'ordre catholique des Salésiens, les engageant à ne pas se décourager et à continuer d'espérer un futur meilleur[107]. Au cours de la conférence de presse en vol entre Istanbul et Rome, le Pape a parlé du progrès de l'œcuménisme entre chrétiens, non pas sur le plan théologique, mais un « œcuménisme du sang » des chrétiens autour de la planète, puisque tous sont persécutés parce qu'ils sont témoins de Jésus-Christ. Leurs persécuteurs ne faisant pas de distinction entre eux, leur sang « *est mélangé* » et par conséquent « *nous sommes unis dans le sang, bien que nous n'ayons pas encore réussi à prendre les mesures nécessaires vers l'unité entre nous.* » a-t-il déclaré[108].

---

[104] Pape Benoît XVI, *Audience générale*, 6 décembre 2006, http://w2. vatican.va/ content/benedict-xvi/en/audiences/2006/documents/hf_benxvi_aud_ 20061206.html.

[105]   *Id.*

[106] Conférence de Presse en vol entre Istanbul et Rome, 30 novembre 2014, http:// w2.vatican.va/content/francesco/en/speeches/2014/november/documents/pa-pa-francesco_20141130_turchia-conferenza-stampa.html.

[107] Pape François, Vœux aux jeunes réfugiés aidés pas les Salésiens, Cathédrale du Saint Esprit, Istanbul, 30 novembre 2014, http://w2.vatican.va/content/ francesco/ en/speeches/2014/november/documents/papa-francesco_20141130_ turchia-orato-rio-salesiano.html.

[108] Andrea Gagliarducci, Pope Francis: Christians worldwide are united in blood (Les Chrétiens du monde sont unis dans le sang), *Catholic News Agency*, 16 dé-

2. Les messages des papes aux ambassadeurs turcs auprès du Saint-Siège

Depuis Paul VI, les papes se sont régulièrement adressés aux ambassadeurs de Turquie auprès le Saint-Siège, évoquant souvent, outre les questions spirituelles, les problèmes de l'Église en Turquie ainsi que la situation de Chypre. Les papes ont insisté sur le rôle spécifique de la Turquie, présenté comme « *un pont entre l'Europe et l'Asie* »[109], et réaffirmant l'importance du « *respect mutuel, de la tolérance et du dialogue interreligieux* » entre les différents groupes religieux présents en Turquie[110]. A cet égard ils ont soutenu le modèle de la Constitution turque[111]. En parallèle, les papes sont devenus plus insistants sur la reconnaissance du droit de liberté de religion et d'un statut juridique pour l'Église. Dans un discours de 2004, le Pape établit un lien entre la question de la reconnaissance du statut de l'Église avec celle de l'admission de la Turquie dans l'Union européenne[112]. Le Pape Benoît XVI, en 2007 et 2010 a rappelé que « *l'Église catholique attend une reconnaissance juridique civile* »[113] et « *aimerait… la création d'un organe de dialogue officiel entre la conférence des évêques et les autorités de l'État afin de pouvoir résoudre les problèmes qui pourraient se présenter, et de maintenir de bonnes relations entre les deux parties.* »[114]

---

cembre 2013, http://www.catholicnewsagency.com/news/pope-francis-christians-worldwide-are-united-in-blood/.

[109] Pape Jean-Paul II à S.E. Altan Güven, Ambassadeur de la République de Turquie au Saint-Siège (6 décembre 1997) disponible à l'adresse suivante http://w2.vatican.va/content/john-paul-ii/fr/speeches/1997/december/documents/ hf_jp-ii_spe_19971206_ambassador-turkey.html.

[110] *Id.*

[111] Pape Jean-Paul II au nouvel ambassadeur de Turquie au Saint-Siège, 7 décembre 2001, http://w2.vatican.va/content/john-paul-ii/en/speeches/2001/ december/documents/hf_jp-ii_spe_20011207_ambassador-turchia.html.

[112] Pape Jean-Paul II, à S.E. Osman Durak, Ambassadeur de Turquie au Saint-Siège, 21 février 2004, http://w2.vatican.va/content/john-paul-ii/en/speeches/ 2004/february/documents/hf_jp-ii_spe_20040221_ambassador-turkey.html.

[113] Pape Benoît XVI, à S.E. Kenan Gürsoy, Ambassadeur de Turquie au Saint-Siège, 7 janvier 2010, http://w2.vatican.va/content/benedict-xvi/en/speeches/ 2010/january/documents/hf_ben-xvi_spe_20100107_ambassador -turkey.html.

[114] Pape Benoît XVI, à S.E. Muammer Dogan Akdur, Ambassadeur de Turquie au Saint-

3. Le Saint-Siège et la question du génocide Arménien

La reconnaissance du génocide arménien est une question sensible pour la Turquie. Le 9 novembre 2000, le Pape Jean-Paul II et Kerekin II, le Patriarche suprême et Catholicos de l'Église apostolique arménienne, ont émis un avis commun condamnant le génocide arménien du début du XXème siècle. S'opposant à la position du gouvernement turc, ils déclarèrent : « *Le génocide arménien, qui a ouvert le siècle, fut un prologue aux horreurs qui devaient suivre. Deux guerres mondiales, d'innombrables conflits régionaux et des campagnes d'extermination délibérément organisées ont fauché la vie de millions de fidèles* »[115]. En 2015, le Pape François, à son tour, déclara que « *le premier génocide du XXème siècle* », a frappé le peuple Arménien.[116]

4. Le Saint-Siège et l'accession de la Turquie à l'Union européenne

Le 13 avril 1987, la Turquie a officiellement demandé à rejoindre l'UE, mais l'histoire de l'entrée de la Turquie dans l'UE commence le 12 septembre 1963, lorsqu'elle est devenue membre associé de la Communauté Economique européenne. Elle intégra l'union douanière le 1er janvier 1996. Le processus d'adhésion se heurta notamment aux critiques soulevées par le Parlement européen qui identifia des « obstacles essentiels » à l'adhésion tels que la non-reconnaissance du génocide Arménien, les conflits avec la Grèce, le maintien de troupes d'occupation à Chypre, l'absence de reconnaissance du peuple kurde, l'absence de démocratie parlementaire et le non-respect de libertés individuelles et collectives, particulièrement les libertés religieuses.

Siège, 19 janvier 2007, http://w2.vatican.va/content/benedict-xvi/en/ speeches/2007/january/documents/hf_ben-xvi_spe_20070119_ambassador-turkey.html.

[115] Pape Jean-Paul II & Catholicos Karekin II, déclaration commune, Rome, 9 novembre 2000, http://w2.vatican.va/content/john-paul-ii/fr/speeches/2000/oct-dec/documents/hf_jp-ii_spe_20001109_john-paul-ii-karekin-ii.html.

[116] Turkey anger at Pope Francis Armenian 'genocide' claim, (La colère de la Turquie à la reconnaissance du génocide arménien par le Pape François) *BBC*, 12 avril 2015, http://www.bbc.com/news/world-europe-32272604.

La question religieuse a aussi une importance, et la position de l'Église catholique a, à cet égard, une grande influence[117]. Bien que le Saint-Siège n'ait pas officiellement pris position sur la question de l'intégration de la Turquie à l'UE, plusieurs personnalités importantes de l'Église se sont exprimées.

En 2004, avant de devenir le Pape Benoît XVI, le Cardinal Ratzinger s'est opposé à deux reprises à l'accession de la Turquie à l'Union européenne. Il a affirmé que l'Europe et la Turquie sont fondées sur des racines religieuses et culturelles différentes[118] et que « *l'entrée de la Turquie dans l'UE serait antihistorique* »[119] « *parce qu'historiquement et culturellement, la Turquie a très peu de choses en commun avec l'Europe, pour cette raison, ce serait une grave erreur de l'intégrer à l'Union européenne* ». D'après le Cardinal Ratzinger, « *il serait préférable que la Turquie devienne un pont entre l'Europe et le monde arabe, ou alors qu'elle forme avec ce monde son propre continent culturel* »[120]. Une fois devenu Pape, Benoît XVI a maintenu tacitement sa position[121].

En mai 2004 également, sous le pontificat du Pape Jean-Paul II, le Cardinal Tauran, le « Ministre des affaires étrangères » du Saint-Siège, a lui aussi exprimé des réserves sur l'adhésion de la Turquie, soulignant que « *l'Europe est chrétienne, quand dans le ciel turc brille le croissant de lune* »[122].

---

[117] *Voir* Erkan Toguslu, "European Churches' Attitudes to Turkey's Membership In EU: The Case of Christian Minorities In Turkey", *Turkish Journal of Politics*, No. 2, hiver 2013, p. 65 ; Michael Minkenberg, "Christian identity? European churches and the issue of Turkey's EU membership", *Comparative European Politics*, N°10, 2012, pp. 149-179; Michael Minkenberg *et al.*, "Turkish membership in the European Union – The role of religion", *Comparative European Politics*, n°10, 2012, pp. 133-148.

[118] Sophie de Ravinel, Entretien, *Le Figaro Magazine*, 13 août 2004.

[119] Conférence sur l'exhortation apostolique de Jean-Paul II « *Ecclesia in Europa* », Velletri, Suisse, 17 septembre 2004.

[120] *Id.*

[121] Pape Benoît XVI, Rencontre avec le corps diplomatique de la République de Turquie, discours du Saint Père à la nonciature apostolique d'Ankara, 28 novembre 2006, disponible sur : http://w2.vatican.va/content/benedict-xvi/en/ speeches/2006/november/documents/hf_ben-xvi_spe_20061128_diplomatic-corps.html.

[122] Sandro Magister, "Europe Is Christian, but Turkey's Crescent Moon Shines in its Skies", *Chiesa.espresso*, 15 octobre 2004, http://chiesa.espresso.repubblica.it/

Différemment, la Commission des Episcopats de la Communauté européenne (COMECE) s'est montrée plus ouverte. Dans une déclaration du 19 novembre 2004, elle a exprimé son espoir que la Turquie continue ses réformes économiques et politiques suivant les recommandations de Bruxelles, soulignant que l'accession de la Turquie est une décision politique et non pas religieuse. Enfin, les évêques et la communauté catholique de Turquie ainsi que le Patriarche orthodoxe de Constantinople se sont prononcés en 2004 en faveur de l'entrée de la Turquie en Europe.

Depuis que le 3 octobre 2004, l'UE a accepté de reprendre les négociations avec la Turquie, l'Église catholique ne s'est plus prononcée sur la question. Dernièrement la Turquie elle-même avait semblé renoncer à rejoindre l'UE[123], alors que des millions de Turcs ont émigré et se sont installés dans des pays européens. Le renouveau islamique actuel, le rôle ambiguë que joue la Turquie dans l'agenda « Néo-Ottoman » du président Erdogan[124], inaugurent une phase nouvelle et imprédictible dans les relations entre la Turquie et l'Église catholique.

* * * * *

Cette brève présentation des rapports entre l'Église et l'Anatolie serait incomplète sans perspective spirituelle, laquelle, d'un point de vue religieux révèle le sens de l'histoire. Or, l'opposition entre la chrétienté et l'Empire ottoman, a une dimension eschatologique. Dans l'Apocalypse relaté par l'apôtre Jean, est présente une image qui fera l'objet d'une grande vénération : celle de la « Vierge de l'Apocalypse ». Elle présente Marie, la mère de Jésus-Christ, à la fin des temps. Elle est vêtue de bleu et sa tête est couronnée de douze étoiles, préfigurant le drapeau

---

articolo/19629?eng=y.

[123] Erdogan's Turkey drifts away from the West, *The Financial Times*, 18 janvier 2015, http://www.ft.com/cms/s/0/fdaa125e-9d7c-11e4-8946-00144feabdc0.html#axzz3TRjlh8m4.

[124] Nicola Nasser, "Syria, Egypt Reveal Erdogan's Hidden 'Neo-Ottoman Agenda,'" *Global Research*, 20 novembre 2013, http://www.globalresearch.ca/syria-egypt-reveal-erdogans-hidden-neo-ottoman-agenda/5358781.

européen. Sous ses pieds sont représentés le croissant de lune, préfigurant le symbole de l'Islam, ainsi que le démon, qu'elle écrase. Les Chrétiens peuvent y voir la promesse de la victoire finale de la Chrétienté sur l'Islam par la Sainte Vierge. Les relations entre l'Église et l'Anatolie ont aussi cette dimension extraordinaire illustrée par les victoires miraculeuses et fondatrices de Constantin au pont Milvius en octobre 312 et de la Sainte Ligue à Lépante en 1571. Dans les deux cas, la Tradition affirme que dans le ciel apparût une croix associée à la promesse : « *In hoc signo vinces* », signifiant *Tu vaincras par ce signe*.